Web Development

Web Development

A Visual-Spatial Approach

CRAIG M. BAEHR

Texas Tech University

Upper Saddle River, New Jersey
Columbus, Ohio

Library of Congress Cataloging-in-Publication Data

Baehr, Craig M.
  Web development : a visual-spatial approach / Craig M. Baehr.—1st ed.
    p. cm.
  Includes bibliographical references and index.
  ISBN 0-13-170122-3
  1. Web site development.   I. Title.
  TK5105.888.B34 2007
  006.7—dc22

                                            2005034624

Senior Acquisitions Editor: Gary Bauer
Editorial Assistant: Jacqueline Knapke
Production Editor: Kevin Happell
Production Coordination: TechBooks/GTS
Design Coordinator: Diane Ernsberger
Cover Designer: Jason Moore
Cover Art: Corbis
Production Manager: Pat Tonneman
Senior Marketing Manager: Leigh Ann Sims
Senior Marketing Coordinator: Elizabeth Farrell
Marketing Coordinator: Alicia Dysert

This book was set in Berkeley Book by TechBooks/GTS. It was printed and bound
by Edwards Brothers, Inc. The cover was printed by Phoenix Color Corp.

Pearson Education Ltd.   Pearson Education Australia Pty. Limited
Pearson Education Singapore Pte. Ltd.   Pearson Education North Asia Ltd.
Pearson Education Canada, Ltd.   Pearson Educación de Mexico, S.A. de C.V.
Pearson Education—Japan   Pearson Education Malaysia Pte. Ltd.

10 9 8 7 6 5 4 3 2 1
ISBN 0-13-170122-3

Preface

Intended Audience

Web Development: A Visual-Spatial Approach provides a comprehensive overview of the Web development process appropriate for beginning to intermediate-level students in both undergraduate and graduate courses and serves as a reference for professionals interested in contemporary approaches to Web design and development. This book might also serve an experienced designer as an informational text on Web development. The material in this book assumes the reader is familiar with basic accessing and browsing of Web sites on the Internet using a Web browser.

Approach

My interest in writing this book evolved from my work as a Web developer and instructor of Web publishing courses. My research in visual-spatial thinking and Web publishing led to the discovery that no single text covered the major tasks and described Web development as an iterative process. After having taught Web publishing using many texts with different approaches, I decided to write a book treating the major aspects of Web development, including planning, structure, navigation, content, design, and usability, as part of an integrated process. My goal in writing this book has been to provide a holistic description of the Web development process, which interconnects these aspects in a meaningful way. This book incorporates both contemporary and traditional theoretical approaches, including rhetorical theory, visual-spatial thinking, and user-centered design.

Research in Web development has evolved beyond basic markup, scripting, and single aspects such as design or structure. This book suggests a process that sees Web sites as wholes, with interconnected parts and unique visual-spatial characteristics. These dynamic relationships between parts of the process can provide a deeper understanding of Web development as a process. For example, structure and navigation directly affect one another; making changes to either in a Web site redesign will cause designers to rethink their approach to both. This suggests that the process of Web development is not linear, but rather more complex and iterative. Making such adjustments to a site may require a designer to revisit previous approaches. Other books have covered individual topics in depth and provide useful modules to instructors in crafting courses, yet there is a need to examine Web development as a holistic process.

Web Development: A Visual-Spatial Approach illustrates how individual tasks relate and contribute to the development of a whole site. Web sites are highly visual, presenting information in a variety of spatial configurations for users to read and interpret. These unique characteristics determine how individual components work together to create dynamic and meaningful relationships to users. They affect how we read, use, and interpret information published on the Web and in other online document forms. Throughout the book, various methods and tasks are grounded in rhetorical theory and user-centered design to keep designers focused on the unique characters of users and contexts within which Web projects are often situated.

Organization

The book is organized into four sections: project planning, content development, structure and design, and usability. Each section provides an in-depth discussion of each stage of the Web development process from start to finish. Each chapter can be taught out of sequence to accommodate slightly different instructional approaches.

The first two chapters address the planning aspect of the development process. Chapter 1 describes the visual-spatial approach and the Web development process. Chapter 2 discusses project planning issues, including defining the rhetorical situation, scope, and methods of handing professional clients. The next two chapters address content development and document markup. Chapter 3 discusses methods of developing, adapting, and writing content for Web projects, including a discussion of style sheets. Chapter 4 discusses document markup and publishing. Chapters 5 and 6 cover the structural aspects of the development process. Chapter 5 covers the process of developing a site structure and methods of organizing and arranging pages in a Web site. Chapter 6 discusses types of navigation systems and methods of developing and labeling those systems. The design phase of the development process is covered in Chapters 7 and 8. Chapter 7 discusses visual design principles and methods of developing graphic content for Web sites. Chapter 8 covers interface design and page layouts. The usability phase of development is covered in Chapter 9. This chapter discusses methods of usability testing and Web accessibility guidelines.

Companion Web Site: www.prenhall.com/baehr

The companion Web site provides chapter summaries, hyperlinks to the actual Web sites featured as illustrative screen captures, ready-to-use PDF versions of worksheets, additional online examples, and additional student exercises. Students can cut and paste detailed summaries of chapter objectives into their notebooks for reference. Downloadable PDF files of worksheets used in each chapter are provided so students can use them in their projects. In addition, links to screen shots of Web sites enable students to explore the sites on their own. Additional chapter examples and exercises encourage application of chapter material to solving problems.

Instructor's Manual

The instructor's manual provides chapter summaries, additional student exercises, sample assignments, PDF versions of worksheets, list of companion Web site resources, and detailed summaries of chapter objectives. The manual provides alternate teaching suggestions for each chapter related to specific chapter objectives. In addition, it provides suggested teaching material in related chapters.

To access the instructors manual online, instructors need to request an instructor access code. Go to **www.prenhall.com,** click the **Instructor Resource Center** link, and then click Register Today for an instructor access code. Within 48 hours of registering you will receive a confirming e-mail including an instructor access code. Once you have received your code, go to the site and log on for full instructions on downloading the materials that you wish to use.

Acknowledgments

Many people have been integral to the development of this book and deserve both credit and thanks for their contributions, support, and helpful advice.

I am grateful and offer thanks to the professional contributors of the Ask a Practitioner feature in each chapter, including Marc Bessent, Andrew Eberhart, Deborah Hess, Brian Jordan, Arthur Oakley, Tommy Petty, Cindy Romero, and Dennis Teske. Their practical advice on solving workplace problems related to Web publishing is a valuable addition to this book.

I would like to thank the reviewers for their help with the revision of the book: Danielle Nicole DeVoss, Michigan State University; Bill Hart-Davidson, Rensselaer Polytechnic Institute; Gary Heba, Bowling Green State University; Michael C. Morgan, Bemidji State University; and Michael Salvo, Purdue University.

I would also like to thank the editorial staff at Prentice Hall for their hard work and contributions to this book: Gary Bauer, Senior Acquisitions Editor; Kevin Happell, Production Editor; Jacqueline Knapke, Editorial Assistant; and Penny Walker, Project Manager for TechBooks/GTS. I offer special thanks to Gary Bauer, for his support of this project and contributing his expertise and suggestions throughout the book's development.

And finally, I am grateful to my colleagues at Texas Tech University, as well as friends and family who have been supportive of my work on this project.

Contents

Note: Every effort has been made to provide accurate and current Internet information in this book. However, the Internet and information posted on it are constantly changing, so it is inevitable that some of the Internet addresses listed in this textbook will change.

Web Development

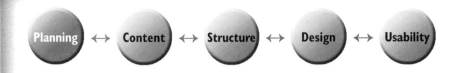

Planning ↔ Content ↔ Structure ↔ Design ↔ Usability

PROCESS of WEB DEVELOPMENT

Introduction

For more than a decade, the World Wide Web has become an important medium for information exchange in business, education, commerce, and personal communication. Collectively, we use the Web to communicate, research, advertise, educate, buy and sell products, and for entertainment. Businesses use Web pages to sell products, services, and communicate globally and internally using corporate Intranets, or internal company networks. Universities and colleges use the Web for research, instruction, and advertisement. Individuals use the Web to make purchases, take courses, read news, play games, communicate with friends and family, and find information on a variety of subjects. As a research tool and source of daily information, the Web has become an integral source of news and information and it serves as a central point for commerce, news, and information exchange for many cultures.

Think of how the Web has affected your daily life. What do you use the Web for daily? How many hours a week do you spend using the Web? What tasks can you perform on the Web from your home computer? Have you taken an online class to learn a new skill or software program? Have you purchased products online? Have you ever performed a Web search on your name to see what information about you is available online? What do you think you will need to use the Web for in the next five years? The answers to these questions help identify the extent to which the Web has become (and will become) an important part of your daily life. As a result of the Web's emerging presence over the past decade, Web development has become an important discipline to our culture to meet the demands of the rapidly growing online publishing and communication industries, as well as online consumers.

The World Wide Web has had many important milestones and players in its rapid development. Many histories of the Web's development have been written, each of which highlight many of the pivotal points and related milestones. The Web as we know it today has been publicly accessible since the early 1990s, but there were many milestones that led up to its current form. In 1945, Vannevar Bush published his famous "As We May Think" article proposing a device called the Memex as an interactive information storage and retrieval mechanized device that bears striking similarities to the Web as we know it today. In the 1960s, Ted Nelson coined the word *hypertext* and conceived the first prototype hypertext product, called Project Xanadu, which he described in his book *Literary Machines*. During the same time period, Douglas Engelbart fully developed the first prototype of his oNLine System, a hypertext system with basic browsing and e-mail sending capabilities. In 1969, after many years of development, Advanced Research Projects Agency (ARPANET), a U.S. Department of Defense project to create the first information sharing computer network, was deployed. During the next decade, ARPANET grew and in the 1980s other information sharing networks CSNET and NSFNET were born to provide equivalent shared computer networking services and access to scientists and universities. In the early 1990s, the World Wide Web became available as a public access resource, with Tim Berners-Lee as its chief developer. Although Berners-Lee is also credited as creating the first Web browser and Hypertext Markup Language (HTML), the National Center for Supercomputing Applications (NCSA) created Mosaic which became the first popular browser created for multiple operating systems. Since then, the Web has grown at an exponential rate, serving as a resource for research, commerce, and online publishing for the world.

Some critics consider the Web to be more than computer networking and communication tools that have evolved over time. Rather, they suggest that the Web is the next evolution in publishing and communication, and that the slowly replacing the printed book and printing press in favor of electronic and online products, such as Web sites. The Web page is gradually becoming as important as the printed book in terms of its use and authority as a source of information. People use the Web for news, entertainment, research, interaction, communication, and much more. As a result, the Web has already changed the ways in which we read, write, and comprehend knowledge on a daily basis. As this change continues, our concept of literacy is changing to include new skills such as browsing and interacting with Web pages, in addition to basic reading and writing. As the Web continues to evolve, our concept of a literate individual may eventually expand to include other skills such as basic scripting and software use. Learning the basics about the Web development process, while somewhat of a choice today, may become integral to a new digital literacy of the future. Due to the Web's integral role in our contemporary lives, it is important to learn about the various technologies, roles, skills, and process involved in creating Web sites and pages.

Web Development: Roles, Skills, and Resources

Developing a Web site is a holistic process that involves many skills, including writing and adapting textual content, graphics, and media into a visually interactive Web site. It includes creating a site structure for individual pages, navigation tools for searching and browsing, and an interface design that organizes elements on the screen for users. Web development draws from a variety of disciplines including technical and professional writing, graphic design, computer science, cognitive psychology, usability engineering, information architecture, and others. As such, Web development might be considered to be a multidisciplinary field. While it may not be necessary to specialize in all of these fields, most Web developers develop skills in at least a handful of these areas. The reality is that companies cannot always afford to hire a team of specialists in each area when they decide to redesign the company home page. As such, Web developers often wear multiple hats in the task of creating Web sites.

Since Web development draws on knowledge from a variety of areas, creating Web sites requires a wide range of skills including writing, editing, graphic design, usability testing, project management, scripting, programming, and computer software use. Whether developing a personal Web site or working on a corporate Web site as part of a development team, an individual's role in Web development will differ depending on personal expertise, resources, and the scope of the project. Table 1-1 shows a variety of roles commonly found on Web development teams.

Although developers may not need to master all of these skills, there are a variety of resources available to help them tackle each of these tasks. The most obvious resources needed include a computer, Web browser, Internet connection, Web server space, software, and reference materials, such as books or useful Web sites with scripting or graphic libraries. On a development team, individuals can learn skills from each other and share resources. When working individually on a Web project, certain tasks can be contracted out, such as the administration of Web server space. For example, most individual users have their own Internet Service Provider (ISP) that provides access to the Internet and provides the Web server and adequate space. As such, a user only has to learn how to upload files to the server in order to publish content on the Web.

TABLE 1-1. Web Development Team Roles

Role	Function
Project manager	Serves as the team leader who establishes and manages the timeline, finances, and resources. May serve as the client's primary point of contact.
Programmer	Oversees the scripting, programming, and other technical issues.
Graphic artist	Acquires and/or develops graphic content.
Writer/editor	Writes and edits content for the Web project and any formal reports required.
Content provider	Provides content to the writer/editor and team to be included in the site. May serve as a reviewer of the project.
Usability tester	Tests the site for usability and accessibility guidelines.
Server administrator	Responsible for publishing and posting files and overall maintenance of a Web server.

The Web serves as a vast resource for developers, providing a wide range of graphic and scripting libraries and software, both free and for a fee. Online libraries provide everything from specific instruction to complete libraries of images and scripts. A basic keyword search on any search portal using terms such as "free Web graphics" or "HTML scripting reference" will produce a wide range of choices. A variety of Web development software programs, such as Microsoft FrontPage, Adobe GoLive, and Macromedia Dreamweaver can be used to develop Web sites quickly and easily and such programs often have their own built-in graphics libraries and scripting capabilities. These programs allow designers to drag and drop content onto Web pages and handle the necessary scripting and programming. For developing graphic content, most designers invest in graphic development software, such as Jasc Paint Shop Pro or Adobe Illustrator, or plan to search the Web for libraries of graphic content. A more detailed discussion of scripting and Web authoring software is provided in Chapter 4 and a discussion of graphics is provided in Chapter 7. So, with a vast array of resources to assist her, a designer does not need to become an expert in every aspect of Web development to develop a basic site. But designers need to learn about the technical aspects of Web design to know which skills to learn and which resources will best assist them.

Important Web Terms and Concepts

In addition to learning the technical aspects of Web design, which includes scripting, available software, graphic design, programming, each designer should be familiar with basic Web terminology. This enables novice designers to understand materials written on these subjects and to be able to ask meaningful questions on the subject. Specifically, some basic terms every designer should know include: hypertext, home page, Web page, hyperlink, visual-spatial thinking, user-centered design, site architecture, navigation, node, and interface. Figure 1-1 provides a definition of each of these terms.

Many of the terms presented in Figure 1-1 were nonexistent a decade ago and were invented to describe the unique aspects of the Web. Some of these modern terms, such as *hypertext*, were only known to theorists a decade ago. These terms and concepts will be discussed in detail throughout the book, but before proceeding, it is important to understand their basic definitions.

Web Site Characteristics

Another aspect of Web development is that Web sites in how they are written, developed, and finally read by there are significant differences among their users. First, the Web can be highly interactive and requires readers to be more active in their selection of paths to take, pages to read, and the overall flow of content. Most people read books in a linear fashion, from page to page and chapter to chapter. Web sites often do not have a linear organization in which they are read. Users can jump around in an electronic text, such as a Web site, using more robust tools such as keyword searching tools, navigation menus, and hyperlinks. Second, a Web site is a highly visual environment and often uses visual graphics and multimedia as primary content. Although printed books have graphics, they are static, or stationary. Third, the structure of Web sites is more complex than that of a printed book in terms of their organization. Users often perceive the Web as an online environment, in which they

HOME PAGE

The first page, or starting page in a Web site

HYPERLINK

Clickable text or visuals that links two related elements, such as pages, content chunks, or headers

HYPERTEXT

Chunks of textual and/or graphic content linked together by hyperlinks

INTERFACE

The whole screen or page a user sees, including the textual, graphic, and interactive content

NAVIGATION TOOLS

Any hyperlinks or buttons used to search, browse, and interact with the site, excluding browser controls

NODE

A single page that acts as a gateway and leads to many related pages

SITE ARCHITECTURE

The overall site structure and arrangement of individual pages that comprise a whole site

USER-CENTERED DESIGN

A design approach that places users' needs at the center of the design process

VISUAL-SPATIAL THINKING

A method in which users conceptualize the whole Web site, by focusing and discerning the function and meaning of visual and spatial objects and their unique characteristics

WEB PAGE

A single page of Web content from a Web site

FIGURE 1-1. Basic Definitions of Web Design Terminology

plan searches and pathways through the site, as if it had a three-dimensional quality. As such, Web sites allow users to interact, contribute, and provide feedback in the online spaces. Fourth, Web sites evolve more quickly than most printed texts. A Web site can be updated daily, whereas printed books require a new printing run. Time sensitivity is still an issue with both Web sites and printed texts, but Web sites tend to have a shorter shelf-life if they are not updated frequently. Often the credibility of content on a Web site may be judged by how frequently it is updated. Finally, Web sites have unique visual and spatial characteristics built into the screen interface, structure, navigation, and other aspects of the site that printed books do not necessarily possess. Because of these unique characteristics, the nature of developing fully functional Web sites is quite different from the process of writing a printed report or book. Not only does it require different developmental methods, but also changes are required in the way we think about creating and using Web sites.

A Visual-Spatial Approach

When thinking of the structure or organization of a book, many people think of an organized table of contents, in which sections are divided into chapters and pages are individually numbered in sequence. We may be aware of the physical and visual characteristics of a book, such as the paper, binding, colors used, or the book's weight. But a Web site is perceived differently. Users often conceptualize Web sites as virtual spaces, where an individual can move from page to page or site to site in a larger, more amorphous spatial structure. Many metaphors associated with describing the Web suggest this, including jump, link, chat room, pathway, and space. When asked to sketch and describe the structure of a Web site, many of us might use arrows, directional lines, flow charts, and other elements to illustrates how we visualize the structure. Many site maps, or Web site directories, often use such elements to help users understand the site's layout. Research that examines how users think visually and spatially when using Web sites has suggested that users perceive and visualize Web sites as spatial structures, rather than linear ones and as a result, think differently than they do when reading and navigating print-based documents (Baehr 2002; Johnson-Sheehan and Baehr 2001).

Users think visually and spatially when they plan which paths to take through a Web site. When visiting a familiar site, they might remember the exact path, or series of clicks, when visualizing how to reach a specific page. Users think visually and spatially when trying to comprehend the organization of the screen interface and individual page layouts. They observe the grouping of text and graphics to understand the relationships between items (how headers suggest the subject of corresponding text) or to determine their function and meaning (as in a searching tool). Users make note of the location of specific items in terms of their visual and spatial characteristics as well. For example, a user might recall the visual characteristics and exact location of the shopping cart icon, which is used to review items for purchase, in an e-commerce site. Figure 1-2 shows an example of how icons and text are used to suggest concepts or meaning for each section of the JetBlue Airways

FIGURE 1-2. JetBlue Airways Navigation Icons

Source: JetBlue Airways, http://www.jetblue.com.

site. Some icons have familiar meanings, whereas others are paired with text to help users perceive their meaning.

To examine the role of visual perception on Web sites, the Stanford Poynter Project conducted eye-tracking studies with Web readers. In reading news Web sites, the studies found users focused most on article text, briefs, and photos in that order (DeVigal 2005). This study suggests users have definite preferences and visual perception habits when choosing what information to read on information-based Web sites. As such, Web development is much more than randomly tossing a handful of pictures and text on a page. It involves careful planning and selection of visual and spatial characteristics that help users perceive, conceptualize, and navigate more efficiently in a site.

Visual-spatial thinking is based on an understanding of how humans perceive and respond to visual elements and their placement, or spatial characteristics, in a visual-textual landscape. Visual thinking, based on the work of Rudolf Arnhiem and founded in Gestalt theory, is one approach to design that considers how users interact with elements in their visual field. This approach is illustrated in Arnheim's principles of visual thinking. These principles describe how users focus and fixate on visual elements to interpret, organize, and use visual information. Five of these principles apply well to our understanding of Web sites. These principles are **vision is selective, fixation solves a problem, discernment in depth, shapes are concepts**, and **complete the incomplete** (Arnheim 1969). Table 1-2 illustrates how visual thinking suggests visual-spatial concepts for Web sites, providing a list of principles, characteristics, and related concepts.

When applied to a Web environment, these principles can help explain how users visualize information and form concepts that lead to specific actions and preferences in Web sites. The Web is a complex environment, incorporating visual information, information structures, navigation tools, multimedia, and interactive features. Site structure, navigation, and interface design are visual-spatial aspects of Web design because each deals with visual information the user sees and how that information is arranged spatially. A site structure, or overall layout, has a specific arrangement of pages that make up the whole site. As users interact with visual navigation tools, site maps, and search the site, they can begin to visualize its arrangement of pages. The interface is comprised of visual tools and graphics that are arranged spatially on the screen to maximize the usability of the site.

Figure 1-3, The WorldSpace® International Satellite Radio Network Web site (http://www.worldspace.com) uses visual elements to help users focus on current location, navigation items, and content areas. The use of shaded boxes, directional arrows, and lines groups content in consistent locations throughout the site, so that users learn where to expect to find information on each page. Directional arrows indicate clickable items and categories of content for the site.

Because of the visual complexity of Web sites, Web browsing requires that users interact with content and make choices. Visual thinking helps us consider how users recognize patterns and respond in similar ways to visual information to make specific choices. For example, users may recognize the list of textual items in the left-hand margin as a navigation toolbar. Also, users might recognize the function of a shopping cart icon on a sales site. Visual thinking offers an approach that considers how users conceptualize, interpret, and respond in similar ways to these elements. Our interaction with visual information starts in the brain, where we visualize possible options, meanings, and solutions before we act. In essence, this is visual thinking.

TABLE 1-2. How Visual Thinking Suggests Visual-Spatial Concepts for Web Sites

Visual Thinking Principle	Characteristics	Visual-Spatial Concepts for Web Sites
Vision is selective	• When something changes in the visual field, the eye is drawn to that element • Repetitious elements are eventually ignored or fade into the background	Visual focus • Visual elements help users focus on important objects • Visuals that change appearance or create good contrast encourage focus
Fixation solves a problem	• Users are actively trying to solve problems • Our focal point is fairly small and we actively focus on elements we believe will help solve problems	Problem solving • Users examine elements closely to determine their function and usefulness • We can override our visual instincts with fixation
Discernment in depth	• When the eye focuses on an object, the background becomes distorted • When focusing on the background, specific objects become unfocused	Contextual • Linked content relates and shares characteristics • Context helps users interpret relation and meaning of content
Shapes are concepts	• Humans recognize familiar shapes and use them to form concepts about other objects • Perception of shape involves interpreting related visual concepts or categories	Conceptual • Grouped elements share characteristics and suggest concepts • Icons and shapes convey specific meaning
Complete the incomplete	• Humans try to conceptualize a whole from elements seen • Process of concept formation, rejection, and reformation	Wholeness • Grouping and arrangement of elements suggest how parts relate to the whole • Contextual clues, perception, and trial and error used to convey as sense of a whole

Sources: Arnheim 1969; Johnson-Sheehan and Baehr 2001; Baehr 2002.

Applying visual thinking to a Web environment requires that we consider the spatial qualities of design with the visual aspects. In Web spaces, perception is as much a spatial activity as it is a visual one, in fact our own perception defies the notion that visual and spatial perception are separate activities (Johnson-Sheehan and Baehr 2001). Designing site structures,

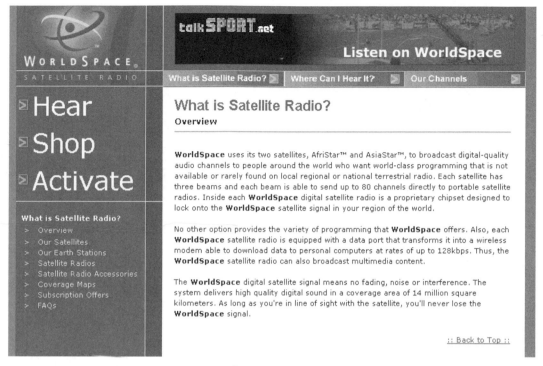

FIGURE 1-3. The WorldSpace® International Satellite Radio Network—What is Satellite Radio Web page

Source: WorldSpace® International Satellite Radio Network, http://www.worldspace.com/whatisit/overview.html.

navigation systems, graphics, and interface page layouts are visual-spatial aspects of Web design. A visual-spatial approach is a user-centered one that focuses design efforts on maximizing the site's usability. By considering both users' needs and their perceptual habits in their work, designers can tailor specific aspects of the site to fit users, rather than having users adapt to an unfamiliar design. Throughout this book, each aspect of the design process, including site structure, navigation, graphic design, interface design, and others, will be examined from a visual-spatial approach to help in the creation of designs that best fit the ways in which users perceive, conceptualize, and navigate Web sites and content. The visual-spatial approach reconceptualizes the traditional Web development process by focusing design not only on how Web sites are used, but also on how their unique visual and spatial qualities are perceived.

Process of Web Development

Following a process approach to designing a Web site provides structure and organization to work on a project. However, the Web development process is more than an assortment of individual tasks; it is a holistic one in which individual tasks interrelate. For example, the site structure affects the design of navigation tools for searching and browsing the site. Interface design includes developing layouts consisting of content

PLANNING

The conceptual phase that involves identifying the subject, audience, purpose, context, scope and functionality of the site

CONTENT

Researching, writing, and adapting content for individual Web pages, including markup and scripting

STRUCTURE

Developing the overall site structure, arrangement of pages, and navigation tools

DESIGN

Designing the visual content, page layouts, and interface elements

USABILITY

Formal comprehensive testing of the site for usability and accessibility prior to publishing the site

FIGURE 1-4. Process of Web Development

chunks, graphics, and navigation tools. The process involves designing a site that incorporates the unique ways in which users perceive and respond to elements of the site. The overall process of Web development involves five major phases, including planning, content development, structure, design, and usability. A summary of each major phase of the Web development process is provided in Figure 1-4. The Web development process is more iterative than linear, like the Web itself. This process can be followed from one phase to the next, and most likely the work in other phases might lead to new ideas and require changes. So, a designer might need to revisit work completed in other phases to make changes or adjustments throughout the overall process. For example, in designing the graphics for the site navigation, a more efficient way of organizing the structure and content of the site may be revealed. This might require a designer to revisit previous work. The usability of a site may be continually tested throughout the process to determine more effective navigation, page layouts, and structures. An iterative process permits this type of flexibility in the design process, accommodating changes throughout the development process.

The planning phase involves developing a concept of the whole site. It includes defining the site's subject and scope, analyzing the audiences, purpose, contextual issues, and constraints. This phase involves analyzing the target users to identify specific needs and functions they require to use the site properly. It involves identifying the site's purpose and specific goals for its design and construction. When designing a project for a client, much of this work will be done in consultation with the client and may result in a written scope of work or contract. Chapter 2 discusses methods of planning and analysis of the project, targeting the user base, defining the scope of the project, and strategies for working with professional clients.

The content phase involves researching, writing, and adapting content for the site. This work involves developing a research plan, writing, editing, and adapting or converting both new and existing content to Web-based formats that users will be able to read. It includes learning basic HTML to help understand how the internal structure of Web pages works and how to mark up and script basic pages. Chapter 3 discusses methods of conducting online research, developing a research plan, developing Web content, including content chunking, document conversion, and methods of adapting content for the Web. Chapter 4 covers the basic structure of an HTML Web page and some basic scripting techniques.

The structure phase involves developing an overall site structure, as well as the organization and labeling of all the pages into a whole site. It includes deciding how to arrange and link individual pages and major sections of the site. The work also entails developing navigation tools for users to browse and search pages, selecting specific navigation types, developing an organizing scheme, creating meaningful labels, and planning their arrangement on individual pages. Chapter 5 discusses types of site structures and a process for developing an effective structure for your site. Chapter 6 covers navigation design, including basic navigation types, labeling, organizing, and methods of arrangement.

The design phase involves developing graphic content and designing page layouts for the site. This includes developing graphics, a style sheet, and selecting which design principles and conventions to use as working guides. It considers the use of a style sheet and design guides to design the screen interface layout of individual pages for the site. This may include developing a single layout for all pages, or creating custom layouts for different sections of the site. Chapter 7 discusses the importance of using design principles and design conventions in creating graphic content and page layouts. Chapter 8 discusses methods of developing the screen interface and individual page layouts.

The usability phase involves performing tests of the site to determine its functionality and fit for the needs of target users. Usability testing will involve designing tests for basic screen and system settings and specific user tests for the site. Finally, testing the site for its conformance to accessibility standards will ensure all types of users have equal access to your site's content, prior to publishing the site. Chapter 9 discusses methods of testing a site for usability, including system settings such as screen resolution, color depth, and browser settings. Chapter 9 discusses how to set up a basic user test. It addresses Web accessibility guidelines from both the World Wide Web Consortium and U.S. Government Section 508 standards. Chapter 10 discusses how to publish the site and develop a basic site maintenance plan.

While each chapter addresses a specific aspect of the design process, each chapter also discusses how each part relates to others in the whole process. For example, Chapter 6 on navigation systems explains how site structure relates to and affects navigation design, and vice versa. Each part in the process examines the unique visual and spatial characteristics of each aspect, such as site structures, navigation, or interface design, and provides methods of adapting work to fit the ways in which users perceive these characteristics. Because the Web development process is an iterative one, after becoming familiar with each phase of the process, each designer can perfect his or her own process through practice and experience.

When I was asked to take on the duties as Web Manager, I didn't fully understand what the job entailed. To my surprise the previous Web manager had no documentation describing the roles and responsibilities of the Web team. So in a sense, I had no idea what I was taking on. Since the team was already working on developing Web pages, I had to look at the structure, note the problems, and try to fix them. The first item I tackled was developing a Web policy letter signed by the Commander in Chief stating the rules of Web design, roles and responsibilities, and the process of approving Web pages. When the Web policy letter was approved, I had to inform my team. Here are the major roles that make up the Albuquerque District team. Keep in mind that many of these roles are done by one person.

Web Manager

Responsible for overall structure and content posted to the entire District website.

System Administrator

Responsible for Web server (hardware/software).

Web Page Developers

Develop Web pages for different offices.

Electronic Management Control Team (EMCT)

Responsible for ensuring submitted information, content, and methods employed and published are reviewed and in compliance with current policies and regulations. Members include Office of Counsel, Public Affairs, Information Management Officer, and the Security and Law Officer. Without the EMCT approval, Web pages will not be posted.

Web Development Process

The most helpful process of Web design is planning. If I don't understand the goal of our project we can easily fail. Knowing the big picture is good but as the Web manager I need to understand every portion of the project. If one portion of the project fails the whole project will fail. One thing I learned is not to be afraid to ask questions. Make sure you fully understand what your customer is wanting. I personally would draw pictures of the different Web pages and have the customer review them. Structure is another important factor when designing a Web site. I use flow-charting to have a visual picture of my Web site. This is very important, especially if you're going to have tools for searching the Web site.

During my career, I have never been able to follow one task after another. I wish it was that cut and dry but I always go back and add new ideas or I find a better, more efficient way of doing something. Plus, most of my revisiting of previous work has been because of customer requests. For example, I created a Web template for our Intranet. During the testing phase I found I could have designed the template better. I think most Web designers revisit completed Web projects. I found most of the times I have revisited Web pages have been due to changes in personnel, or technology, or were because I simply didn't like the functionality of the design.

Improving Web Development Skills

Although every person has different methods of preferred learning, there are three sources that will be the most beneficial to improving Web development skills, besides this book. The first is taking courses specifically geared toward Web development. Courses provide an opportunity to study under an expert and to share experiences with other students. They provide a formal curriculum, access to materials, and specialized training. These courses can be academic courses, workplace training, and seminars. The second method of improving skills is self-study. This may include self-paced training, reading books, and browsing Web sites. A good book on JavaScript might help in learning some advanced scripting techniques. A Web-based training (WBT) course might also help learn and improve a novice designer's skill. The third method of improving skills is practice, whether it is on an actual project or designing a personal Web page. Web development is similar to learning a foreign language, in that practice is essential to work toward continually improving skills. Without practice, any formal training or self-study will be easily forgotten. Practice allows designers test skills and to combine what has already been learned in new ways. After completing a course or book on Cascading Style Sheets (CSS), it might be useful to try setting up a basic style sheet for a site as practice. Practice is always the best teacher, but shouldn't be the only one. A combination of the other methods will provide an introduction to new skills and theories that can be used to improve Web development skills.

A combination of these three methods will be effective in helping improve Web development skills. Each is important in its own way. Formal training will help in learning new skills from an expert, see them in practice, and get immediate help during the learning process. Self-study allows an individual to work at his or her own pace and select specialized topics that may not be offered as fully developed courses. Practice permits the testing and perfecting of both Web development and basic problem solving skills within the context of your work. Ultimately, it is up to each Web designer to decide what combination is best, since each individual prefers different learning methods.

Conclusion

Web development has become increasingly important to our online publishing and communication industries over the past decade. The Web itself has evolved into a visually interactive environment, or virtual space, in which we work, buy and sell products, conduct research, learn new skills, and communicate with friends and family. Although the history of the Web's use as a public resource is relatively short, the roles, skills, and technology required to maintain its growth matches its rapid pace of evolution. A starting point for anyone interested in becoming a Web developer is to become familiar with the technologies used and the basic skills needed. Equally important is a clear understanding of the development process and how users think and react differently to content in Web sites.

Chapter Summary

- The development and increasing use of the World Wide Web for business, education, entertainment, and personal use has contributed to the evolution of Web development as important discipline in online publishing and communication.

- Web development requires a wide range of skills including writing, editing, graphic design, usability testing, project management, scripting, programming, and computer software use. A designer need not master every skill; there are a wide variety of online resources, software tools, and specialists that can help.

- Web development teams often include a wide range of roles, including project manager, programmer, graphic artist, writer/editor, content provider, usability tester, and server administrator.

- Web sites have unique characteristics that distinguish them from print-based documents, such as their interactivity, use of visuals and media, complex structures, rapid evolution, and unique visual and spatial characteristics.

- A visual-spatial approach is important to the Web development process because it considers the ways in which users perceive and conceptualize visual and spatial aspects of Web sites.

- Five principles of visual thinking that apply well to our understanding of Web sites are: vision is selective, fixation solves a problem, discernment in depth, shapes are concepts, and complete the incomplete.

- The process of Web development is both a holistic and iterative one, which involves five major phases: planning, content, structure, design, and usability.

- Ten important Web development terms every designer should be familiar with are home page, hypertext, hyperlink, interface, navigation, node, site architecture, user-centered design, visual-spatial thinking, and Web page.

- Three methods of improving Web development skills include formal training, self-study, and practice.

Exercises

1. Select a familiar Web site, such as an organization's site, company site, or school site and contact the Web site's support team. Inquire what roles make up the ongoing Web development team and define these roles. Then ask what types of resources were used to develop and maintain the site, such as software programs, online libraries, or Internet Service Provider.

2. Select an important figure from the introduction and research their other works and significant contributions using the Web. Make a list of significant publications, contributions, work, or other important details that pertain to Web development. Prepare a short five-minute presentation that summarizes his or her involvement with the field.

3. Select a Web site that is used for purchasing and browsing products. Identify how visuals are used to catch the users' eyes and help them learn how the site is organized

and used. Then, browse the site for several minutes to become familiar with the layout of the site. Finally, using just a sheet of paper and writing utensil, sketch the general layout of major sections of the site. Identify the visual and spatial characteristics used in creating the sketch that might suggest how users might think visually, spatially, or in a different way when attempting to sketch its layout or structure.

4. Using a popular search portal, such as Google or Yahoo, locate three free Web graphics sites and three free scripting library sites that would be useful in developing a basic personal Web site. Some sites will be more useful in terms of the quality and quantity of their offerings, so search a handful of sites until you locate sites that have both.

2

Planning ←→ Content ←→ Structure ←→ Design ←→ Usability

PROJECT PLANNING

Learning
Objectives

After completing this chapter, you will understand:

- Important aspects of the Web project planning process

- How to develop project goals based on visual-spatial thinking

- Strategies for writing a scope of work

- Developing a project schedule based on goals and tasks

- Developing a site maintenance plan

- Planning issues for working with professional clients

Introduction

The initial phase of the Web development process is project planning, during which decisions will be made to conceptualize the site. This work will involve defining the site's audience, purpose, and specific constraints that may need to be considered. The project planning phase involves identifying specific development goals and tasks to be accomplished, based on user needs and the visual-spatial approach. These goals will lead to the development of a written scope of work that documents specific technical and design requirements for developing the site. In turn, the scope of work serves as a consistent blueprint or set of requirements that define the entire development process. Project planning involves developing a timeline to schedule individual tasks, set significant milestones, and deadlines for deliverables. Finally, a site maintenance plan should be developed to account for subsequent changes to the project over time. The scope of work, schedule, and site maintenance plan serve as comprehensive blueprints for developing the Web project. A process diagram for Web project planning is provided in Figure 2-1 to provide an overview of the work involved. For professional client projects, the planning process includes developing goals, needs, and strategies in consultation with a client to identify specific deliverables, costs, and billing for services.

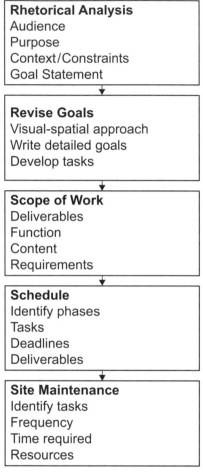

FIGURE 2-1.   Process Diagram for Web Project Planning

Analysis of the Rhetorical Situation

The first part of project planning is an analysis of the rhetorical aspects of the project, which include audience or users, purpose, and contextual issues or constraints. These elements define the rhetorical situation of the project and can contribute to a more user-centered design. Whether your product is a Web site, online report, help system, or other electronic product, considering these rhetorical aspects is important and helps contribute to good usability.

The first rhetorical element to consider is audience analysis. A Web site's target audience includes the site's primary and secondary users. Primary users include individuals who will have a specific use for the content of the site. They may use the site for research, information, or to complete a task, such as purchasing a product. Secondary users include users who may have interest in the site, but not a specific need or use for its content. This might include managers, members of the development team, colleagues, friends, and perhaps

TABLE 2-1. User Analysis Matrix

User Group	Needs	Values	Characteristics
Primary			
Potential customers	Information on pricing, services, benefits, and points of contact	Accurate information, samples of projects, reasonable pricing	Any demographic, commercial focus, shrewd
Secondary			
Sales staff/employees	An informative site that provides reference material to refer to clients	Accurate information, useful sales tool	Technically savvy, knowledge of company operations
Competition	Information on pricing, services, benefits, and points of contact	Accuracy, collecting information to use for benchmarking	Web design consultants or businesses

the competition. Consider the competition when deciding what types of data should be disclosed or shared. If the site is being published on the Internet without any access restrictions, secondary users could include any random viewer. Although it is improbable to try to plan for anyone as a potential user, there may be important issues to consider, nevertheless.

Audiences are more complex than just a demographic group or label, such as "customers" or "teenagers." They have unique needs, values, and characteristics. Each user group may have specific needs or uses for a Web site. In turn, each group will have different concepts of value, credibility, and what they find to be most important. And finally, each group has its own unique characteristics, such as demographic information, experience, background, or abilities that should be considered in the analysis. Identifying these details is important to give developers a more complex sense with how users will interact with and use a Web site. Table 2-1 is a user analysis matrix that can be used to identify specific aspects of user groups for a Web site designed to advertise a freelance Web design and consulting business. Throughout this chapter, each worksheet will provide sample data based on a single sample project scenario.

Identifying the site's purpose is the next important aspect of rhetorical analysis because it serves as the foundation for defining specific goals for the site. The purpose addresses the development goals for the site. A clear statement of purpose serves as a focus for subsequent development work and addresses specific needs that users have. Answer these three questions to help write the site's purpose statement:

- Why is the site being developed?
- What response do I want from users of the site?
- What specific needs does the site serve?

LEGAL AND ETHICAL ISSUES

Copyright, citation, intellectual property, use of proprietary or sensitive information, accuracy of data and information graphics

CULTURAL AND SOCIAL ISSUES

Language, user demographics, cultural norms and values, use of color, writing style

USABILITY AND ACCESSIBILITY ISSUES

Physical disabilities, visual and auditory impairments, color blindness

TECHNICAL ISSUES

Browser type, operating system, hardware, software, Internet connection speed

FIGURE 2-2.   Contextual Issues to Consider in Web Project Planning

Based on the answers to the three questions, draft a written statement of the site's purpose. As part of this statement, make a list of related goals that will help achieve the statement of purpose. Later in the planning process, this statement and list of preliminary goals will help define specific goals and tasks related to the project.

The third aspect of the rhetorical situation is identifying contextual issues and constraints. These include legal, ethical, cultural, social, usability, accessibility, or technical constraints that pertain to the site. Some specific contextual issues to consider are summarized in Figure 2-2.

For example, a financial consulting firm's site would be ethically constrained to provide accurate information of services and prices. A computer business that sold new systems would be constrained by legal limitations with regard to licensing software. If either site had international customers, it would be important to be conscious of cultural issues that require the site to be developed in different languages or with alternate content. There might be competitive issues, such as not disclosing internal proprietary data on a public site. Make a list of all important contextual issues to use as a guide when developing content, graphics, and other aspects of the Web site. The information gathered during this initial analysis will help design a Web site tailored to the site users, their unique needs, as well as other important project constraints. Table 2-2 is a sample worksheet that summarizes the collective data on the rhetorical situation, including audience, purpose, and contextual issues.

Setting and Revising Goals: A Visual-Spatial Approach

After analyzing and identifying specific elements of the rhetorical situation, specific goals need to be developed to help define the overall scope of the project. Since the majority of a site is comprised of visual and interactive content, it is important to consider user perception in setting goals for development and identifying tasks. Developing goals using a visual-spatial approach helps designers focus on specific methods and techniques that

TABLE 2-2.   Rhetorical Situation Summary

Audience (target users)

Primary users	Potential clients, small businesses, and/or individuals interested in having a Web site designed for them
Secondary users	Other Web design businesses and independent consultants
Statement of purpose	To advertise a freelance Web design and consulting business that provides information on services and past projects
Goals	• Describe mission and purpose of business • Provide list of services and fees • Provide sample projects for potential clients to view • Provide contact information

Contextual issues and constraints

Legal and ethical	Provide legal disclaimers and copyright statements for samples Provide clear description of services and competitive fees
Cultural and social	Foreign language translations for international clients and offices Research related cultural norms and values
Usability and accessibility	Test site using set of established accessibility guidelines for users with disabilities Provide textual equivalents for audio and visual media
Technical	Develop site without the need for specialized viewers or software tools to maximize access to site

consider the unique ways users interact, search, and understand Web sites. Considering visual-spatial thinking early on in the development process has two advantages: (1) it saves time from having to change a finished design to better fit users, and (2) it establishes a precedent for incorporating visual-spatial thinking into future design and development tasks. As a result, effective planning should consider ways in which users think visually and spatially in a Web site to help focus and identify specific goals and project tasks.

Considering visual-spatial thinking during initial goal setting requires the designer to consider user behaviors and needs throughout the development process, which is a process is known as **user-centered design**. This approach is widely used in software development companies and government agencies to develop products suited to user preferences and habits. Usability specialists Jakob Nielsen, Donald Norman, and Robert R. Johnson stress the importance of focusing on the user throughout the process of planning and development of technical products and Web sites (Johnson S. 1997; Nielsen 2000; Norman 2002). Developing project goals from the perspective of the user will help maximize the usability and accessibility of the finished product. Setting goals from this perspective will help avoid costly redesign efforts in later stages of the product. Table 2-3 provides a list of specific questions to assist in developing initial planning goals based on Arnheim's five principles of visual thinking and the visual-spatial concepts introduced in Chapter 1.

TABLE 2-3. Planning Questions that Incorporate Visual-Spatial Thinking

Concept	Related Questions to Ask
Visual focus	• What should users notice first when visiting the site? • What aspects of the site's content and design should be emphasized for users to help them notice useful tools and content more easily? • What goals should be set to help account for these aspects?
Problem solving	• What problems might users have that site can help them solve? • What functions might users need to perform on the site? • How should content be organized to facilitate easy location and retrieval? • What development goals should be set to provide users with multiple ways of solving problems, finding content, and performing tasks on the site?
Contextual	• What methods of contextualizing content should be used to improve the speed and accuracy of finding content and performing tasks? • What goals should govern the development of content and context for the site?
Conceptual	• What shapes, icons, or visuals would help users understand key concepts, sections, or functions used in the site? • What development goals should outline the use of these important elements?
Wholeness	• What guidelines or principles should be followed in the design process to facilitate understanding and ease of use of the site? • What development goals will help outline and explain content sections and functions for users?

Review the initial list of project goals and use this list of questions to focus and revise them. The final written goals should identify specific tasks related to content development, structure, design, and usability—all important development phases of Web projects. Under each goal, write a list of specific tasks that are required to achieve the goal. Later, these goals and tasks will be incorporated into the written scope of work. Table 2-4 lists some of the development goals and specific related tasks for the Web design consulting business sample project.

Writing a Scope of Work

After identifying specific goals and tasks for a project, the next stage of planning involves writing a scope of work. A written scope of work documents the specific information on the site's anticipated users, purpose, context, and goals. It is a document that identifies the specifications for a project, including a project summary, technical requirements, design requirements, deliverables, schedules, due dates, and other issues. The scope of work acts as

TABLE 2-4. Development Goals and Specific Tasks for Web Projects

Goal #1	Describe mission, purpose, services, fees, and contact information.
Task	Write clear descriptions of each. Use headers and hyperlinks to outline content and provide links to supplemental information.
Task	Develop a consistent visual theme that conveys professionalism, organization, and minimizes flashy graphics for readability.
Task	Use icons to pair with headers of each section to help users scan and quickly locate relevant information.
Goal #2	Provide a section of the site that displays sample projects.
Task	Organize a projects page that helps users visualize range of projects that provides titles, short descriptions, screen shots, and links to sample projects.
Task	Provide a drop-down list of projects at the top of the page to allow users to select which project to view.
Goal #3	Provide flexible navigation for the site to help users locate information more quickly.
Task	Develop a main navigation toolbar that outlines the site content and major sections.
Task	Develop a keyword search feature that allows users to quickly search for answers to specific inquiries.

a contractual document between the developer and the client that outlines details and specifics of the work to be completed. It should be referred to at all stages of developing a site to ensure that every aspect of the work conforms to the project's unique goals, requirements, users, and needs. It ensures that the developer provides the client with a product that meets these specifications and helps to avoid costly assumptions and mistakes during the development process. Table 2-5 is a sample written scope of work that contains important details for the Web design consulting business sample project.

Some of this information can be finalized from the earlier analyses of users and draft statements of purpose, context, goals, client, or other source. The remainder must be carefully identified based on what it known about the project or received from the client.

The project title, purpose statement, and project summary provide an overview and in a broad sense, focus for the entire project. They serve as the project mission statement that describes the work to be performed. The audience profile succinctly describes the primary and secondary users, including how they will use the site and their specific needs for both content and function. Defining specific goals and deliverables is important because they dictate the specific tasks that need to be performed. Clearly written goals lead to clear and specifically defined tasks. Listing major content sections help the designer conceptualize how the site's content and functions will be organized on a broad scale, which will assist the designer in the structure phase of the project. Describing

TABLE 2-5. Sample Written Scope of Work for Web Projects

Project title

SpiderWeb Design

Project purpose statement

To advertise a freelance Web design and consulting business that provides information on services and past projects

Project summary

Develop a site with a professional and organized design to advertise a new cutting-edge Web design business. The site should provide information on services, fees, past projects, and how to contact the owner. The site should be easy to navigate, use, and read, while showing off the diverse range of services and products available.

Audience profile

Primary users

Potential clients, small businesses, and/or individuals interested in having a Web site designed for them

Secondary users

Other Web design businesses and independent consultants

Specific goals

- Describe mission, purpose, services, fees, and contact information
- Provide a section of the site that displays sample projects
- Provide flexible navigation for the site to help users locate information more quickly

Deliverables

- Fully-developed Web site delivered on CD-ROM
- Two progress reports with screen shots of work in progress
- Access to site online during bimonthly meetings

Major content sections

Home page, services, projects, fees, contact information

Functions and navigation tools

Main navigation toolbar that outlines major content areas
Keyword search feature that allows users to search site content

Content

Existing content

- Written descriptions to be provided by client
- Uniform resource locators (URLs) of past projects provided by client
- Company logo graphics to be provided by client

Research needs

- Collect benchmarking research on content, design, and fees by competition
- Test and verify past project Web site URLs exist

(Continued)

Technical requirements

Design platform: Viewable on PC and MAC
Screen size: Design for 1024 × 768 screen resolution
Browser compatibility: Latest versions of Internet Explorer and Safari
Graphic formats: JPG or PNG for screen shots
File formats: No special requirements
Development software: Any
Other issues: None

Design requirements

Theme: No specific theme required
Colors: Subtle colors with good contrast
Graphics: Company logo used in a banner on every page
Tone: Professional and organized
Other: None

Other requirements

Bimonthly phone meetings to discuss progress, ideas, and questions

functions and navigation tools that will be used will help the designer plan tasks to develop each of these requirements for the site. Including these elements in the scope will lead to less guesswork later on when developing navigation systems and other functions for the site.

Identifying existing sources of content gives the designer a broad sense of what content should be included, where it is located, and what content must be researched and added to the project in the content development phase of the project. In some cases, there might be a very specific need to develop a detailed content inventory at this phase. Chapter 3 addresses developing a detailed inventory of content sources, which will be based on the major content sections and sources of content identified in the scope of work. Determine whether a shorter summary of content or a more detailed inventory will be most useful during planning and select the method that will be most useful.

Defining specific technical, design, and other requirements is essential in the scope of work because they identify specific constraints that must be observed in the project. Technical requirements include client preferences regarding the design platform, screen size, compatible browsers, file formats for documents and graphics, and development software. The developer should consider the technological limitations of some computer systems that may be used to access the site. These limitations may require the project to be limited to certain system settings and features such as screen resolution, software plug-ins, Internet connection speed, and security settings. Design requirements might also include ideas about the overall theme, use of graphics, colors, and tone. Other requirements include miscellaneous requirements or guidelines that are unique to the project, which must be observed. These might relate to the usability and accessibility of site content. These issues are especially important in order to provide equal access to all users, including those with limited access or disabilities. For instance, many sites provide text equivalents for graphic content to improve accessibility for all users.

The scope of work must be clear in its description-specific goals and requirements of the project to ensure delivery of the product as expected. Although a scope of work is a written document, it may need to be changed as the project evolves. If any changes are required, they should be documented in a revised version of the scope of work to ensure the final product conforms accordingly to specifications.

Developing a Project Schedule

Once the scope of work is in place, scheduling a detailed breakdown of specific tasks is the next step. A project schedule, or timeline, provides details about what work must be accomplished, when, and what specific deliverables are required at various phases of the work. From the written set of goals, determine which phase of the development process each set of tasks best fits. In some cases, tasks may span multiple phases, so include them in each area where applicable. In addition to the five development phases, project completion is included to list the final due date and deliverables. For each task, estimate the duration, start date, and completion date. Then, for each phase of work, identify any deliverables, such as reports, drafts, mock-ups for testing, and follow-up meetings. When working on development teams, include a list of roles and responsibilities, and identify who will perform each task. Figure 2-3 provides a sample graphic timeline that documents tasks and deliverables, as well as duration, start dates, and completion dates for the Web design consulting business sample project.

This basic timeline should help the work progress more smoothly, since it provides specific tasks and dates for completion. At each phase, the list of specific deliverables serves as a reminder of what items must be submitted, reviewed, and/or tested after an entire phase of work has been completed. When developing the schedule, identify tasks that are dependent on other tasks when setting deadlines. One advantage of using a graphic chart is that it helps illustrate visually how tasks fit together in the project development process. Sometimes, it may be necessary to capture costs as part of the timeline, particularly for sites developed for companies. These types of costs are discussed in the Costs and Billing section of this chapter.

Developing a Site Maintenance Plan

Site maintenance occurs after a site has been completed, but it is important to incorporate these tasks as part of project planning. Since Web sites often change over time, it is important to address how a site will be maintained as it evolves. Site maintenance issues include specific tasks, frequency, resources, and responsibilities. These specifics are determined in part by the project purpose, nature of content, and specific requirements of the project. Considering these important issues will help determine the best methods of maintaining a Web site after its initial publication. In some cases, developing a Web site may only be one phase of the work on a Web development project. Most Web sites are evolving documents that need to be updated and maintained on a regular basis, depending on their purpose

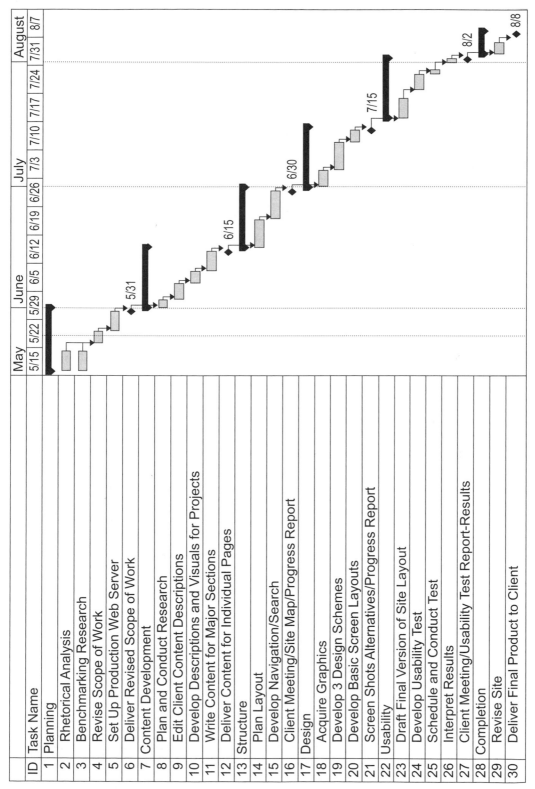

FIGURE 2-3. Timeline Worksheet for Web Projects

and content, and become part the next phase in site development. Planning site mainte-nance involves three steps:

1. Identify maintenance issues
2. Develop a site maintenance matrix
3. Write the maintenance plan

Identifying Maintenance Issues

The first step is to identify what elements of the site require routine updating and mainte-nance. This usually pertains to specific time-sensitive content, such as schedules, products, services, and so on. If the site provides a date of when it was last updated, users will expect that the content will be modified regularly. For sites with longevity that use multiple file formats for downloadable files or documents, these items may need to be periodically updated to newer versions. Of course, there may be other reasons for maintaining and up-dating content based on the site's purpose and other issues. Start working on the site main-tenance plan by making a list of content that requires periodic updating. Then, identify the frequency for updating each item.

Developing a Site Maintenance Matrix

The next step is to schedule each maintenance issue, identifying the task, frequency, time required, and resources required that make up the site maintenance matrix. Each mainte-nance issue or task should be described in sufficient detail so the assigned person can com-plete the work. Identify the page name and/or file name where the content resides. The frequency should specify how often the task needs to be performed, that is, first Monday of each month, last day of each month, and so on. Estimate the time required to complete each task. If the time varies for a task, try to quantify the amount or add explanatory notes. Identify all required resources, including equipment and the individual(s) responsible for the task, if working on a team. Table 2-6 is a sample site maintenance matrix for a company Web site that has maintenance needs for its news section, quarterly newsletter, and contact information. This form can be adapted and used in developing a matrix that can be used for any Web project.

Writing the Site Maintenance Plan

The final step involves writing the actual plan, which includes the site maintenance ma-trix and a few other important details. The plan should address details regarding the fol-lowing issues: purpose, content providers, responsible parties, summary of resources needed, site maintenance schedule and period, and any costs or service charges. If the up-dates are being performed as part of a contractual obligation for an external client, then it is important to specify fees for services and delivery dates for services. The final written plan can be in the form of a memorandum or a detailed report, depending on the specific requirements or needs of either the project or client. Figure 2-4 provides a sample site maintenance plan for the previous example to illustrate one way a plan can be written and organized.

TABLE 2-6. Sample Site Maintenance Matrix

Maintenance Issue/Task	Page/File Name	Frequency	Time Required	Required Resources
Update news section on home page	home.htm	1st Monday of each month	1–2 hours	Obtain news from public relations (PR)
Add quarterly newsletter to newsletter page	news.htm	Mar 1, Jun 1, Sep 1, Dec 1	15–20 minutes	Obtain newsletter from PR in PDF format
Remove newsletters from last year	news.htm	Mar 1, Jun 1, Sep 1, Dec 1	15–20 minutes	Write files to archive CD-ROM
Update contact information page	help.htm	As needed	15–20 minutes	E-mail from HR

SITE MAINTENANCE PLAN FOR ABC COMPANY

PURPOSE

The purpose of this plan is to outline the specific responsibilities, resources, tasks, timeline, and charges to maintain the ABC Company Web site.

CONTENT PROVIDERS

Updated content for the site can be acquired through both the public relations and human resources departments.

RESPONSIBLE PARTIES

The Web site technical support manager will be responsible for requesting content from the content providers, updating the Web site as outlined in the site maintenance matrix, and publishing files to the Web server.

RESOURCES NEEDED

The following resources will be needed to perform site maintenance tasks: computer, Web development software, desktop publishing software, and access to the company Web server. These resources and any additional equipment will be provided to the Web site technical support manager as needed.

(Continued)

SITE MAINTENANCE SCHEDULE AND PERIOD

The service period for this site maintenance plan is one year from the date the plan is signed and approved. The following matrix summaries the major maintenance tasks, file names, frequency, estimated time required, and resources for each site maintenance task.

Maintenance Issue/Task	Page/File Name	Frequency	Time Required	Required Resources
Update news section on home page	home.htm	1st Monday of each month	1–2 hours	Obtain news from public relations (PR)
Add quarterly newsletter to newsletter page	news.htm	Mar 1, Jun 1, Sep 1, Dec 1	15–20 minutes	Obtain newsletter from PR in PDF format
Remove newsletters from last year	news.htm	Mar 1, Jun 1, Sep 1, Dec 1	15–20 minutes	Write files to archive CD-ROM
Update contact information page	help.htm	As needed	15–20 minutes	E-mail from HR

COSTS AND SERVICE CHARGES

The charges for performing maintenance tasks and for the purchase of additional equipment will be paid out of departmental overhead accounts.

FIGURE 2-4.   Sample Site Maintenance Plan

Although this plan is shorter, a longer, more detailed plan can be developed based on the project and/or client needs. The site maintenance plan should serve as documentation of the specific requirements and guidelines that define the work, schedule, and responsibilities of each party. Addressing the six major issues outlined above will help ensure the plan is comprehensive and covers the essentials.

Planning Issues for Client Projects

A professional client project adds one more layer of complexity to the process. In addition to considering user needs, the needs of the client must be considered as equally important to the planning and development process. Working with a client is a two-way street: Clients provide designers with their needs and expectations for a product, and designers work to provide the client with a product that meets their specifications. Although the overall development process is the same, one important added role to the project is the client. The developer must clearly understand and incorporate the needs, goals, and design aesthetic of the client as part of the process. Often, consistent communication is essential to identifying and refining goals and needs. Below, suggested guidelines are provided on both designer and client perspectives that are important additions to developing and managing projects for professional clients. Specific questions to ask based on each guideline are provided to help designers and clients address important project concerns.

Designer's Perspective

- **Communicate on a consistent basis, using a single point of contact.** Early on in the project, determine rules that govern communication between the design team and the client, including the frequency, acceptable method, and contact person. Establishing an open line of communication and basic rules will make subsequent contact between the design team and client easier and help to avoid misunderstandings. Determine how often regular meetings or informal updates should be made to ensure goals and site work conform to the client's needs. Select methods of communication favorable to both the design team and the client. Identify a single point of contact on either side to ensure consistency and accuracy in the exchange of information between design team and client. These details should be added to the scope of work.

> **QUESTIONS TO ASK**
>
> Who is the design team point of contact?
> Who is the client point of contact?
> What methods of communication should be used?
> How frequently should meetings be held with the client?

- **Ask specific questions to help clarify client needs, goals, and expectations.** Often, after an initial meeting with the client after the project has been assigned, the design team is left to sort out the specifics. Because of time, budget, or sheer enthusiasm, the design team may be eager to begin work on the project. At this early stage of development, the team should develop a list of specific questions for the client to clarify any task or goal that is unclear in any way. This method of clarification helps avoid making guesses and misinterpreting the client's needs in later work. Asking questions for purposes of clarification is also important throughout the entire process for the same reason. For clients with broad ideas, develop specific questions and provide samples of work for their comment. For clients with specific ideas, create a log of comments and ask questions about any inconsistencies to ensure needs are met. Any clarification or changes to the project should be documented in a revised scope of work.

QUESTIONS TO ASK

What content will the client provide and when?

What file formats should be used for documents?

What preferences does the client have with regard to development software or methods?

Are there samples of work that help illustrate the client's design concept or ideas?

- **Explain design terms and concepts in the language the client understands.** The design team communicates with the client in a variety of forms, including phone calls, meetings, e-mails, progress reports, and other methods. Designers possess unique knowledge of methods used to develop and describe each aspect of a Web site, such as its content chunking, structure, navigation, interface, and usability. Often, they may use such terms in communicating with the client, which may be clear to designers but not to clients. Clients may interpret these concepts quite differently, or may be confused by them. Designers can ensure clients understand their ideas by explaining and defining terms and concepts in language that the client understands.

QUESTIONS TO ASK

What terms need to be defined for the client?

How can these terms be explained to a nontechnical audience?

What methods of illustration can be used to help the client understand specific concepts or terms?

- **Provide clients with visual forms of work to illustrate concepts.** The best way to help clients visualize a design, concept, or layout is to provide them with a visual representation, such as a screen shot or prototype of the site. A scope of work or progress report describes specifications, tasks, and goals, but does not capture the unique visual and spatial characteristics of a page layout, graphic feature, or design theme. When a client requests that their new real estate office site uses a buzzing bee in its design theme, a designer and client will undoubtedly have different concepts of its application in the site design.

QUESTIONS TO ASK

What samples can the client provide to help designers visualize their design concept?

What types of sketches or graphics can be developed and provided to the client to help them visualize and track progress on the project better?

- **Meet the schedule, deliver the product as ordered, but allow for flexibility.** The design team's credibility and success will rely heavily on its ability to meet the scheduled deadlines and deliver the product as ordered. For a variety of reasons, clients may request changes to the design, content, functionality, or other aspects of the site. Sometimes this might be a result of budget, time, technical limitations, or new ideas discovered during the project's development. As a rule, follow the guidelines for schedule and deliverables, but be willing to negotiate changes with the client based on some of these issues that may arise. Any modifications to the project should be documented in a revised scope of work to ensure the final product is delivered as expected. Remember the old adage that says the customer is always right.

QUESTIONS TO ASK

When is the final deadline for the project?

What deliverables are required and when are they due?

If changes arise, what methods will be used to negotiate and revise the schedule and project deliverables?

Client's Perspective

- **Establish clearly written goals, expectations, and outcomes.** Clients often have a concept of the site including specific features, goals, design themes, organizational ideas, and what tone should be conveyed. Designers may have their own interpretations of that concept and how to achieve specific goals. The most effective way to ensure clients and designers have a clear concept of the project, its goals, and other aspects is to write the goals, expectations, and desired outcomes in a scope of work, contract, or other written form.

QUESTIONS TO ASK

What are the project goals?

What expectations do clients and designers have for the project?

What are the desired outcomes and deliverables?

- **Review the design work and communicate on a routine basis.** Often, clients have other work priorities competing for their time, some of which do not intersect with the Web site project. As such, they may have insufficient time to review work on the Web project as routinely and thoroughly as needed. Sometimes, clients place their trust in the design team in lieu of reviewing their work consistently. Design teams may be so involved with the work itself that they fail to submit their work for periodic review and comment. Any of these factors can lead to a misunderstanding and failure to meet project expectations on both sides. The best way to ensure a quality product is to invest the time to review work and communication on a routine basis. Establish a preferred point of contact, regular meeting time, and preferred method of communication. Developing a detailed and clearly written scope of work, samples of designs, written reviews, and regular meetings all contribute to better communication between the developer and client.

QUESTIONS TO ASK

How frequently should work-in-progress be reviewed?

What method and criteria should be used to evaluate the work?

How should the review results be documented and presented?

How will action items be identified, implemented, and communicated?

- **Provide designers with a clear understanding of the company.** In order for the design team to develop a quality product, they will need some background information on the company—its products, services, and mission. Clients should provide the design team with marketing materials, mission statement, company profiles, descriptions of products and services, and other documents to inform them about the business. Without sufficient background, the design team may find it difficult to ask the right questions and tailor the Web project to the unique aspects of the business. This information needs to reflect the standards of the client's business and not the development team's interpretation or concept of the business.

QUESTIONS TO ASK

What information on the company or business will the client provide?

What research is required to learn more about the company and its competitors?

- **Request periodic reviews of design alternatives for pages and important graphics.** In most cases, periodic progress reports and design reviews may be scheduled as the project develops. Design is often the most difficult aspect of meeting the client's concept of the site, because it involves aesthetics, which are highly subjective. What the designer may consider elegant and professional, the client might consider flashy and inappropriate. Unless the designer is given a precise picture of how the site design should appear, it is unlikely the client will be happy with every aspect of the final product. To ensure the site design conforms to the client's overall concept, request periodic reviews at major stages of the project for page layouts, design themes, and important graphics such as logos and banners. A few scheduled reviews benefit both the client and the designer by ensuring work is progressing as expected. It saves time and frustration in last-minute redesign work at the end of a project. As a designer, invest the time in reviews to ensure a better overall product.

- **Consider the expertise of the design team in developing the site.** The client employs the design team to produce a product to a certain set of specifications. Although the client may have very specific ideas of its design, content, organization, and function, they may not always have the user in mind. The design team most likely has a wide range of expertise, including writing, programming, scripting, design, and usability. This knowledge can be useful in helping maximize the ease of use, accessibility, function, and subsequent maintenance tasks, when the site is delivered and published. As such, this expertise should be considered when developing the site's concept and making changes to the site.

Based on personal experience on past projects, each designer will undoubtedly have other important guidelines to add. The essential lessons learned here are not new lessons for experienced designers, but are often forgotten. These ten guidelines examine important issues from both perspectives that can help designers see the other side of project development. In combination with other important lessons learned from past projects, these guidelines can lead to a better working relationship with clients and a more successful and usable end product.

Written Documentation

In terms of written documentation, typically, clients will expect the same items discussed earlier in this chapter, including a written scope of work, project schedule, and site maintenance plan. In addition, clients will often expect an itemized billing sheet that defines how money and resources will be used. Often, these deliverables are compiled into a written project proposal. A formal written proposal helps persuade the client that the developer or team has a clear understanding of the project, reasonable expertise in performing the work, and is used to negotiate the project goals, scope, and cost. Written proposals identify the problem or need, detailed discussion of the project goals and features, qualifications of the developer and/or team, brief discussion of costs, and discussion of competitive benefits. Many good books on writing proposals are available that provide a detailed discussion of techniques and strategies, including the following:

- Richard Johnson-Sheehan, *Writing Proposals: Rhetoric for Managing Change*
- William Pfeiffer and Charles Keller, Jr., *Proposal Writing: The Art of Friendly and Winning Persuasion*
- Brian Holloway, *Proposal Writing Across the Disciplines*
- Richard Freed and Joe Romano, *Writing Winning Business Proposals*

Preparing documentation for a client project usually occurs in a series of stages. First, a scope of work and/or request for proposals statements are prepared by the client. These documents can range from extremely detailed to very general in their level of description. The information is often advertised in journals, magazines, newspapers, online databases, or on Web sites. Then, developers prepare and submit a written proposal that explains how the work will be done, their qualifications, and cost for completing the work. In turn, the client will review proposals and award the project to a developer. Then, the client and developer will meet to negotiate the finer points of the project and cost. The result will be a detailed and revised scope of work, schedule, and/or contract, which serves as the written plan that specifies work to be completed on the project.

Costs and Billing

Part of the written proposal is a section that addresses specific project development costs. Most Web developers use one of three methods of billing for professional projects: single-fee, per-page fee, and hourly fee. Each billing method has its advantages and disadvantages and selecting the right method will be important. A single-fee is a flat fee for all services to be performed, which can be based on the total number of pages, functionality, and other issues. The single-fee method often requires a breakdown of individual costs, so the client understands how the total cost is calculated. A per-page fee is usually a set rate for each page in the site. This method of calculation does not usually apply to sites that require the development of databases, since it would be difficult to assess the equivalent number of pages a database has. This method often requires defining what comprises a single page, such as number of graphics, word count, or other method of defining a page. An hourly rate is based on the total number of hours spent on the project, which folds in costs for materials and other resources. This method often requires a breakdown of specific tasks and hours required to complete each task. If the project entails site maintenance, a separate fee should be negotiated based on tasks or hours of work required.

Some factors to consider in determining what fee to charge include labor, equipment, and overhead costs. Labor can be calculated based on number of hours multiplied by rate to estimate a total cost per task. Subdividing labor into individual tasks or phases might be a good strategy for showing the cost breakdown. Equipment costs might include the purchase or rental of software, hardware, domain names, and basic supplies. For equipment purchases, specify which party owns the equipment after the project is complete.

TABLE 2-7. Summary Cost Worksheet

	Site Development (one-time cost, $)	Site Maintenance (annual cost, $)
Labor		
Content writing and editing	1,000.00	200.00
Design and graphic production	750.00	100.00
Usability testing	500.00	50.00
Publishing and uploading	250.00	50.00
SUBTOTAL	2,500.00	400.00
Equipment		
Software purchases	500.00	N/A
Domain name purchase	50.00	50.00
Rental (document scanner)	250.00	N/A
Supplies (CDs, disks, paper)	50.00	20.00
SUBTOTAL	850.00	60.00
Overhead expenses (10% rate)	335.00	47.00
Tax (7% rate)	234.50	32.90
TOTAL	3,584.50	502.90

Sometimes charging a lower overall rate can be favorable if the scanner purchased for the project is retained by the designer. Overhead incorporates the cost of doing business, including utilities, rent, and operating expenses, which can be billed as a percentage of total cost or at a specific rate. Be sure that what you charge is reasonable and competitive with the competition. Each developer may have a specified rate to charge for profit that may differ, but be sure not to exceed the competition by too high a margin, or you may risk losing the contract. Table 2-7 provides summarized cost breakdown for a Web project. It is important to capture both site development and site maintenance costs for projects that require both the development of a site and continuing maintenance. For projects that only require the development of the site, maintenance costs may be left off or negotiated with the client at a later time.

Specific amounts to charge will vary based on a number of factors, most important of which is geographic location. To determine the rate to charge, research what other Web developers and companies charge for services. Some sources include local advertisements, computer magazines, and the Internet. This information will help in determining what rate to charge in order to be competitive. Some clients will seek out other bids for the same job, so it is equally important to select a competitive rate. Developing an itemized list of costs is important to show clients precisely what they are paying for. In addition to a breakdown of labor, equipment, and profit, include the local tax rate in the itemized cost breakdown. Itemizing costs helps clients see the value of the work being performed by identifying how the money will be spent on the project.

ADVICE from PRACTITIONERS

Dennis Teske • Engineering Manager
Major Aerospace Corporation

Essential Planning Tasks for Client Web Projects

Establish clear, concise, and unambiguous requirements for the end product at the beginning of the project. Nothing leads to confusion on a project like requirements that are open to interpretation. There needs to be an established baseline for the requirements that are formally reviewed by both parties. It is natural that requirements may change during the course of the project, but with an established baseline, those changes can be more easily managed and understood.

Plan for Communication

Maintain open and honest communication. This can be in both a formal and an informal setting. Design reviews are a more formal approach, with storyboards and proposed layouts reviewed in a formal meeting prior to the contractor moving on to the implementation stage of the project. So many contractors want to dive right into the creation of the Web site without having a review with their customer. I insist on reviews to give me the confidence that they are working toward the product that I envisioned. It may seem like extra work, but in the long run it saves the contractor from having to do a lot of expensive rework because the contractor hasn't met my expectations, and it saves me from schedule delays and not being completely satisfied with the end product. Besides the formal reviews, we establish weekly program reviews in which we view prototype sites and look at program metrics to ensure that there are no surprises like schedule and cost overruns. These can take the form of a quick meeting or telephone conversation.

Plan for Periodic Review and Testing

Perform adequate testing of the product prior to its delivery. When I receive my product, I want it to be ready to publish on the server and be immediately functional. There is nothing worse than getting to the "end" of the program only to find that I am continuing to spend money and experiencing delays due to broken links, typos, and shoddy work. Working on a project is costly and time consuming—I expect a high-quality product at the end. It pays off for the contractor also, as follow-up and maintenance work are normally set up as a separate contract. If poor-quality work is performed on the original contract, I am going to put bids out to someone else for future projects.

Set Up a Payment Schedule for Projects

I would recommend having project milestones tied to a series of scheduled payments for larger projects. That ensures that it isn't an "all or nothing" payment that can be held up at the end due to minor issues. This also forces periodic reviews of the work as it progresses, ensuring communication is maintained and no one is going off track from what the original intent of the project was. It is beneficial to the development team, as they are not cash strapped for any extended period of time while waiting for one lump sum payment at the end of the project. It is also, beneficial to the team purchasing their services, as they are kept abreast of the nature of developments and can identify any issues well before they turn into full-scale show stopper problems.

Conclusion

Effective project planning is important to the development process because it helps designers conceptualize the site, and identify specific goals, constraints, and guidelines for the project. It involves writing clear statements of purpose, audience, context, and clearly written goals. A written scope of work serves as the designer's blueprint for how work should be conducted, whereas the schedule serves as a reminder of important deadlines, deliverables, and site maintenance issues. When working for a professional client, planning includes developing strategies for successful communication and project management. Professional project planning may also include developing a written proposal, scope of work, timeline, and discussion of costs in consultation with the client.

Chapter Summary

- Planning requires identifying the site's audience, purpose, context, project goals, tasks, scope of work, schedule, and site maintenance issues.
- Initial planning involves analysis of the rhetorical aspects of a project, which include purpose, audience (target users), as well as contextual issues and constraints. Drafting general planning goals is an important part of developing an early concept of the project.
- Visual-spatial thinking can help developers revise planning goals that are aligned with user perceptual needs and habits. It is a user-centered design approach that focuses on the user at every point of the design process.
- Developing a written scope of work is essential to project planning. It identifies the specifications for a project, including target users, statement of purpose, context, project summary, specific goals, content inventory, technical requirements, design requirements, and other important issues to guide later development and design tasks.
- A project schedule, or timeline, provides details about what work must be accomplished, when, and what specific deliverables are required at various phases of the work.
- Developing a site maintenance plan involves three important steps: (1) identify maintenance issues, (2) develop a site maintenance matrix, and (3) write the site maintenance plan.
- A site maintenance matrix identifies essential maintenance issues or tasks, page/file names, frequency of updates, estimated duration, and resources required for keeping a Web project updated.
- A written site maintenance plan should include the purpose, content providers, responsible parties, summary of resources needed, site maintenance schedule and period, and any applicable service charges.
- Professional client projects involve incorporating specific needs, goals, and design aesthetics that satisfy the client and users.
- A professional project proposal includes a written scope of work, project schedule, site maintenance plan, and itemized costs.
- Web projects are typically billed using one of three billing methods: single-fee, per-page fee, and hourly fee. Specific fees should be researched and benchmarked to ensure the use of competitive rates. Fees are calculated based on labor, equipment, utilities, and profit.

Exercises

1. Select a Web site and examine any pages to determine the site's purpose, mission, intent, and any legal or other important notices. Most of this information can be found on the site's home page or by following a link from this page. Perform an analysis of the site's audience, purpose, and contextual issues or constraints. Use Table 2-2 to record the findings. Afterward, return to the site and note any content or visual information that appears to contradict the findings.

2. Select a Web site that seems to favor the use of visual information over textual content. Then, using Figure 2-1, answer as many questions as possible about the site's design. Determine how effective the site appears to be in terms of planning for the visual-spatial thinking habits of its users. What suggestions for planning a redesign of the site should be considered based on these findings?

3. Based on the findings from Exercise #2, develop a list of goals and specific tasks that address the suggestions for planning a redesign of the site. Use Table 2-4 to record these goals and tasks. Verify that each list of tasks will successfully achieve each goal identified.

4. Research the Internet to find at least two Web sites that have a similar purpose to a current project you are developing. Perform an analysis of the rhetorical situation and identify specific features of the site that address specific user needs, values, or characteristics. Then, identify any specific features that seem to be used consistently between the sites.

5. Select a Web site that uses a page last updated feature or has time-sensitive content. Select a single page in the site and identify specific content that may require periodic updates or changes. Then, estimate the frequency and time required to update each item on the list. Develop a site maintenance matrix for your findings.

6. Review the list of guidelines for Designers on Clients and Clients on Designers. Working in a small group, brainstorm other suggestions based on work each group member has in working on professional projects, whether Web-based or not. Pick one perspective, either Designers on Clients or Clients on Designers, and make a list of the group's collective lessons learned.

7. Using the Internet, visit three separate Web development consulting business sites that list services and fees for performing site maintenance. Compare and contrast the services provided and fees charged. Based on the results, identify any consistencies or trends in how services are described or billed.

8. Research three different local Web development service providers in the local or regional area to determine what rates and methods of billing used. Then, based on this information determine what a competitive rate to charge would be for a 15-page Web site for a local business, such as a bookstore or specialty store. Calculate the average rate charged for single-fee, per-page fee, and hourly fee.

3

Planning ↔ Content ↔ Structure ↔ Design ↔ Usability

RESEARCH and CONTENT DEVELOPMENT

Learning Objectives

After completing this chapter, you will understand:

- Fundamental differences in writing Web content

- How users read content and think visually and spatially about content

- Guidelines for content analysis and conducting online research

- Guidelines for writing Web content

- Methods of adapting content for the Web

- How to develop a style sheet using Cascading Style Sheets (CSS)

- Important document conversion and file format issues

Introduction

The second phase in creating a Web site is content development, which includes researching, writing, editing, and adapting textual and graphic content for a Web environment. It involves interlinking and converting content into formats that can be read by Web browsers. Because of fundamental differences between printed documents and Web sites, the process of developing content requires much more than a copy and paste approach. Content development often begins with conducting research using a combination of conventional methods, and may extend to the Web to include search portals and online libraries. Due to the visual, interactive, and interlinking nature of the Web, users think visually and spatially about Web content, which is different from how they think when reading printed books and documents. As such, in their work, developers must consider how users read, learn, and think differently in Web environments. They need to account for the level of detail and size of individual content chunks as well as how to best link content in meaningful ways. Developers must adapt content for the Web, develop style guidelines and style sheets, thoroughly edit, and consider how best to convert content into readable and printable files and formats. The entire process of developing content for the Web is a complex set of tasks that matches our understanding of user thinking with carefully planned writing.

How Users Read Web Content

To write and develop useful Web content, it is important to understand how users read Web content differently than they do with print-based sources. Because of the unique nature of Web sites, users approach reading and thinking about them much differently than other types of documents. Web content authors Irene Hammerich and Claire Harrison pinpoint the complexity of writing for the Web, suggesting that pages must be written so they stand alone and are both flexible and readable across a broad user base (2002). Because users can search and browse individual pages in a site in virtually any order, it is important that each page can stand alone. Since users have different reading habits, browsers, and system settings, it is equally important to develop content that is also flexible to meet these demands as much as possible. The use of hyperlinks creates an added challenge for Web content writers. Hypertext theorist George Landow argues that forms of hypertext, such as Web pages, are often read in a nonsequential order, based on associative relationships between linked pages and content chunks (1997). The use of hyperlinks and navigation tools requires active reading of the text, where users must select their pathway through Web content. A challenge to writers is to provide meaningful labels for links and associations between linked pages and text chunks. The highly visual nature of Web sites makes visual content have a much more prominent role in reading and making meaning of content. Visual content, including multimedia video and audio, allows users to visualize concepts and interact with content on the screen. The unique aspects of Web sites require us to think, develop, and construct content in ways quite different from print-based text (Baehr and Logie 2005). This is precisely how visual-spatial thinking can help writers understand how users think and read Web sites in new and different ways.

Much research on reading user habits suggests users tend to scan, skim, filter, and raid Web sites to find relevant information (Baehr 2002; Johnson-Sheehan and Baehr 2001). They tend to dislike excessive scrolling and longer chunks of text. Their actions are governed by their visual perception and trial and error instincts. Users think differently when navigating and reading Web content. While these instincts govern their choices, such as responding to what is familiar or most visually distinctive, users can ignore instinct, such as avoiding flashing advertising banners or pop-up windows. Users have to weigh the importance of the need for information with the level of investment they're willing to make, with regard to time and resources. Users also have different preferred learning methods and reading habits that govern how they interact with Web content. Usability researcher Jakob Nielsen stresses the importance of user choice in selecting and customizing content found in Web sites (2001). Users learn from what they see in other sites, such as how to use a search feature or fill out a form. In turn, they tend to repeat these learned behaviors in other sites that use similar features. Because users read and think differently about Web content, the guidelines for writing Web content differ from writing printed materials.

How Users Think Visually and Spatially about Content and Context

Reading and making meaning out of a Web page involves active reading and thinking. Visual-spatial principles help explain user actions and reading habits in Web sites. Because of the visual nature of Web sites and their interactivity, users read sites for more than just content. They must think visually and spatially to understand the meaning of content as well as the context in which it is placed. Content is primarily information such as text and/or graphics. Contextual information includes elements that suggest the organization, grouping, and important concepts that outline the site's content. This includes the use of shapes, visuals, headers, navigation tools, and repeated elements. Several of Rudolf Arnheim's visual thinking principles, described in Chapter 1, help explain how users interact and form concepts about these elements, which guide their browsing and searching.

The principle *discernment in depth* explains how users perceive content and context in a Web site. At any one time, we focus on specific details of content or context. For example, when looking at a painting of a landscape, we can focus on the characteristics of a single object, such as a tree, or on details present in the entire landscape. In a Web site, users may focus on a particular text chunk, header, or graphic, but when examining the entire screen, each of these elements become visual objects arranged in a single space. Users might notice the background, overall layout grid, and identify general locations of graphics and text chunks. When examining the Web site as a whole, the site context is in focus. These contextual details tell users details about the overall layout and organization, but not information about specific text chunks. When specific content is in focus, users become aware of that element's specific characteristics. In doing so, they become less aware of overall contextual details of the site. Figure 3-1 shows a screen shot of the United States Library of Congress Accessibility page, which helps illustrate the use of content and context in a Web page. Visual elements, such as boldface headers and a separate bulleted list of hyperlinks (left margin) help users discern the context of information on the page. In the center of the page, blue headers are used to outline the different accessibility technologies available to users. Understanding the context helps users discern how content is arranged on this page and in deeper layers of the site.

Users actively seek out to discover elements that will help solve a specific need or problem, explained by the principle *fixation solves a problem*. These objects might include a navigation menu, hyperlink, form, search field, header, or specific text chunk. In Figure 3-1, users can identify the site's content, which is comprised of textual headers, content chunks, a picture of the library building, a keyword search box, and a labeled bulleted list of navigation links. Elements that help users discern the context include the use of bolded headers to outline content chunks, a blue banner to group the title and search feature, black shading to group the bulleted list of navigation links, and the use of blank space between elements to show relationships between individual elements.

Once users discover objects that are useful, they focus on reading and examining these specific text chunks or graphics and their details. This active examination helps users to determine the meaning, function, and usefulness of screen elements, suggested by the principle, *vision is selective*. Words, images, shapes, and icons all suggest specific meanings to users within the site's context. Users try to comprehend the meaning and function of shapes and visuals as part of this activity, which is suggested by the principle, *shapes are concepts*. Since context affects the ways in which users comprehend these elements, it holds equal importance to content in terms of user perception. Understanding the meaning or concept of shapes helps users make decisions about navigation and strategies for filtering and sifting through content on the site.

The entire process of how users discern, fixate, focus, and form concepts about site content is an attempt to construct a meaningful whole picture of the site. This activity is

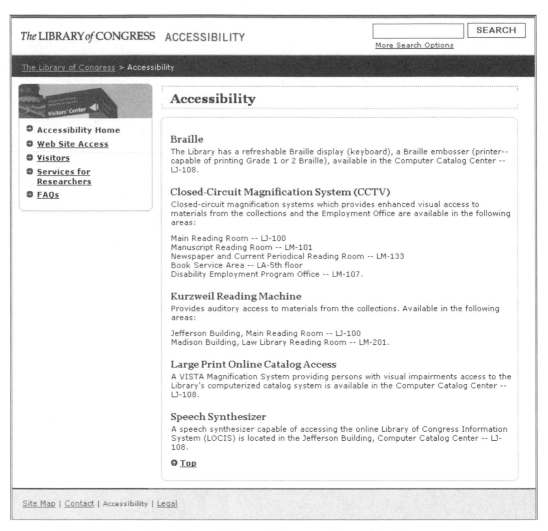

FIGURE 3-1.   United States Library of Congress Accessibility Statement Page

Source: Accessibility (Library of Congress), http://www.loc.gov/access.

suggested by the principle, *complete the incomplete.* Table 3-1 summarizes this process of how users act and think both visually and spatially with regard to Web content and when reading Web pages.

This process is an iterative one, as well, where users may need to rethink initial conceptions as they continue to learn and explore a Web site. Visual-spatial principles help designers understand the process by which users perceive Web content and interact with it. Users perceive content as more than words and images; they think visually and spatially about the meaning, location, and function of content to help act, read, and interpret content. As such, as part of the methods of developing and arranging content for the Web, consider the visual-spatial process of how users read and think about Web content.

TABLE 3-1. User Actions that Suggest Visual and Spatial Thinking

Visual Thinking Principle	User Actions
Discernment in depth	Examination of contextual details and specific content to help guide user actions and navigation of the page and site
Fixation solves a problem	Actively seek and select screen elements to help solve the current problem, task, or information need
Vision is selective	Close examination of screen elements to determine their meaning, function, and basic concept
Shapes are concepts	Analysis of shapes and other visuals to determine their meaning and function within the context of their location and the site
Complete the incomplete	Construction of a conceptual framework, or whole picture, of the site based on the analysis and perceived meaning of visual objects, their spatial location, and distinguishing characteristics

Content Planning and Research

Before the actual writing and arranging of content, often the first step of developing Web content involves identifying existing content and research sources of content to be used in the site. This includes making a list of content sources, such as existing documents, descriptions, graphics, scripts, and other sources. From an analysis of existing content, a developer can identify what content is missing and plan research goals to help fill in the gaps. This list will help in planning what resources, methods, and tools will help achieve those research goals. Developers will want to use a variety of research tools and methods, including databases, library searches, and online search portals to locate the content needed to develop a Web site.

Content Analysis

The first part of developing content is to analyze sources of content by performing a content analysis. The purpose of a content analysis is to look at the type, format, subject and purpose of each source of content to determine patterns or relationships between them. Usability experts Jakob Nielsen and Mark Pearrow, and information architect researchers Louis Rosenfeld and Peter Morville stress the importance of using content analysis as a method of organizing and evaluating content sources, from both development and usability perspectives. A content analysis helps developers to analyze the relationships between sources of content and to identify gaps that might suggest specific research needs. Sources of content to include in a content analysis might include documents, forms, reports, instructions, graphics, and Web sites.

To conduct a content analysis, write a one-sentence description of each content artifact, describing its subject and purpose. Identify content types, such as descriptions,

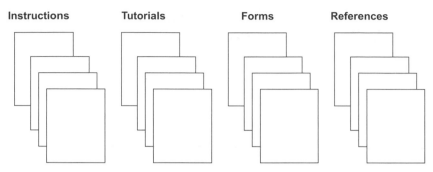

FIGURE 3-2.   Sample Visual Content Map

definitions, instructions, lists, and forms. Then, determine the different document formats that will be used, such as HTML, DOC, JPG, GIF, PDF, and so on. Examine the patterns or relationships between individual artifacts to determine how they might best fit together into a section or group. Group documents that are related based on their subject or purpose. Set aside documents that don't seem to fit in any group or category. Sort the remaining artifacts into an existing or new group. Label each group with a name that accurately describes each group. The main task is to classify each artifact into categories that will represent the major content areas of the site. Figure 3-2 shows an example of a basic visual content map that shows the sorting of content documents into categories based on their use, such as instructions, tutorials, forms, and references.

Continue to develop the map by labeling each document with a title, document format, and any other important details. Building a visual content map helps developers visualize important relationships between major content areas and individual documents within each section. Web researchers Robert Lynch and Sarah Horton stress the importance of creating these types of conceptual maps in content planning and site layout (2002). It also helps developers see content from a much broader perspective. This map can be expanded and developed as new sources of content are created and changes are made. It may take several iterations before perfecting the process. A content analysis gives developers a general idea of how to group and organize content into sections or functions, and how to plan the linking of individual content chunks later in development. Eventually, the results of the content analysis will become part of the process of developing a site structure, which is described in Chapter 5, Site Structure.

Planning Effective Web Searches

A content analysis helps developers organize existing content and helps them identify specific needs for researching and locating new sources of information for a Web site. As part of the content development, it is important that developers know how to find, access, and retrieve information online as part of their work. The Web is a virtually limitless resource of textual content, graphics, and scripts that can be used to develop and enrich a site's content. In preparing to conduct research using the Web, developers should identify key words and methods that fit specific goals or needs. For example, a developer may need a set of graphic icons and a script to handle form data. Or the developer might need to compile a list of sites or content on a specific subject. Regardless of the specific goals or needs, make a list of relevant key words for each source of information or element. Doing so in advance will save time in random guessing and browsing. Keep in mind these seven important guidelines to assist in conducting effective Web research:

1. Identify important key words and terms to help narrow search parameters.
2. When using search portals, select at least three to perform searches, since there is variation in indexed content on each portal.
3. Use basic keyword search to begin basic searches.
4. Use advanced search to refine the results of searches.
5. Use a subject index for serendipitous browsing, since it may help locate related subjects in the index.
6. Assess the credibility of online sources.
7. Make note of important bibliographic information for later citation and reference.

The next three short sections explain how to use some important online research tools, including search portals, subject indices, graphic libraries, and scripting libraries as sources to assist in locating sources of information on the Web.

Search Portals and Subject Indices   The most important tools to conducting online research are search portals and online databases on specific subjects. These sites use a variety of methods to index pages published on the Web into searchable databases. Search portals are easy to use, because users can type in keywords or questions into a text box, click a button, and receive a list of relevant results, or hits. Many have advanced searching options that allow users to include or exclude certain words, specify a location, language, site, or when the page the information was found on was last modified as criteria for the search. Figure 3-3, shows the advanced search page on the U.S. Geological Survey Web site, which allows users to customize searches based on phrasing, date last modified, and other criteria to help narrow the search results.

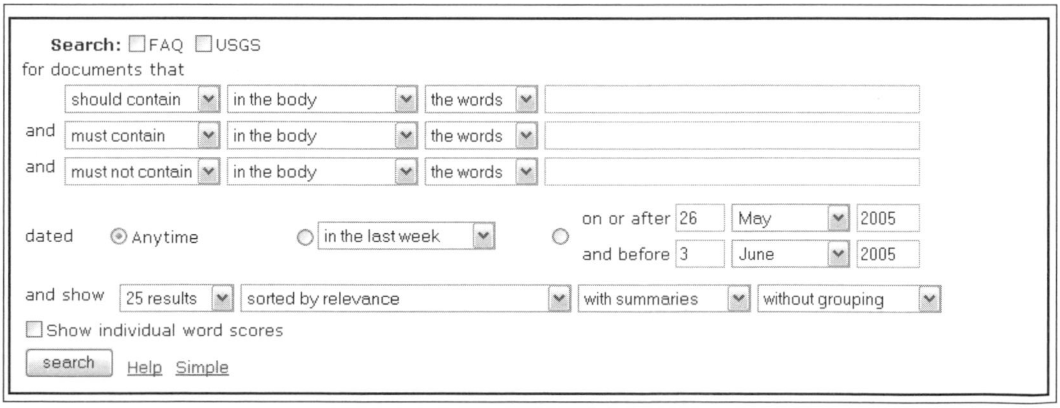

FIGURE 3-3.   U.S. Geological Survey Advanced Search Page

Source: U.S. Geological Survey, http://www.search.usgs.gov/search.

Most Web users are familiar with at least one search portal that they use to search the Web for information. Many search portal sites are available on the Web, some of which have more limited databases and more are available every day. When performing online searches, it is important to use at least two or three popular search portal sites, since each produces slightly different results. Smaller and more specialized search portals and sites can be useful in narrowing searches as well. Professional organizations and online libraries are two examples of sites that offer search utilities and databases on more specialized subjects. Often, they offer lists of other sites to visit that contain related information. From a Web design standpoint, two important types of sites developers may find useful are graphic libraries and scripting libraries.

Many of these search portal sites have a subject index, organized into general and specific topics for users to browse. Users can click on a general topic, then select from a list of subtopics that lead to a list of relevant Web pages and sources. Searching through a subject index may take more time but it can help eliminate random and unrelated hits generated by a keyword search. Figure 3-4 illustrates a site index from the Yahoo search portal, which helps users visualize how content is organized into topics and subtopics and helps them use it as a navigation tool to narrow their searches.

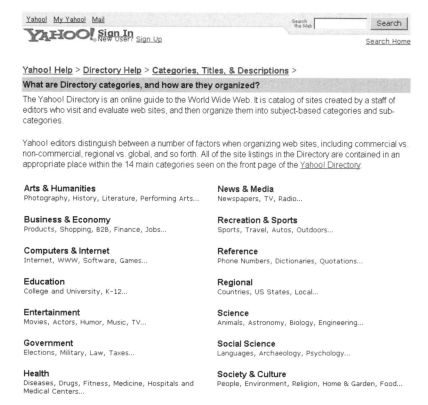

FIGURE 3-4.   Yahoo Web Directory

Source: Yahoo, http://help.yahoo.com/help/us/dir/ctd/ctd-07.html.

Graphic Libraries   Conducting research for Web sites is not exclusive to searching for textual content. Graphic content searches are often necessary to help developers supplement the site design or account for limited graphic support. Graphic library sites are collections of graphic content that can be downloaded or saved for use in Web design work. They offer collections of background images, clip art, photographs, buttons, icons, animations, and other visuals. Some of the more sophisticated sites allow users to generate custom graphic banners and navigation toolbar menus. Many of these sites provide indexes and search features to help designers locate specific graphic content. These sites range from completely free to pay for use. Many sites will offer some content for free and some for a fee. Some sites request a reference to them on the site that uses the content.

One common problem with graphic library sites is they often have a short life on the Web, so it is important to search for new sites periodically and update your list of favorites. Another problem deals with the large number and varying quality of graphic libraries on the Web. Any user can find these sites by typing in graphic libraries in any search portal for a list of hits. The tough task will be sorting through the list of results and refining search parameters to find sites that will meet specific needs, in terms of cost, quantity, quality, format, and usefulness. In some cases, CD libraries, graphic software, and Web authoring software may be helpful sources, as these have their own sets of graphics that can be used. For a more detailed discussion of types of graphics, graphic formats, and their use, see Chapter 7, Visual Design.

Scripting Libraries   Sometimes research involves finding the right script to create a dynamic action for a Web site, such as a scrolling banner or rollover navigation toolbar. Scripting library sites offer scripts in a variety of scripting languages that can be downloaded, modified, and included in Web pages. Many offer indexes or search features to locate specific scripts. These scripts can be used to create custom navigation toolbar menus, pop-up windows, advertising banners, animations, process form data, detect user settings, and other actions. Many sites provide working samples to test. They will often have descriptions of how to modify scripts. These sites are useful for designers that have insufficient time, resources, or experience in writing and testing scripts. Some scripts are available without cost while others require a fee to be paid. Some will require a reference to their site as part of the script. Some sites will even offer basic instruction on learning how to script. Learning a bit about scripting languages can make understanding and modifying them a bit easier. Scripting libraries usually have a longer shelf life on the Web than graphic libraries. Use search portals and keyword searches to find scripting libraries. One drawback is that some sites fail to guarantee the functionality of scripts and may have scripts that fail to work properly. Another problem deals with the compatibility of scripts with the designer's operating system, Web development software, browser, or other system settings. Before using a script, check it for compatibility and test it thoroughly for functionality.

Credibility and Permissions   Part of content development and research involves determining the credibility of sources and citing sources where appropriate. Determining the credibility of Web content is still a difficult task, due to the newness of the Web and the lack of formally established standards or guidelines. Web credibility expert B. J. Fogg suggests that credibility on the Web involves perceived trustworthiness and expertise of the site's contributors, content, and design (2003). As a result, Web credibility often involves considering many factors, which include the following:

- Date (dates of last update, date on page)
- Affiliation (reputation of the organization, company, or agency responsible for the content)
- Style (level of editing, language and grammar use, clean design)
- Content (accuracy, correctness, completeness)
- Functionality (how well forms, links, and other interactive features work)

While not all of this information may be available on every Web site, gather as much of it as possible in assessing the overall credibility of the information found, whether the intent is to incorporate content or merely link to it in the site. Then, based on that information, determine whether it should be included in the site. Content providers, clients, and experts on specific subjects might help make determinations on credibility and use of specific content. Their input can be valuable in the assessment process as well.

Acquiring permissions for online content is important since graphic and textual content used on Web sites is often copyrighted and requires specific citation for its use. In terms of intellectual property rights, the same basic rules for print-based citation apply to Web content. For graphic content, many sites have specific citation requirements posted on their sites that govern their use. For example, graphic and scripting libraries often require users to post a link on their site and appropriate reference citation back to the site from which the content has been obtained. Intellectual property rights apply to both graphic and textual content. As a rule of thumb, to ensure appropriate citation is used, be sure to read a site's permissions statement or rules of use before incorporating text, graphics, or scripts in site content. It is important to note that even though graphics may be easily downloaded, they may only be used if proper permissions are obtained and paid for in accordance with a site's legal statements.

ADVICE from PRACTITIONERS

Developing Content for Client Projects: What to Ask and What to Know

Brian Jordan • Project Manager & Chemist
Civilian Government Agency

These are some important issues when dealing with content issues and contractors hired to produce Web site projects, based on my experience:

- Clients should prepare a plan to supply content to the team for the project.
- Know what you are expecting from the contractor. If possible, find examples of projects you feel presented similar content effectively or projects that may have similar audiences.
- Spend the time to develop your big picture goal for the project, including a concise statement of those goals.
- Take time to think about who the ultimate audience is for the project and be willing to listen to other suggestions about who that audience might be.
- Take the time to listen to new ideas or concerns raised by the development team. This is why you hire a contractor: to improve on your ideas and ultimately develop a better project.

Try to obtain as much upfront information related to audience and ultimate functionality from the client as possible and leave lesser issues, such as the background color and home page logo, for after a site concept or theme has been developed. Then, put together a well thought out storyboard presentation for the client's review with options from which to choose. Try to give the client options to choose from related to content, layout, and functionality. This may be the only time you get with the client prior to a draft version of the site, so make this an organized and useful part of your work. Attempt to get a definitive decision on content, layout, and functionality prior to starting the actual development and coding of pages.

Avoid needing to dismantle a fully developed product that does not meet the client's goal. Ultimately the choice is the client's and one design may provide an inherent benefit to the client that has not been previously discussed or presented to the development team. For example, a project that quickly lays out a contact list or registration form may be preferable to a very detailed home page with many layers of complexity.

One final piece of advice: Make sure the goal is satisfied when the project is complete. Nothing is more frustrating to a client than a partially completed project with a few bells and whistles that took most of the time and resources, with part of the goal missing.

Guidelines for Writing Web Content

Based on what is known about user learning preferences, reading habits, and thinking, we can develop and apply strategies for writing Web content to fit these needs. Developing and writing content for the Web involves different strategies and methods, but just like print-based documents, it must be written, edited, and rewritten until it suits the information needs and habits of site users. Web content is composed of textual and graphic elements. The basic written unit of content on a Web page is a **content chunk**, which can be a stand-alone unit of text and/or graphics. An individual content chunk is often separated from others by spacing, graphic elements, or by its arrangement on a page. Content chunks can vary in size, depending on their purpose, screen layout, or specific project style guidelines. Generally, an acceptable size for a content chunk can range from five to seven wrapping lines of text. If a chunk includes graphics, it could be as large as what fits on the user's screen.

Often, content chunks are written and then pieced together into individual Web pages. Content chunks are arranged onto individual pages and interconnected using hyperlinks. Sometimes, content chunks are stored in database tables, and based on user input, page content is constructed dynamically. For example, a keyword search sends the request to a database that retrieves related content and hyperlinks. The goal of content chunking is not to reduce everything to a short description but rather to write content so it is more readable and more likely to be read. Since content chunks tend to be shorter than essays or paragraphs, writers must not compromise detail or thoroughness when writing them. Writing content chunks requires saying more with less. The process of writing effective chunks requires succinct, detailed writing and careful editing. The content chunk is the basic unit of Web pages, not the paragraph or essay as in printed books and documents, for a variety of reasons:

- Users prefer reading shorter passages on Web pages.
- Content chunks are read and put together based on how they relate.
- Web content suggests immediacy to users.
- Reading onscreen may cause eye strain.

One unique characteristic of Web content that helps users create meaningful associations between chunks is the use of hyperlinks, which is discussed in the next section. Hyperlinks provide instant access to other related content chunks. They create a sense of immediacy and suggest meaningful relationships between linked chunks. Smaller linked content chunks tend to fit better with the information needs and expectations of Web site users. Since eye strain is often a complaint of frequent computer use, reading information on bright computer screens over time can account for limited attention spans. This does not mean that level of detail needs to be compromised in favor of smaller chunk size. Interconnecting chunks with hyperlinks can accommodate more detailed and lengthy descriptions than most printed books. In addition to these suggestions, Figure 3-5 provides some important guidelines for writing Web content based on user needs.

These general writing guidelines, based on the visual-spatial approach, focus on writing content chunks that best fit the users' reading habits. As part of writing content, be certain to follow proper use of grammar and punctuation as with any printed document.

- Provide a summary of important points first, followed by specifics. Web readers tend to look for results up front, and then search for related detail.
- Organize content chunks into main content areas or categories that might serve as navigation links, headers, or sections of the Web site, to provide the basic context and organization of site content and functions.
- Identify each content chunk or sections of chunks with meaningful headers to match users' habits of scanning documents.
- Rewrite and reformat paragraphs that use lists into bulleted or numbered lists, which help users easily visualize major points and concepts.
- Reduce the size of individual chunks to fit on a single screen when possible, since users tend to prefer less scrolling and shorter documents. This amount should be determined by the screen resolution settings for which the site is designed (see Chapters 7 and 8 for a discussion of this).
- Break up larger chunks into smaller ones that can be linked using hyperlinks. Providing "more information" links with summaries is one good method.
- Provide links to individual sections on longer pages with horizontal scrolling to aid users in searching and navigating more quickly.
- Develop a style sheet that establishes the sizes, font faces, colors, and spacing for headers, chunks, graphics and text. Consistency in the visual style of text chunks helps establish credibility with users.
- Consider the site's primary audience, purpose, and contextual issues in writing content chunks.
- Edit content with a careful eye since every mistake can compromise a work's credibility.

FIGURE 3-5. Writing Guidelines for Web Content

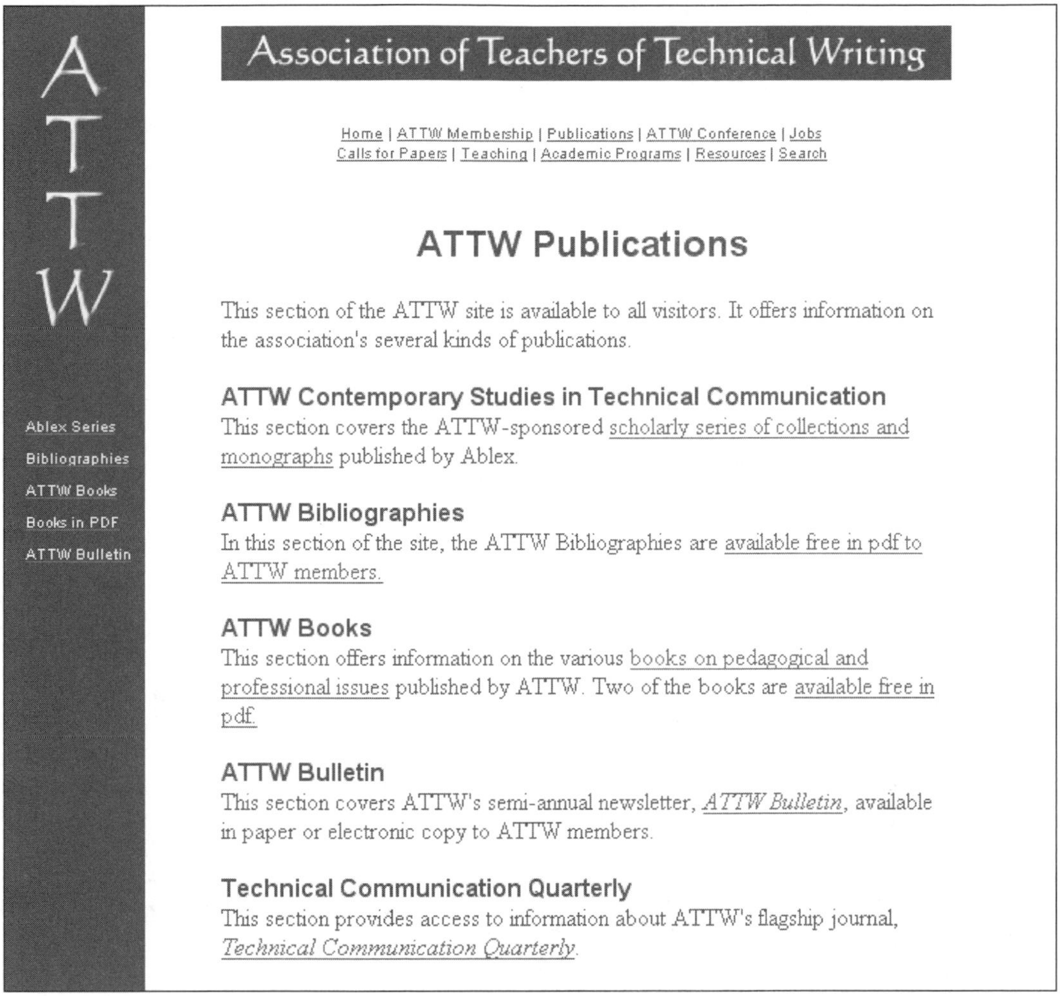

Association of Teachers of Technical Writing

Home | ATTW Membership | Publications | ATTW Conference | Jobs
Calls for Papers | Teaching | Academic Programs | Resources | Search

ATTW Publications

This section of the ATTW site is available to all visitors. It offers information on the association's several kinds of publications.

ATTW Contemporary Studies in Technical Communication

This section covers the ATTW-sponsored scholarly series of collections and monographs published by Ablex.

ATTW Bibliographies

In this section of the site, the ATTW Bibliographies are available free in pdf to ATTW members.

ATTW Books

This section offers information on the various books on pedagogical and professional issues published by ATTW. Two of the books are available free in pdf.

ATTW Bulletin

This section covers ATTW's semi-annual newsletter, *ATTW Bulletin*, available in paper or electronic copy to ATTW members.

Technical Communication Quarterly

This section provides access to information about ATTW's flagship journal, *Technical Communication Quarterly*.

Sidebar navigation:
Ablex Series
Bibliographies
ATTW Books
Books in PDF
ATTW Bulletin

FIGURE 3-6. The Association of Teachers of Technical Writing Publications Page

Source: ATTW – ATTW Publications, http://www.attw.org/publications/ATTWPubs.asp.

Well-written chunks will help make the process of linking them together in meaningful ways much easier. Figure 3-6, a screenshot of the Publications Page of the Association of Teachers of Technical Writing Web site, http://www.attw.org, uses many of the writing guidelines for Web content.

Creating Effective Hyperlinks

Virtually all Web content deals with the use of hyperlinks to create a meaningful structure of content used in the site. Hyperlinks are clickable text or visuals that link two related pages, content chunks, or headers. They can perform functions, such as sending email, form data, or other information to the server. As such, they are integral to both content development and navigation in Web sites. Hyperlinks serve important functions when used to link Web content, which include the following:

- Outline content
- Show relationships
- Suggest concepts
- Indicate function

Hyperlinks also outline content by serving as headers, labels, or navigation. Ideally, a hyperlink label should adequately describe the content to which it points or links and be meaningful within the context used. The often used label "click here" in most cases leaves the user to determine its meaning from the context in which it is used. Groups of hyperlinks work together to outline content when they serve as an index, site map, or navigation menu. Hyperlinks show relationships between the content chunk and page in which they are found and the chunk or page to which they link. This is precisely why using a meaningful label is important: It suggests the relatedness of two chunks or pages. A poor, yet often used, label to connect content chunks is the "click here" link. Some variations include "read more" or "next page." In many cases, these labels suggest a function but fail to suggest a meaningful relationship between pages or chunks. Using key words that give a reader a sense of the subject of the linked material would be a more effective approach.

One unique aspect of Web pages and hypertexts is that they sequence or link documents associatively. When a user sees the link label "definition of hypertext" he expects the content or page it links to will have associated or related information. Hyperlinks suggest concepts or relationships visually just as icons, shapes, and graphics do. The link suggests whether it will lead to another page, definition, or perform a function, such as submitting a response through a form. Its distinguishing visual qualities, textual label, or spatial arrangement might help users determine the concept it represents. Figure 3-7 shows an example of

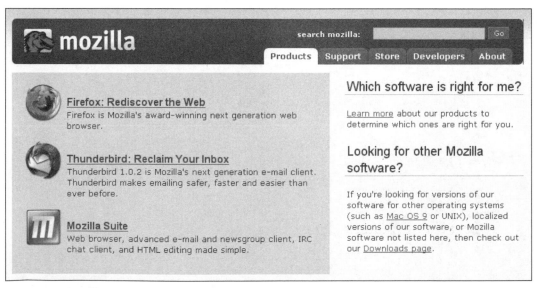

FIGURE 3-7.   The Mozilla Products Page

Source: Mozilla Products, http://www.mozilla.org/products.

FIGURE 3-8. The U.S. Library of Congress Site Image Map

Source: Library of Congress, http://www.loc.gov.

the Mozilla Web site Products page, which uses hyperlinks to outline content and show relationships between chunks and pages. Across the right-hand top margin, textual hyperlinks are used to outline the site content, that is, products, support, store, developers, about. On the left-hand side of the page, icons, hyperlinked headers, and short text descriptions outline the different product sections of the site. Hyperlinks embedded in paragraphs in the right margin suggest a relationship between the paragraph and the linked pages.

For example, a hyperlink of a shopping cart icon labeled "my items" might suggest the overall concept and use of such a feature. In a similar way, a hyperlink can indicate its function. It tells users something about the concept or meaning, but these characteristics also can indicate the function the link serves. That function can be one of many things, including displaying another page or chunk, sending feedback or form data, or opening a new page or window. Concept is a bit different from function in that it suggests a hyperlink's meaning whereas function suggests what type of action the link performs. The Library of Congress Web site, shown in Figure 3-8, pairs graphic images with text descriptors to suggest concepts and themes for major sections of the online collection. An image of global maps is paired with the "Global Gateway" link and is used to suggest the global or multicultural resource section of the site. Pairing textual links with visuals sometimes helps users understand the concept better.

Hyperlinks should be used for a specific purpose and to enhance the readability of a page or chunk. Using too many hyperlinks in a chunk or page can confuse readers, especially if every other word is a link. Consider carefully their use and function before using them. When developing hyperlinks for use in Web content, keep in mind these important guidelines:

- Group hyperlinks to outline site content and functions.
- Choose meaningful labels that suggest the relatedness of chunks.
- Use icons, shapes, and graphics that suggest meaningful concepts.
- Ensure hyperlinks make sense in the context of the page or content chunk.
- Use hyperlinks for a specific purpose and to enhance readability, not impede it.

Hyperlinks are often grouped and used in toolbars, menus, site maps, and indexes to create navigation systems to aid searching and browsing. For a more detailed discussion of how hyperlinks are used to develop more complex navigation tools and menus, see Chapter 6, Navigation Systems.

Adapting Content for the Web

Once content is written for a Web site, it must be adapted for optimum viewing and reading. Adapting content for the Web involves three major steps: developing a style sheet for textual content, editing the content, and converting documents to appropriate file formats. Style sheets establish consistent style guidelines for content in a site. Consistency leads to better understanding and greater credibility. Thorough editing is essential to credibility, but is also the mark of good writing. Web content should be edited with the same rigor as any printed book or document to ensure its usefulness. File conversion and formatting is important so that the document can be displayed in electronic formats that can be read in Web browsers. While most Web content will be in one format, such as Hypertext Markup Language (HTML), there may be specific reasons for using alternate formats to satisfy a certain purpose or user population.

Step 1: Create a Style Sheet

Style sheets comprise a list of rules that govern the consistent markup, format, and display of textual and graphic content for a Web site. They include any internal style guidelines unique to the organization and/or project, such as fonts, colors, alignments, spacing, size, and formatting. Using consistent styles throughout a document will make it more professional, readable, and usable. Table 3-2 identifies some important stylistic elements that should be considered in Web development. The associated HTML tags used for each style element are placed in parenthesis. HTML tags are discussed in detail in Chapter 4, Document Markup and Publishing.

Cascading Style Sheets (CSS)

In many Web sites, style sheets are developed using Cascading Style Sheets (CSS) to single-source and apply consistent styles both globally and locally in a site. CSS is a scripting language that can be used develop style sheets and position elements consistently in Web pages. As such, CSS can be used to control both visual styles and spatial arrangement of elements on a page. It sets visual styles for text, hyperlinks, backgrounds, tables, and graphics. CSS can also be used to position and add space around elements by specifying margins, borders, and padding around text, graphics, and entire sections of documents. So, using CSS can help developers create style sheets and layouts that fit their visual-spatial goals in the development and layout of pages. For example, CSS could be used to create visual contrast around a set of navigation links by setting the background color, spacing, and text colors to emphasize these elements. Table 3-3 provides some sample selectors, values, and examples are provided as an introduction to basic style and formatting elements used in scripting basic CSS.

While this is only a short list of some CSS selectors, properties, values, and examples, it provides some basic elements that can be used to create simple styles. A variety of books and Web sites are available that provide comprehensive coverage of CSS scripting. Along with a good reference guide and additional practice, developers can improve their scripting skills to develop more complex style sheets.

Specific rules apply to the syntax and scripting of CSS. Lines of CSS can be applied to specific HTML tags and document divisions or sections. For more information on using

TABLE 3-2. Style Elements Used in Web Development

Style Element	Style Specification
Font faces, sizes, and colors	
Heading level 1 (H1)	Arial, 18 point, red
Heading level 2 (H2)	Times New Roman, 14 point, black
Textual content (P)	Times New Roman, 12 point, black
Text-based hyperlinks (A)	
Unvisited links	Times New Roman, 12 point, red, underlined
Visited links	Times New Roman, 12 point, purple, underlined
Bullet point symbols (LI)	Times New Roman, 12 point, black
Spacing and alignment	
Headers (H1, H2)	Left justification
Content chunks (P)	Full justification, left-indent 10 pixels, double-space between paragraphs. Content chunks will not exceed five wrapping lines.
Rules (HR)	Standard size horizontal rules used beneath major section headers, with 400-pixel widths.
Color use	
Background (BODY)	White
Table cells (TD)	Background cell colors, light grey
Bullet point symbols (LI)	Black

HTML tags, see Chapter 4, Document Markup and Publishing. Some of the rules that govern the use of CSS include the following:

- CSS uses selectors, which are often HTML tags, to which to apply styles.
- CSS uses declarations, which are composed of a paired property and value.
- Properties are specific style elements that are assigned specific values.
- Individual declarations are separated by a colon.
- Multiple declarations can be used in a single line of CSS script, as long as they are separated by semicolons.
- Each line of CSS is contained between braces (the squiggly variety of brackets).

The following line of CSS would apply to all paragraphs, or , <P> tags, used in a document. This line sets paragraph textual content to Times font, 12 point size, and black color. The P is the selector. The example uses three properties: font-family, font-size, and color. Each selector has a specific value, Times, 12pt, and black, respectively. Braces are used to start and end the series of declarations. Each declaration is separated by a semicolon.

```
P {font-family: Times; font-size:12pt; color:black;}
```

TABLE 3-3. List of Sample CSS Selectors

Selector	Values
Background color	Specific color name or hexadecimal value
Border	Specifies width (in pixels or inches), style (dashed, dotted, solid), and color (color name or hexadecimal)
Color	Specific color name or hexadecimal value
Font-family	Font face name, i.e., Arial
Font-size	Point size, i.e., 12pt
Font-weight	Normal, bold, bolder, lighter
Height	Specified in pixels, i.e., 100px
Margin	Specified in pixels, i.e., 10px; –left, –right, –top, –bottom, can be used to format specific margins
Padding	Specified in pixels, i.e., 10px; –left, –right, –top, –bottom, can be used to add spacing around elements
Text-align	Specifies justification for text, i.e., center, justify, left, right
Text-decoration	None, underline, strikethrough
Width	Specified in pixels, i.e., 100px

Sometimes, there may be a specific reason to use different styles for two different paragraphs. The example above applies the same styles to all paragraphs in a document. If there was a separate paragraph that uses Courier font instead of Times, CSS can be used to set a separate style class for that paragraph. CSS classes allow users to create exceptions or set multiple styles for elements such as paragraphs. Each class requires a unique name that must be used in the line of CSS and the HTML tag. The example below uses a class called "style1" to change the font to Courier for paragraph tags that use that class.

```
P.style1 {font-family: Courier; font-size:12pt; color:black;}
```

In the body of the HTML document, each paragraph for which the "style1" is used class would need it to be specified as an attribute as follows:

```
<P CLASS="style1">
```

Placement of CSS in the Document Markup   Lines of CSS script can be placed in three locations in the document markup:

- Externally, in a separate file that is referenced in the document header
- Embedded in the header between <STYLE> and </STYLE> tags
- Inline, where style information is placed inside individual HTML tags, as STYLE attributes

External CSS   External CSS scripts are lines of CSS script placed in an external file and referenced into every page to which the styles should be applied. External CSS files have a .css extension and can be created in a text editor or Web authoring program and saved. As an example, using the style specifications set in Table 3-2, an external CSS file has been created in Figure 3-9. While typical CSS style sheets can be quite lengthy and seem complex to the first glance, they start out simple and are typically developed one line and one element at time.

```
H1 {
font-family: Arial;
font-size: 18pt;
color: red;
text-align: left;
}
H2 {
font-family: Times;
font-size: 14pt;
color: black;
text-align: left;
}
P {
font-family: Times;
font-size: 12pt;
color: black;
text-align: justify;
text-indent: 10px;
}
A:link {
font-family: Times;
font-size: 12pt;
color: red;
text-decoration: underline;
}
A:visited {
font-family: Times;
font-size: 12pt;
color: purple;
text-decoration: underline;
}
HR {
width: 400px;
}
BODY {
background-color: white;
}
TD {
background-color: grey;
}
LI {
font-family: Times;
font-size: 12pt;
color: black;
}
```

FIGURE 3-9. The mystyle.css File

To reference in this external CSS file, a single HTML tag is required in the document header, as follows:

```
<LINK REL="STYLESHEET" TYPE="TEXT/CSS" SRC="mystyle.css">
```

This single tag can be placed on multiple pages in a site to reference in a global set of styles for the entire site.

Embedded CSS   Embedded lines of CSS script are placed between <STYLE> and </STYLE> tags in the document header. These styles apply only to the page in which they appear. The first three style declarations of CSS script used in Figure 3-8 are used below.

```
<HEAD>

<STYLE TYPE="TEXT/CSS">

H1 {font-family: Arial; font-size: 18pt; color: red;
text-align: left;}
H2 {font-family: Times; font-size: 14pt; color: black;
text-align: left;}
P {font-family: Times; font-size: 12pt; color: black;
text-align: justify; text-indent: 10px;}

</STYLE>

</HEAD>
```

Embedded styles can override or be used to add additional lines of style that apply to a specific page.

Inline CSS   Inline CSS scripts are placed inside individual HTML tags and apply only to those specific tags on the page. As a result, inline CSS scripts only appear in the <BODY> section. The first three style declarations of CSS script used in Figure 3-8 are used below.

```
<BODY>

<H1 STYLE="font-family: Arial; font-size: 18pt; color: red;
text-align: left">Heading Level 1</H1>
<H2 STYLE="font-family: Times; font-size: 14pt; color:
black; text-align: left">Heading Level 2</H1>
<P STYLE="font-family: Times; font-size: 12pt; color: black;
text-align: justify; text-indent: 10px">Textual Content</P>

</BODY>
```

Inline CSS scripts override any external or embedded CSS scripts by creating single line exceptions to those styles. They only apply to single tags in which they are used. The following rules apply to the hierarchy of CSS scripting types:

- External CSS scripts are overridden by Embedded CSS scripts
- Embedded CSS scripts are overridden by Inline CSS scripts

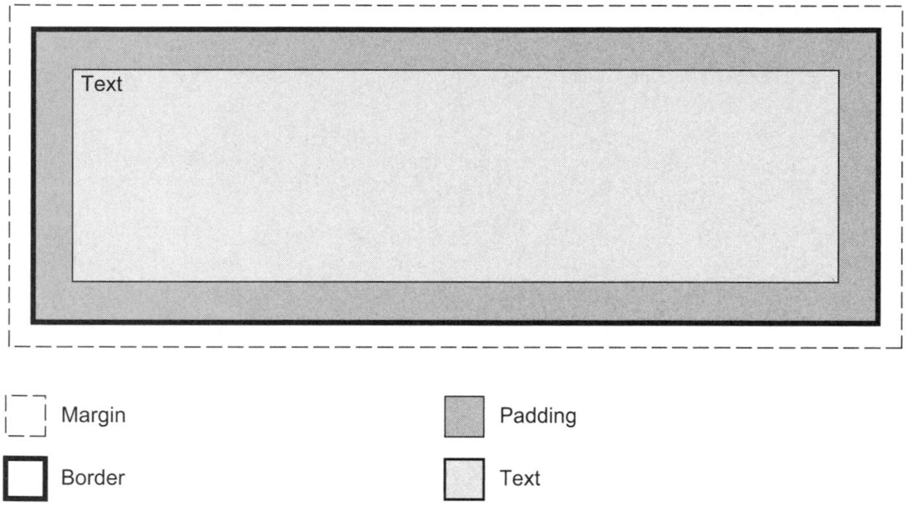

FIGURE 3-10.   CSS Box Model

Positional CSS   Cascading Style Sheets can also be used for creating positional page layouts using document divisions or sections, using the HTML <DIV> tag, and specific positional elements. Positional elements in CSS include margin, border, and padding. These elements comprise what is commonly known in CSS as the box model, shown in Figure 3-10.

The margin is the invisible border around an element, such as a paragraph <P>, document section <DIV>, or selection of text. The border is the visible border around an element, inside the margin. Padding is the spacing inside the border, between the border and the element itself. CSS script can be used to specify the height and width of elements as well as the amount of space around them. Figure 3-11 shows an example of using a single line of CSS to format a paragraph of text. It sets 20 pixels of left-margin spacing, places a 2-pixel, solid black border around the paragraph, and 10 pixels of spacing between the border and the paragraph text.

As with any markup or scripting language, the best way to learn more about using CSS to create more complex styles and layouts is to find a comprehensive guide and to practice. A quick search for "CSS reference guide" on any major search portal site (such as Yahoo or Google) will yield a number of Web site references. Three useful online references are

```
P {margin-left:20px; border: 2px solid black; padding:10px;}

    This is a paragraph of text with a 20 pixel left
    margin, 2 pixel solid black border, and 10 pixels of
    padding around all sides of the text.
```

FIGURE 3-11.   Using CSS to Format a Paragraph

Webmonkey (http://www.webmonkey.com), W3Schools (http://www.w3schools.com), and the World Wide Web Consortium (http://www.w3.org). Courses, libraries, and bookstores are other helpful sources to find guides to help learn more about using CSS.

Step 2: Edit Content Thoroughly

Take a detailed approach to editing each content chunk and page to ensure it conforms to the specific style sheet guidelines. Use the style sheet as an editing checklist to evaluate its use of style. Be equally detailed in editing the content, spelling, and grammar of each chunk just as with any printed document. Read through each chunk to ensure each is well written, edited, and uses appropriate style. Although the use of spelling and grammar may seem somewhat lax in email communication and some Web sites, a well-edited and written document still has much more credibility than one that is poorly developed. On the Web, remember the old saying that it is important to say more with less, whenever possible.

Step 3: Document Conversion Issues and File Formats

Part of adapting content for the Web involves deciding which electronic formats to use for optimum viewing in Web browsers. Converting content into electronic format will make it easier to cut and paste content chunks into Web page templates, layouts, and tables. Most Web content should be formatted in Hypertext Markup Language (HTML), a basic markup language used to structure and notate content so it can be read by a Web browser. This can be done with the help of Web authoring software, such as Adobe GoLive, Macromedia Dreamweaver, Microsoft FrontPage, or other programs. Some developers prefer to mark up content using HTML and other scripting and programming languages to manually mark up using a text editor or other program. However, if a Web site uses a large number of checklists, worksheets, fact sheets, or other such documents, it may be easier to convert these into file formats that are easily downloadable or printable. Some of these formats include Adobe Portable Document Format (.PDF), Microsoft Word (.DOC), and Rich Text Format (.RTF). For larger printed documents, such as long reports, consider using Web authoring software or a word processing program to convert them directly to HTML files or other formats. Table 3-4 provides a list of some common file formats and their use.

Select file formats that are most commonly used or provide documents in multiple formats to accommodate the widest user base. Some file formats are more likely to be used by the target audience and should be considered. Conduct research to see what software users have on their systems. If they have Microsoft Word, then they can view documents in that format (.DOC files). Using file formats that are readable with free document viewers, such as the Adobe PDF, can save users the additional expense of purchasing software. Provide a link to the free downloads on the site to assist users. If it is not feasible to use a single format for reference documents, provide multiple formats to accommodate users. Some sites will provide one version in HTML format and an alternate version for printing. Save text-based documents as Rich Text Format (.RTF) or as Text Files (.TXT), viewable

TABLE 3-4. Commonly Used File Formats and Use		
File Format(s)	**Purpose**	**Benefits**
DOC	Provide a document that can be viewed, downloaded, and edited.	Provides easy editing for users with the appropriate viewer or program.
GIF, JPG, PNG, etc.	Display textual and/or graphic content in a static form.	Allows users without specialized viewers or programs to see a snapshot of content.
HTM or HTML	Display content in a format viewable by Web browsers.	Content is viewable by any Web browser.
PDF	Display a printable version of a printed document.	Provides a downloadable version of a document that can be read with a free viewer.
RTF, TXT	Provide a text-only document without complex graphics or formatting.	Provides a downloadable text-only version with typically small file sizes for fast download.

by most basic word processing programs and text editing programs. These file types are good for basic text documents that don't require complex formatting, tables or graphics. Alternately, scan documents and save them as images, or graphic formats, which are viewable by most Web browsers, such as .JPG, .GIF, or .PNG files. Though typically used for graphic images, these file types serve as quick snapshots of documents as images. However, they have some limitations. For example, they can be difficult to modify and can have larger file sizes, longer download times, and poor readability. Let the purpose of the document dictate the format used. For a large and diverse group of users, provide two to three different formats of documents as a good rule of thumb. When providing a link to non-HTML document formats, be sure to include the file name, information on the program or viewer needed, and the file size. This will ensure users can properly download and view alternative file formats.

Conclusion

Developing Web content is a complex set of tasks that involves an understanding of user behavior and carefully planned research and writing. Research is a more robust task than a simple key word search, just as content writing is more than simple copying and pasting. Since users think and interact differently in Web environments, it is important to consider this knowledge in the development of Web content. The visual-spatial approach can help developers integrate what is known about user interaction throughout the process of researching, writing, assessing credibility, and adapting content for the Web.

Chapter Summary

- Content development involves writing content chunks, adapting existing content, and converting documents to Web-viewable formats.

- Users read and think differently in Web sites, which requires different approaches in how we write Web content. The visual, associative, and interactive nature of Web sites is one cause of this. Users have different learning preferences and reading habits that affect their reading and thinking.

- Users think visually and spatially when reading and interacting with Web content, which affects their reading of Web content. Visual-spatial principles help explain how users perceive and interact with content to focus, fixate, solve problems, and comprehend Web content.

- Conducting Web research involves identifying goals, searching methods, assessing credibility, and analyzing content.

- Writing Web content involves developing meaningful chunks of information that support user learning preferences, reading habits, and methods of thinking visually and spatially in Web sites.

- The basic written unit of a Web page is a content chunk, which can be a stand-alone unit of text and graphics. Developing effective chunks requires succinct, detailed writing and careful editing.

- Hyperlinks serve four very important functions in developing content: to outline content, show relationships, suggest concepts, and indicate function.

- Adapting content for the Web includes developing a style sheet, thorough editing, and converting documents to appropriate file formats.

- Developing a style sheet is useful for establishing guidelines that govern the use of consistent styles for Web content used in a site.

- Cascading Style Sheets (CSS) is a scripting language that can be used to develop style sheets, apply visual styles and create spatial layouts of Web pages.

- Editing web content should be as detailed as editing any printed document. Read through each chunk to ensure each is well written, edited, and uses appropriate style.

- When selecting file formats for documents, select those that are most commonly used or provide documents in multiple formats to accommodate the widest user base, such as .PDF, .RTF, .HTM. Let the purpose of the document dictate the format used.

Exercises

1. Select a commercial Web site that sells products and search for a specific product, such as a music album or movie. Keep in mind the ways in which users think visually and spatially in Web sites and review Table 3-1. Use this to evaluate how well content is written, displayed, and organized in the site. How well does it match how users think visually and spatially about content? In what ways is it successful and in what ways does it fail?

2. Using a Web project topic of your choice, perform a content analysis using the process described in the chapter. Carefully consider the relationships between individual content artifacts and sort them into major content areas for the site. Select meaningful labels for each content area and draw a visual content map to illustrate your work.

3. Use a search portal to find a listing of free graphic libraries on the Web. Select one at random and use the list of credibility guidelines to assess the site. Observe the dates, affiliation, style, content, and function. Then, determine an overall credibility rating for the site and list three to five suggestions for improving the credibility of the site's content.

4. Search the Web for a free scripting library site. Browse and search the site for a useful script you might consider using in developing a Web site. Using a Web software authoring program or basic text editor, customize and test the script. Based on experience with using the scripting library, would it be one to recommend to others? What aspects make the site easy to use?

5. Select a short article from a popular magazine or newsletter and rewrite it for the Web using the writing guidelines for Web content. Consider the use of visuals, hyperlinks, and styles to make the article both usable and enticing for a Web reader.

6. Find a Web site and analyze the use of hyperlinks found on the home page. Categorize individual links, or if more helpful, groups of links based on whether they outline content, show relationships, suggest concepts, or indicate a specific function. Identify any patterns or techniques used with hyperlinks on the page.

7. Choose a corporate Web site and analyze its use of stylistic elements using the list of style elements in Table 3-2. Examine a few of the site's pages to see how individual styles are used. Observe any inconsistencies and note any exceptions. What styles seem to work best in the site and which ones could use improvement?

8. Create an external CSS file to develop a global style sheet for either Exercise 6 or for your current Web project. Then, identify specific pages where exceptions to the global style sheet are needed. Use either classes, embedded, or inline styles, write lines, of CSS to account for these exceptions.

9. Select a government agency Web site (federal, state or local) and make note of the types of content (i.e., descriptions, definitions, forms, pamphlets, etc.) that are used. Also, make note of the file format types used (i.e., HTML, DOC, PDF, etc.). How effective is the organization of the content? Is it easy to discern the organization? Are multiple formats used for downloadable or printable documents? Are there clarity or readability issues with documents? List three to five suggestions to improve the organization, readability, and/or overall accessibility of the content.

4

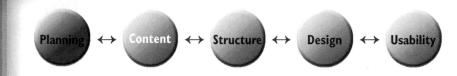

Planning ↔ Content ↔ Structure ↔ Design ↔ Usability

DOCUMENT MARKUP and PUBLISHING

Learning Objectives

After completing this chapter, you will understand:

- Document markup

- Advantages of using manual markup and Web authoring software

- The basic structure and syntax of document markup

- Basic HTML syntax and guidelines

- Availability of markup and scripting references

- Process for publishing Web pages and sites

- Guidelines for listing sites on search portals

Introduction

Creating a Web site involves more than researching, writing content, designing graphics, and using software. All content, whether visual or textual, must be marked up for Web browsers to display content properly. Document markup languages specify and set styles, formatting, hyperlinks, graphics, and structure. Every Web developer should have at least a basic knowledge of Hypertext Markup Language (HTML) to understand how to mark up content in Web sites. HTML is a markup language that governs the syntax, layout, and inner structure of Web documents. It uses tags that specify how content such as headers, titles, body text, divisions, hyperlinks, and graphics will be viewed. This chapter will discuss document markup structure, syntax, specific guidelines, layout, references, and publishing pages.

Some developers use Web authoring software that marks up content automatically. These programs allow developers to drag, drop, and place content on a blank page, as they would in a word processing software program, while the program generates the markup. These software programs can make the development process much easier since they provide graphical tools and buttons to develop page layouts, format text, create navigation toolbars, and add interactive graphics, forms and features. Some of these include Microsoft FrontPage, Macromedia Dreamweaver, and Adobe GoLive. Knowledge of at least one Web software authoring tool is useful in Web development whether a developer prefers using such software or manually marking up content. Table 4-1 lists some advantages of using each method.

TABLE 4-1. Advantages of Web Authoring Software and Manual Markup

Web Authoring Software	Manual Markup
• User drags and drops content onto pages while program marks up content for user	• Greater control over placement of elements
• Basic pages can be quickly created	• More customization options than most Web authoring software
• Built-in design templates and graphic libraries	• Can edit markup generated by Web authoring software
• Easy to convert electronic document and content to HTML	• User markup generally easier to read than markup generated by software programs

Learning a Web authoring software program provides an idea of its limitations and a clearer sense of what can and can't be done easily. Knowledge of manual markup might be useful in helping to customize a design that can't easily be achieved with a program. For example, manual markup can be used to customize designs and pages when limitations of Web authoring software have been reached. The needs of each developer and project will help determine the choice of development tools and methods. Often, using a combination of both methods will offer developers the greatest flexibility in Web site development.

Other markup and scripting languages can be used with HTML to add global style sheets and interactive forms and graphics to Web pages. Some of these include Cascading Style Sheets (CSS), discussed in Chapter 3, JavaScript, and Hypertext Preprocessor (PHP). A working knowledge of some of these languages can be used to create more dynamic features and interactive Web pages. Many useful books on a wide variety markup and scripting languages are widely available in the computer section of most bookstores to help developers learn these languages to add interactive features to their pages.

After pages have gone through markup, they are published or uploaded to a Web server, so the features, functions, and layout of pages can be viewed and tested. The publication process involves obtaining specific information about the files, folders, Web server, Uniform Resource Locator (URL), and selecting a method of uploading pages.

Document Structure

While site architecture governs the structure of content of a Web site, HTML markup specifies the structure, styles, and layout of individual content pages. These elements are visual-spatial aspects of document markup. The structure of an entire Web site as a whole is discussed in Chapter 5, Site Structure. A basic Web page has two major structural sections, a header <HEAD> and a body <BODY>. The header contains information displayed in the browser window and any embedded scripts that add styles or specific functions to a page. The body contains the textual and graphic content, including hyperlinks, which the page contains. Figure 4-1 shows a basic HTML document markup with these structural elements in place.

The first line indicates that HTML is used as the document markup language. Web pages should begin with an <HTML> tag and end with a </HTML> tag. Some pages use the

```
<HTML>
<HEAD>
<TITLE>Main Site Title</TITLE>
```
<!-- Cascading Style Sheet (CSS) scripts, some JavaScript function scripts, and other scripts may sometimes be found in the header section. --!>
```
</HEAD>
<BODY>
```
The body section contains the main Web site textual content, hyperlinks, and references that load graphics and multimedia. Various HTML tags are used to mark up and reference content and hyperlinks. In addition, some Cascading Style Sheet (CSS) scripts, some JavaScript function scripts, and other scripts may sometimes be found here.
```
</BODY>
</HTML>
```

FIGURE 4-1.   Document Markup Structure of a Web Page

<DOCTYPE> tag to specify which version of HTML is being used to mark up a page. HTML is widely used as the primary document markup language by Web authoring software. Extensible HTML (XHTML), a stricter version of markup and variation of HTML, can also be used for document markup and works better with some languages such as Extensible Markup Language (XML). While XHTML has been recommended for use by the World Wide Web Consortium (W3C), many developers still use basic HTML to markup basic Web pages. Many reference guides on both HTML and XHTML can be found in bookstores and online. The Document Markup Section of this chapter lists some useful resources and methods of locating such guides.

The first major structural section of an HTML document is the header <HEAD>, which contains the site title and any embedded scripting, such as CSS or JavaScript, used to format styles or add specific functions to the page. The <TITLE> tag specifies the main site title that is displayed at the very top of the browser window with the program name. For example, if Microsoft Internet Explorer was used to view the sample markup used in Figure 4-1, the title "Main Site Title" is displayed at the very top of the browser window as shown in Figure 4-2. The header section starts with the <HEAD> tag and ends with the </HEAD> tag.

The second structural section is the body <BODY>, which contains the main Web site textual content, hyperlinks, and references that load graphics and multimedia on the page. In

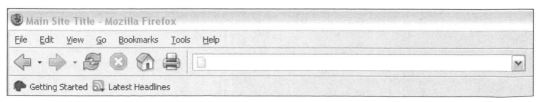

FIGURE 4-2.   Screenshot Showing the TITLE from the Sample Markup in Figure 4-1

addition, other scripting languages may be used to set styles or add function to HTML elements in the body. The body section starts with the <BODY> tag and ends with the </BODY> tag.

Understanding the internal structure allows designers and users to easily locate components of Web pages, such as headers, titles, functions, textual content, and other important elements that make up the page. It familiarizes the designer and user with the basics of the markup and scripting languages used to compose a page. Learning something about the actual language is one component of digital literacy. Since all Web authoring software uses existing markup and scripting languages such as HTML, learning them can be useful knowledge that can be applied when working with a broad range of software or text markup utilities.

HTML Markup

HTML is composed of tags that mark and reference specific content and major sections of documents. For most tags, an opening tag and a closing tag are required to indicate where the markup should start and end. For example, the <B> tag is used around text to create boldface and the </B> closing tag tells the browser to stop using boldface. <B> starts the markup instruction and </B> stops the markup instruction. It is important to use the closing tag that stops the markup instruction to avoid applying styles and markups to other content. For example, a section header on a page may require boldface text, but not the subsequent paragraphs of text. The following line of HTML markup makes only the word "Hello" appear in boldface:

```
<B>Hello</B> and Welcome.
```

Some tags have attributes that customize the style, such as the color, font face, or appearance of the text. Others have attributes that allow external graphic files or other Web pages to be loaded or linked to. For example, the <FONT> tag can be used to specify certain font faces, colors, and sizes. The following line of HTML markup makes the sentence appear in Courier font face and blue color:

```
<FONT FACE="COURIER" COLOR="BLUE">Welcome to my Web site.
</FONT>
```

Attributes are used with tags and each attribute has a specific value that is placed in quotes, such as a font name or color. For colors, a complete listing can be found in many scripting guides and reference Web sites by searching for "Web safe color chart" in any search portal site. Colors can be specified by name or hexadecimal value. Table 4-2 provides a short list of selected HTML tags and attributes.

These basic tags are useful to practice creating basic pages and learning how to use HTML markup. Once a developer becomes comfortable with these basic tags, it is time to seek out a more comprehensive guide. While this list provides only a sampling of tags and attributes, there are entire books and Web sites that serve as comprehensive guides on markup and scripting. See the last section of this chapter for some recommendations and suggestions for finding the right guide based on individual needs. Once the basics have been learned and practiced, the best way to learn more HTML is to find a useful guide and continue practicing.

TABLE 4-2. Selected HTML Tags

<HTML>	Initial tag that tells the browser the document is in HTML
<HEAD>	Marks the document header, which contains the <TITLE> and any embedded scripting
<TITLE>	Specifies the title of the page located at the top of the browser window
<BODY>	Marks the document body, which contains the textual and graphic content (and hyperlinks) used to compose the page. The BGCOLOR attribute used with this tag can specify a color for the page background. The BACKGROUND attribute can specify a picture to repeat in the background of a page.
<H1>, <H2>, <H3>, <H4>, <H5>, <H6>	Header tags that apply relative text sizes. <H1> uses very large text, while <H6> uses very small text. <H4> is set at the browser's default text size.
<B>	Boldface text
<I>	Italicized text
<U>	Underlined text
<FONT>	With the use of specific attributes, specifies font FACE, COLOR, and SIZE. FACE is specified using the font face name. COLOR is specified using either a color name or hexadecimal value. SIZE is specified as an integer, with 2 being the value of the default browser font size.
 	Line break
<HR>	Creates a horizontal rule, or line. The WIDTH attribute can specify the line length in pixels, and the SIZE attribute specifies the thickness, i.e., SIZE=1 is a thin line the size used in this table. The ALIGN attribute can be set to align it with a margin using LEFT, RIGHT, or CENTER.
<P>	Marks a paragraph of text. The ALIGN attribute can be set to align text as LEFT, RIGHT, CENTER, or JUSTIFY (full justification). It can also be used to create a double-spaced line break.
<A>	Commonly used with the HREF attribute to create a hyperlink to another Web page, as follows: <A HREF="home.htm">
<IMG>	Commonly used with the SRC attribute to display a graphic on a Web page, as follows: <IMG SRC="tree.jpg">
<TABLE>	Creates a table. The HEIGHT and WIDTH attributes specify the dimensions of the table in pixels. The BORDER attribute sets line thickness, with 1 as the default value (i.e., BORDER=0 removes the appearance of the border lines). BGCOLOR can set the background color of a table.
<TR>	Specifies a table row. Uses same attributes as <TABLE>.
<TD>	Specifies a table cell within a row. Uses same attributes as <TABLE>.

To create a basic HTML page, three types of applications can be used: plain text editors, HTML editors, and Web authoring software. Plain text editors, such as Windows Notepad, allow the user to type lines of markup manually. Plain text editors are installed as features of most operating systems. HTML editors, such as Arachnophilia, Bluefish, and HotDog, provide users with buttons and features to automatically add repeated tags or elements to markup typed by users. Some HTML editors are freeware and others require the user to purchase them. Web authoring software programs have a script view that works like a plain text editor, but also provides buttons and features the user can select and the program will automatically generate the markup. Web authoring software is generally for purchase and will be the most expensive option of the three. Based on need and availability, select the tool that will work best for a project. Most basic shorter pages can be easily created using a plain text editor, while longer pages might be more easily developed using the other applications.

Figure 4-3 provides an example of HTML markup for a basic Web page. This sample page uses HTML markup tags from Figure 4-2 to create page that uses a header, horizontal rule, textual content, and a hyperlink.

Welcome to My Web Site

This site uses very basic HTML markup created using a text editor. The color of this text is a medium grey color and its hexadecimal value is #999999. Below is a link to the search engine if you would like to search the Web.

Link to Search Engine

```
<HTML>
<HEAD>
<TITLE>Sample Web Page</TITLE>
</HEAD>
<BODY BGCOLOR="#FFFFFF">
<H1>Welcome to My Web Site</H1>
<HR WIDTH=400 ALIGN=LEFT>
<P ALIGN="JUSTIFY">
<FONT COLOR="#999999">
This site uses very basic HTML markup created using a text
editor. The color of this text is a medium grey color and
its hexadecimal value is #999999. Below is a link to the
search engine if you would like to search the Web.
</FONT>
</P>
<A HREF="http://www.someurl.com">Link to Search Engine</A>
</BODY>
</HTML>
```

FIGURE 4-3.   Sample Web Page Using HTML Markup Tags

Creating a basic Web page using manual HTML markup helps developers understand the markup language, its capabilities, and basic structure. The best way to learn markup is to practice. Many Web authoring software programs allow developers to view the source markup code and manually edit it. A basic knowledge of HTML can be useful when trying to troubleshoot basic problems that may occur when using these programs to design Web pages.

The steps used to create this basic page are provided below in Tutorial #1.

TUTORIAL #1: Using HTML to Create a Basic Web Page

1. Using the application of choice, create a new file and then add basic structural elements for a Web page, including <HTML>, <HEAD>, and <BODY> tags.

2. In the <HEAD> section, place a title between <TITLE> and </TITLE> tags to appear at the top of the browser window (see Figure 4-2 for an example).

3. Inside the <BODY> tag, assign a BGCOLOR attribute that sets the background color to white (#FFFFFF).

4. After the <BODY> tag, add a text header by typing "Welcome to My Web Site" between <H1> and </H1> tags. The <H1> tag will use large boldface text as the default text style.

5. Next, add a horizontal rule, using the <HR> tag. Assign attributes to give it a 400 pixel width (WIDTH=400) and left margin alignment (ALIGN=LEFT).

6. Begin a new paragraph by adding a <P> tag and assign full justification by using the ALIGN="JUSTIFY" attribute.

7. Add a <FONT> tag and COLOR attribute to set the text color to dark grey using a hexadecimal value of #999999.

8. Enter a few sentences of text.

9. Add the </FONT> and </P> closing tags to mark the end of the font style and paragraph settings.

10. Set a hyperlink by adding an <A> tag and the HREF attribute to specify the Uniform Resource Locator (URL) in quotes.

11. Type a text name for your link and then add the </A> closing tag to end the hyperlink. Anything between the <A> and </A> tags will be the hyperlink the user sees on the screen.

12. Finally, add the </BODY> and </HTML> closing tags to mark the end of the document body and end of the HTML document.

13. Once the lines of markup are entered, then the file can be saved and viewed in a Web browser. HTML pages should be saved as .htm or .html files, which are formats viewable by Web browsers. A basic file might be named "default.htm" or "test.htm." When prompted to select type of files when saving, select "All Files" or "Web Page" and if asked for the encoding method, select "ANSI" to ensure proper saving.

14. Open the saved file in a Web browser to view the marked-up page.

15. To continue making changes, reopen the file in a text editor and continue to make changes using other HTML markup tags and scripts to enhance the design.

Document Markup Guidelines

There are some important guidelines that should be followed to create what is known as "clean script," or "easy-to-read markup." Creating clean markup makes it easier for developers to troubleshoot, edit, and modify markup and scripts as needed. As such, there is a usability aspect to using clean script for developers and programmers. Unfortunately, many Web authoring software programs create script that is much more difficult to read and discern. As a result, it may take a bit longer to interpret and troubleshoot the markup used. Some important guidelines in creating clean markup include the following:

- Use spacing between lines to make it easier to read.
- Use consistent case and spacing between elements.
- Use closing tags for each tag that requires one.
- Properly nest tags by closing tags in the reverse order they are opened.
- Select simple names for referenced files using lowercase letters and omitting spaces.

All of the markup and scripting examples used in this chapter are examples of clean markup and scripting. These guidelines support the visual-spatial approach, in that the use of spacing, consistent elements, and styles help users to more easily interpret the markup and scripting, focus on problem areas, and solve those problems when viewing the actual markup or script. Using consistent styles and spacing aids the overall readability of markup and script. Using closing tags and properly nesting them helps signify where specific markup and styles begin and end. Using simple file names with lowercase letters and omitting spaces in referenced files makes it easier to remember file names and locate them when sorting files. For example, it might be easier to remember and reference the name of the news page if it is named "news.htm" as opposed to naming it "Current_News_January.htm." Individuals should develop their own guidelines for creating clean script to supplement these tips. Following these simple guidelines will make troubleshooting, editing, and customizing markup easier in the development process.

ADVICE from PRACTITIONERS

Marc Bessent • Senior Operations Support Specialist
Major Internet Service Provider

Markup and Scripting Are Handled Differently

A team of Web designers, developers, and administrators handles markup and scripting for our main product. They redesign the site based on user feedback and issues reported by customers and internal reviewers. The main Web site receives a new look approximately every six months. It has been, and remains today, one of the most visited Web sites on the Internet for both the company's customers and people who enjoy the freely available content. The scripting for the .com portal is done using a customized product developed by the company.

The scripting and programming of the internal department and group level Web sites is typically handled by a person or small group of people in that department that have some skills with

Web development. This can leave room for improvement, but permits those departments to get a customized product they can use without waiting for cycles from a team of developers that have higher priorities.

Importance of Markup and Scripting Knowledge

In our company, scripting is done in Hypertext Markup Language (HTML), Hypertext Preprocessor (PHP), JavaScript, and ActionScript, just to name a few. The scripting is used to maintain and query databases, create dynamic Web pages, organize the page, determine browser capabilities, and many more tasks. Scripts give the developer the ability to create content that the user can interact with. In the design phase it is good if a few people present have a rough knowledge of the abilities and limitations of scripts to ensure that expectations placed on the final product will not exceed results. Some knowledge of what scripts can do gives a sense of capabilities and limitations of what can and cannot be done. This helps avoid adding time to the development cycle and subsequent project delays. During development, it is crucial that the Web developers be proficient in several scripting languages. It is better to have a strong understanding of programming in general and the ability to quickly learn another programming/scripting language than to be strong in only a single language.

Using Document Markup for Layout

HTML markup can be used to create page layouts in addition to basic markup of text and graphic content. The most common HTML method uses tables to create invisible grids to position and arrange content. Many Web authoring software programs use customized table grids that allow users to modify the height and width of cells, rows, and columns using the mouse pointer. These values can be set manually using specific attributes of the <TABLE> tag. Tables set their border attributes to a value of zero so the lines of the table appear invisible. Then, content can be placed inside each cell of a table to create a basic page layout. Figure 4-4 shows an example of setting up a basic three-pane layout using tables.

This example uses two tables to create a three-pane layout. Within each <TABLE>, <TR> tags mark the start of individual table rows within a table, while the <TD> tags mark individual table cells. Each row and cell can specify the WIDTH and HEIGHT in number of pixels. The steps used to create this basic page are provided in Tutorial #2.

Another method of document markup to create layouts is the use of frames. Frames allow developers to display multiple pages of content in a single Web browser. In the example above, frames could be used to load three separate pages for the banner, navigation, and content, instead of using tables. The use of an internal frame, or <IFRAME>, allows one page to be displayed within or on top of another. While there are compatibility issues with viewing pages that use frames, some developers still use them in creating complex layouts. The document markup resources mentioned in the next section include some useful guides for learning how to use frames in designing page layouts.

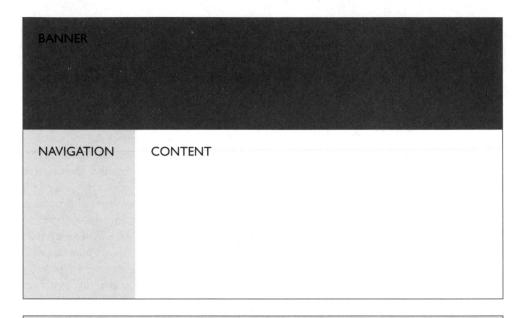

```
<HTML>
<HEAD>
<TITLE>HTML Sample</TITLE>
</HEAD>
<BODY>
<TABLE BORDER=0 WIDTH=800 HEIGHT=200>
<TR>
<TD BGCOLOR ="#999999" VALIGN="TOP">BANNER</TD>
</TR>
</TABLE>
<TABLE BORDER=0 WIDTH=800 HEIGHT=400>
<TR>
<TD WIDTH=200 BGCOLOR="#CCCCCC"
VALIGN="TOP">NAVIGATION</TD>
<TD WIDTH=600 BGCOLOR="#FFFFFF" VALIGN="TOP">CONTENT</TD>
</TR>
</TABLE>
</BODY>
</HTML>
```

FIGURE 4-4.   Using Tables to Create a Three-Frame Layout with HTML Markup

TUTORIAL #2: Using HTML Tables to Create a Layout

1. Using the application of choice, create a new file and then add basic structural elements for a Web page, including <HTML>, <HEAD>, and <BODY> tags.

2. In the <HEAD> section, place a title between <TITLE> and </TITLE> tags to appear at the top of the browser window (see Figure 4-2 for an example).

3. After the <BODY> tag, start a new table using the <TABLE> tag. Set the BORDER attribute to 0, WIDTH to 800 pixels, and HEIGHT to 200 pixels.

4. Add a <TR> tag to start a new table row.

5. Add a <TD> tag to start a new table cell within the first row. Add a BGCOLOR attribute to set the background color to dark grey (hexadecimal value #999999). Set the VALIGN attribute to TOP to align text placed inside the cell with the top left margin.

6. Type the word BANNER. Other text or graphics can be added as desired.

7. Add </TD>, </TR>, and </TABLE> closing tags to mark the end of the table cell, table row, and table, respectively.

8. Begin a new table, using the <TABLE> tag. This second table will be nested, or rendered inside the first one. For this new table, set the BORDER attribute to 0, WIDTH to 800 pixels, and HEIGHT to 600 pixels.

9. Add a <TR> tag to start a new table row.

10. Add a <TD> tag to start a new table cell within the first row. Add a BGCOLOR attribute to set the background color to light grey (hexadecimal value #CCCCCC). Set the VALIGN attribute to TOP to align text placed inside the cell with the top left margin.

11. Type the word NAVIGATION. Other text, graphics, or links can be added as desired.

12. Add a </TD> tag to mark the end of the table cell.

13. Begin the second table cell in this row by adding another <TD> tag. Set the BGCOLOR attribute to white (#FFFFFF). Set the VALIGN attribute to TOP to align text with the top left margin.

14. Type the word CONTENT. Other text, graphics, or links can be added as desired.

15. Add </TD>, </TR>, and </TABLE> closing tags to mark the end of the table cell, table row, and table, respectively.

16. Finally, add the </BODY> and </HTML> closing tags to mark the end of the document body and end of the HTML document.

17. Once the lines of markup are entered, then the file can be saved and viewed in a Web browser. HTML pages should be saved as .htm or .html files, which are formats viewable by Web browsers. A basic file might be named "default.htm" or "test.htm." When prompted to select type of files when saving, select "All Files" or "Web Page" and if asked for the encoding method, select "ANSI" to ensure proper saving.

18. Open the saved file in a Web browser to view the marked-up page.

19. To continue making changes, reopen the file in a text editor and continue to make changes using other HTML markup tags and scripts to enhance the design.

TABLE 4-3. Useful Online Markup and Scripting Resources

Online Resource	URL
HTML Writer's Guild	http://www.hwg.org
W3Schools	http://www.w3schools.com
WebMonkey	http://www.webmonkey.com
World Wide Web Consortium	http://www.w3.org

Document Markup Resources

A wide variety of useful markup and scripting references are available. Many books are available on every markup and scripting language at most bookstores. These guides are written at different levels of expertise and some require specific prior knowledge and training for them to be useful. What a printed resource offers is a reference guide for troubleshooting problems and a tool for self-study to improve skills. Computer training centers and continuing education programs now widely offer introductory courses in HTML and other scripting languages. One good book, reference Web site, or introductory course is usually enough of a start to gain a basic understanding of the syntax, structure, and tags used in developing a Web page.

For online resources, a simple keyword search in any search portal site will produce a varied range of results. A quick search for "HTML reference guide" on any major search portal site (such as Yahoo or Google) will yield a number of Web sites. As with any online search, each will have to be evaluated to determine usefulness and relevance to each designer's specific needs. Table 4-3 provides a short list of four useful online markup and scripting resources.

These sites offer a wide range of materials including scripting guides, online training, examples, design suggestions, and accessibility guidelines. The HTML Writer's Guild offers online training and certification in a wide range of markup and scripting languages and Web authoring software programs. W3Schools has a combination of reference guides, online course, examples, and certification programs for developers. WebMonkey provides a how-to library and quick reference guides based on the level of the developer, whether beginner, intermediate, or advanced. The World Wide Web Consortium provides reference guides and sets of guidelines on a wide variety of markup and scripting languages. While these suggestions may provide a starting point in building a collection of useful references, each developer should supplement this list with books, courses, and guides that will best suit individual skills levels and preferences. A combination of these sources will help a developer expand the working knowledge of markup and scripting languages to aid in the Web development process.

Process of Publishing a Web Site

Once content pages have gone through markup, the next step is to publish them. Publishing a Web site involves uploading pages, or an entire site, to a Web server so it is accessible over the World Wide Web. Typically, this includes uploading all pages, graphic content, and other supporting files that make up the site. In some cases, it may involve uploading the site to a company server for internal company access or the site may be written to CD-ROM for distribution. The method of publication will depend on who needs access to the information and the site's purpose. The process of publishing a site involves a Web developer, uploading program, Web server, and often, a technical support person, such as a systems administrator.

The first part of the process involves obtaining specific information and resources, which are addressed in detail in the following sections. Whether uploading an entire site or a few pages, prior to publishing a Web site, there are four important steps that must be followed, which include the following:

- Identify the location and size of project files to be published.
- Create a method of managing files and folders.
- Obtain the process for accessing the server and address of the host server.
- Obtain a Uniform Resource Locator (URL) or Web address.

Once this information is obtained, the second part of the process involves the actual uploading of files to the Web server so the site can be viewed on the World Wide Web. The following sections will address each part of the process of publishing a Web site.

Identifying Project Files

As described in Chapter 2, maintaining an inventory of project files will make this part of the process very easy. The inventory should identify where all files needed to be published are located. Without an inventory of files, it will be necessary to create one in order to identify the location, size, and format of all files that make up the site. Once this information has been obtained, the next step is to begin publishing the files to the Web server so it can be shared with users over the Internet or other network. It is also important to determine the size of all files that make up the site. If all files are placed in a single location or folder, the size can be determined by examining the properties of that folder. It should offer the number of files and total size of those files. Otherwise, the total size of the site will have to be calculated by adding the values of all of the various files and folders. The total size needs to be known for the next step, part of which involves knowing how much space will be required on the server on which the site will be published.

Folder and File Management

One important goal that should be incorporated into every Web project is to keep track of all the files that comprise the site. This involves knowing their exact location, size, and file format. Many designers will keep all files for a Web site project in a single folder on a computer or server. This makes finding the files and publishing them much easier later on in the development process. In some cases, it may not be possible to do so, which is why it is important to maintain an updated inventory of files as one of the project development goals. Organizing files into a single folder, or multiple folders, will help make the process of uploading and adding pages easier during site development. For simple sites with less than ten pages, placing all files in a single folder is recommended. This makes linking and referencing easy, since specifying a folder name or pathway is unnecessary. For more complex

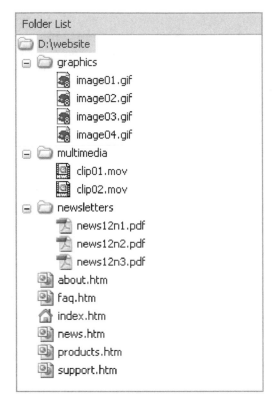

FIGURE 4-5.   A Basic Web Site Folder and File Management Structure

sites with large volumes of content, organizing sections of the site into a series of separate folders is helpful. For example, some sites might place all graphic files in a folder called "Graphics" so that linking or referencing them on pages is easier to remember. Creating file naming conventions can assist developers in organizing and locating files more easily. Using all lowercase letters, no spaces, and no special characters can make it easier to recall names when using them to create hyperlinks. Sometimes, files may be time sensitive or belong to a group. These relationships can be used to create consistent and meaningful naming conventions. For example, a series of newsletters might be named based on the volume and number, such as, "news12n1.htm." Using some of these folder and file management strategies will help in locating, updating, and uploading files as a site is developed and maintained. Figure 4-5 illustrates a sample folder and file management structure for a Web site. In the example, graphic images, media clips, and newsletters are placed in separate folders. Main site pages are placed in the root directory.

Obtaining the Process for Server Access and Address

This step involves contacting a server administrator or technical support department to acquire the specific location and process for accessing the Web server, its address, and successful methods used to upload Web site files. This includes obtaining dedicated storage space on a Web server. Most likely, the designer or team has determined where the site will be published in advance of publishing. Usually, this requires a Web server, which is provided through an Internet Service Provider (ISP), used to connect to the Web, such as a company or school Web server. In almost all cases, with access comes some allocation of space on a dedicated Web server. Contact the technical support department or service provider to find out how much space is available. This will enable the designer and/or team to determine if the size of the site will fit on the space available on the Web server. Verify the total size of the Web site does not exceed the available storage space. In many cases, additional space will need to be requested or an alternate Web server used to post the site. In the case of an ISP, most sell additional server space for a fee. Obtaining the host server address along with a username and password is necessary to access the server and upload files. Depending on what software program used to upload the site files, this information will normally be required to login to the server.

Obtaining a Uniform Resource Locator

Normally, your ISP or system administrator will assign a URL for the site. If a custom URL is required, it can be purchased over the Internet by searching for companies that sell them. For the Google Search Engine Site, the URL is http://www.google.com. Depending on how the files will be posted on the server, the URL may vary in length and its designation. Most users have dedicated Web server space provided under each user account and as a result, each user account will have a slightly different URL assigned to it. For example, assume an ISP has a standard URL as shown below.

http://www.myisp.com

If the user account name is "sample," then the standard URL for a site published to that account might be as follows:

http://www.myisp.com/sample

Depending on how folders and files are named and arranged on the server, and the file name of the home page, the URL might be slightly different. For example, if the same user in the example above uploaded a folder called "test" with all the site files in it, then the URL to access it would be:

http://www.myisp.com/sample/test

With regard to the file name of the home page, the above URLs assume that it is called either "default.htm" or "index.htm" (either file extension could be replaced with .html as well). A browser will automatically look for and load either of these files, so it is unnecessary to include the home page file name as part of the URL. If both files exist, index.htm will be loaded and not default.htm. If the home page file name is "home.htm," then it must be added to the URL. The result would be:

http://www.myisp.com/sample/test/home.htm

If problems occur at any point in the process, consult a technical support or a systems administrator for assistance. Once this last piece of information is obtained, the good news is that the site is ready to be uploaded to the Web server.

Uploading the Site

The second part of the process involves uploading the files to a Web server. A site can be published, or uploaded, to a Web server in two ways: (1) upload it using the built-in component of Web authoring software; or (2) by using a File Transfer Protocol (FTP) program. Contacting technical support or a system administrator may be advisable when unfamiliar with these programs or to obtain specific guidance. The Web authoring software used to develop the site should have a manual or help system that can provide instructions on using the uploading feature. FTP software can be purchased or downloaded from the Internet, and some is provided free of charge for a limited period. Performing a basic search on any search engine site for FTP software will provide a list of possible programs that can be used to upload the site. Many ISPs will have Web pages that provide detailed instructions on publishing and uploading files to their Web servers. Some ISPs may even recommend specific utilities and provide a link to download them from their main Web site. For corporate sponsored sites or companies, a system administrator will upload the site or at least provide assistance. In such a case, the entire site can be handed over to the system administrator, who can upload the site.

After publishing the site, one important issue to keep in mind concerns maintaining project files. Keep a protected copy of the site on a computer or disk after it is published in case specific problems arise with the uploaded version. This copy can also serve as a working copy for future changes to the site and be used to upload the new version. If there are specific security issues with regard to access and editing pages and files, the server manager or systems administrator can assist in password protecting and access control to specific folders and files.

ADVICE from PRACTITIONERS

Deborah Hess • Information Technology Engineer
Major Telecommunications Corporation

Top Five Things a System Administrator Needs from a Design Team

System administrators require specific information from the Web design team in order to help minimize problems when publishing a site.

(1) **Development and Production Server Space** Having a dedicated testing or development server or location of files separate from the full production Web server is important during the site development. This will save the systems administrator from needing to restore files on the main production server and subsequent changes the design team may require, such as fixing broken links. All testing and last minute changes can be done and tested on the development server. Once it is looking and working correctly the site can be moved to the production server.

(2) **Web Services Required** System administrators need to get ideas of what functions and viewers used in the site to know what requirements will be needed for hardware and software of the

Web Server. A major determinant for hardware and software configuration is the operating system (OS) used and any preference for the server software (i.e., Apache or Microsoft IIS).

(3) Graphics The system administrator needs to know specifically how graphic intensive the site will be, including audio/video files and animated graphics. Graphics will dictate the amount of memory, network card speed requirements, and sometimes even video hardware components required on the Web server and client system. Graphics also will determine what software that would need to be installed. For example, Macromedia Shockwave Player or Apple QuickTime software may need to be installed on the system.

(4) Total Size of Data and (5) Types of Data Used The type of data, and if/what type of database used, can influence what OS has to be used and also helps the systems administrator with disk sizing and configuration. Another consideration to think about with data would be the other types and amount of files such as videos, music, pictures, large spreadsheets, Adobe PDF Files, and so on. All of the previous examples would require considerable disk space especially if there are large file sizes and/or a large quantity of such files.

All of these items are important for the system administrator to be able to get the Web server set up for initial use by the design team. If any of these items have not been discussed, problems may occur after it has gone into production.

Listing a New Site on a Search Portal

Once a site has been published, developers might consider listing the newly published site on search portal sites, such as Google or Yahoo. Most search portal sites will have a link for users to add their site to the search portal's database. Usually the process is as simple as entering the URL of the site and pressing a button. Most of the work is done by software robots that search for all pages that comprise a site's URL and adding those pages to their index of sites. In some cases, search portal sites will automatically search the Web and index new content. Once a site is added to their index, usually a site will be reindexed on a regular basis to account for changes and updates. Particularly with commercial sites, it is important to consider listing a site on a few search portal sites to reach a larger audience. Many large portal sites share database indexes, so it may not be necessary to ensure a site is listed with every search portal site.

Three important content elements a search portal needs to index a new site are a title, description, and keywords, described in Table 4-4. Each page in a Web site can use a unique title, description, and set of keywords, or they can be repeated on all pages in a site. These content elements can be added using manual HTML markup, META tag software utilities, or Web authoring software.

<META> and <TITLE> tags are found in the HTML markup in the header section, or <HEAD>. From the examples used in Table 4-4, the following would be a typical listing for the site:

SpiderWeb Creations

SpiderWeb Creations is a Web Development Company focused on creating innovative Web site designs for clients. **http://www.myurl.com.**

TABLE 4-4. Indexed Content Elements

Content Element	Location and Example
Title	The HTML markup <TITLE> tag, which lists the title for a page and displays it in the top line of the browser window. <TITLE>SpiderWeb Creations</TITLE>
Description	A textual description found in the HTML markup <META> tags. <META NAME="DESCRIPTION" CONTENT="SpiderWeb Creations is a Web development company focused on creating innovative Web site designs for clients.">
Keywords	A list of key words associated with the site's content found in the HTML markup <META> tags. <META NAME="KEYWORDS" CONTENT=" Web site development, site designs, client Web sites">

If these tags are not used, a search portal may use content found on pages to build titles, descriptions, and keyword lists. Since the results may not be as expected, it is important to be sure to provide them so pages and sites can be indexed and listed properly.

Conclusion

Document markup and scripting is important to Web development because they make content viewable and usable in a Web browser interface. While Web authoring software can mark up and script content for a Web developer, it is useful to have a basic working knowledge of the structure, syntax, and methods of these languages. A working knowledge of both provides the greatest flexibility to the developer in choosing which method or combination of methods works best for a project. Knowledge of markup and scripting can assist in creating custom elements and in solving basic problems. In turn, familiarity with Web authoring software can aid in production, complex scripting, and markup of larger documents. A variety of tools can be used for markup and publishing based on developer and project needs. As such, each developer should research and choose the right combination of methods and tools that will work best.

Chapter Summary

- Web developers should have at least a basic knowledge of Hypertext Markup Language (HTML) to understand the basic structure, language, syntax, and layout of Web pages.
- As a rule, Web developers should have knowledge of markup and scripting languages and Web authoring programs to allow for greater flexibility in development methods.

- A basic Web page has two major structural sections, a header and a body.
- The header contains the site title and any embedded scripting, such as CSS or JavaScript, used to format styles or add specific functions to the page.
- The body contains the main Web site textual content, hyperlinks, references that load graphics and multimedia, and any inline scripts on the page.
- Three types of development tools can be used in HTML markup: plain text editors, HTML editors, and Web authoring software programs.
- Creating clean markup makes it easier for developers to troubleshoot, edit, and modify markup and scripts as needed.
- HTML markup can be used to create page layouts. The most common HTML methods are using tables and frames.
- Many useful markup and scripting references are available, which can be found in books or by using a keyword search in any search portal site. They offer a wide range of references including online training, help guides, examples, certification programs and specific guidelines.
- Each developer should select a variety of books, courses, and guides that will best suit individual skills levels and preferences.
- Prior to publishing a Web site, three important steps to follow include the following: (1) identify the location and size of project files to be published; (2) obtain the process for accessing the server and address of the host server; and (3) obtain a Uniform Resource Locator (URL) or Web address.
- A site can be published, or uploaded, to a Web server in two ways: (1) upload it using the built-in component of Web authoring software; or (2) by using a File Transfer Protocol (FTP) program. In many cases, a systems administrator or technical support personnel can assist with this process.

Exercises

1. Select a one-page printed document, such as a memorandum or advertisement and use HTML to compose the markup for a Web page version.
2. Using the same task in the first exercise, complete the task using a Web authoring software program of your choice, such as, Microsoft FrontPage, Macromedia Dreamweaver, Adobe GoLive, and so on. Then, compare the markup and scripting developed by the program to the result from the first exercise.
3. Review the guidelines for effective HTML markup from the chapter. Then, evaluate the quality of the markup and scripting created by the Web authoring software to complete the task for the previous exercise. Identify what guidelines, if any, are violated, and what changes should be made to the markup and scripting.
4. Search the Web for HTML reference guides using appropriate keywords in a few search portal sites. Examine at least six to ten sites and make a list of strengths and weaknesses of each. Then, select the top three sites based on your research and share your results.

5. Select an ISP Web site and research the site to obtain as much information as possible about the process for uploading a Web site to their server, including amount of space available, specific requirements for publishing, recommended programs to use, and any other important details.

6. Use the Internet to search for at least two downloadable FTP programs for either a PC or Mac platform. Select programs that are available for trial download or are free of charge. Compare and contrast the features each provides and test upload a page or two as part of your analysis.

5

SITE STRUCTURE

Introduction

The design of site structures deals with arranging individual pages of a Web site into an organized collection, or whole structure. The process of organizing individual Web pages into a structure is known as *information* (or site) *architecture*. Developing the site structure involves more than arranging pages into hierarchies, categories and subcategories. The site designer must find ways to establish meaningful relationships between individual pages and sections in planning the arrangement of pages in a site. This task involves selecting meaningful labels and titles for pages, navigation links, and often indices or site maps. The designer must find ways to communicate the site structure to users by using contextual cues that suggest the arrangement of pages and content. Site structures should be tested to see how well they fit users' mental models or expectations they might have about the organization of information. The site structure becomes the blueprint for later work, including designing navigation tools, organizing content, and developing the interface.

Site structure considers how content chunks and visuals are structured and interconnected by hyperlinks. The Web requires us to see this structure of information in layers, whether it is layers of pages we navigate in a site, content chunks from a database, or layers of graphics and text as they are arranged into what the user sees on the screen. Information architecture experts Rosenfeld and Morville suggest site structures are "logical structures that help us find answers and complete tasks" (3). The visual and spatial layouts of Web site structures are often illustrated for users through the use of site maps, indices, and navigational toolbars. Developing a site structure considers how content and context work together to create a comprehensible structure. The process is one in which designers plan information pathways for the site and its users. For example, structures that provide more contextual cues for users at higher levels and more content in deeper levels support user expectations of a logical structure.

Developing a Site Structure

Site structure is important to Web development for many reasons. Developing a site structure involves much more than organizing pages into a simple hierarchy. Just as any writer would plan the order of individual chapters in a book or sections in a report, a Web designer must plan the arrangement of pages and documents in a Web site. Users form visual models of how information is arranged based on their reading experiences and common stylistic conventions. For example, in print-based publications, users expect to see certain conventions, such as a table of contents, headers or indices that explain how the document is organized. Web sites are more dynamic documents than their print-based counterparts because they use hyperlinks, multimedia, and interactive features. Since the same stylistic conventions do not apply to Web sites, users must rely more on their reading and browsing experiences to form a visual model of how the site is organized. Once users understand the site's structure and organization, they can plan more efficient information searches in a Web site. It is equally important to find ways of helping users comprehend the site structure as part of the development process. While the organization and structure of a site may not be obvious to a new user, providing redundant navigation, site maps, indices, headers, and other descriptors would all be effective ways of communicating the structure to users.

The process of developing a Web site structure involves five major steps: analysis, labeling, design, testing, and revising (see Table 5-1). Analysis involves examining the textual and graphic content to be used in the site, including paper documents, digital files, and Web pages. The analysis will involve using visual-spatial principles to evaluate and identify methods of improving an existing structure and developing a new one that fits user perception and needs. Selecting meaningful labels for the site helps organize and define each major content area and function of the site. In designing the structure, the task involves sketching a structure that considers how to best organize content sections and considers the unique visual and spatial relationships between each content artifact in the structure. Testing helps determine how well the structure fits their needs and expectations. Revision will involve editing and condensing the structure-based results. If more than minor changes are made, it may be necessary to retest. Since each step of the process builds on the previous one, it is important to follow them in the proper progression.

Analysis and Identifying Content Areas

This first step is based partly on the research, analysis, and evaluation from developing the site's content. If written content for the site exists, this will save some time in the overall process. The purpose of analysis is to determine the types of content that will be used and

TABLE 5-1. The Process of Developing a Site Structure		
Process	**Purpose**	**Tasks**
Step 1: Analysis	To determine major content areas and types of content used in the site	• Examine textual and graphic content • Use visual-spatial principles for analysis and planning site structure
Step 2: Labeling	To select meaningful labels for node pages and content pages	• Identify major content areas and functions of the site • Develop labels that match site content areas and function
Step 3: Design	To design a site structure that best fits the nature of content and to plan methods of communicating the structure to users	• Develop sketch of site structure based on content areas and functions • Consider spatial relationships inherent in the structure
Step 4: Testing	To evaluate the site structure to determine how well it conforms to users' mental models	• Use tests such as card sorts and mock-ups to evaluate the structure • Evaluate how the site structure fits user needs
Step 5: Revising	To edit and improve the structure based on the results from testing	• Edit and revise the structure based on testing results • Retest the structure after revisions are made

how best to organize it. This initial step involves determining the site's major content areas and functions. Typically, each major content area serves as a node page in the site structure. Node pages are found at higher levels in the site structure and typically represent a major content area and often have their own internal navigation. These pages typically serve as gateways to more detailed information and pages on a specific subject. For example, a site that sells a specific brand of car might have a node page called "models", which lists all the types of models of cars. That same page might have its own local navigation toolbar that provides links to individual pages for each model. Each content area is essentially a separate information pathway. Users follow an information pathway through a site to find more specific types of information. Visual-spatial thinking suggests that as users search deeper levels of the site structure, they expect to find more specific types of content (Johnson-Sheehan and Baehr 2001). Part of the process of analyzing content is to determine the site's major content areas, or information pathways will be that users can follow in the site. Two useful methods of analysis are content analysis and visual-spatial analysis.

Content Analysis

The purpose of a content analysis is to look at the type, format, subject, and purpose of each content artifact in order to determine patterns or relationships between them. For new sites, make a list of content that will be used in the site. For site redesign projects, examine how content is arranged to determine what changes need to be made, including a list of new content to be added. In either case, there will most likely be existing documents, descriptions, or graphics to add to the list. The main task is to classify each artifact into categories that will represent the major content areas of the site. The process of creating a content inventory and content analysis is described in detail in Chapter 3, Research and Content Development.

As part of the content analysis, write a one-sentence description of each content artifact, describing its subject and purpose. Identify content types, such as descriptions, definitions, instructions, lists, and forms. Then, determine the different document formats that will be used, such as HTML, DOC, JPG, GIF, PDF, and so on. Examine the patterns or relationships between individual artifacts to determine how they might best fit together into a section or group. Group documents that are related based on their subject and/or purpose. Set aside documents that do not seem to fit in any group or category. Sort the remaining artifacts into an existing or new group. Label each group with a name that accurately describes each group. After completing the process, examine the results to see what changes need to be made. It may take several iterations before perfecting the sorting process.

Visual-Spatial Analysis

A visual-spatial analysis of a site structure can be important for two reasons: (1) it measures how well the site structure and related features help users comprehend the organization and layout of the site; (2) it helps identify areas of improvement in designing a more effective structure to fit user perception and need. Two visual thinking principles that can be used to analyze the site structure are Arnheim's visual thinking principles: discernment in depth and completing the incomplete. Discernment in depth suggests that context and content are mutually exclusive in a Web site (Johnson-Sheehan and Baehr 2001). In Web sites, users expect more contextual information in higher levels of the site structure, while more specific detail is found in deeper levels. Contextual cues serve to outline content and show relation between individual elements on the screen. Some methods of providing context include the use of headers, redundant navigation, breadcrumb links, ALT attribute tags, and site maps or indices. The principle of completing the incomplete suggests that users attempt to create conceptual wholes, or mental models, of elements in their visual field to discern how the whole is collectively organized (Arnheim 1969). A good site structure is organized so that users can easily comprehend and navigate the site's contents. Some site structures are more difficult to comprehend, so the most effective ones tend to make the whole structure more obvious

CONTEXTUAL AND STRUCTURE

- What contextual cues does the site provide that help users understand the structure and organization of the site?
- How useful are the site's navigation labels in suggesting how content is outlined or organized?
- Are site maps or indices provided that help users understand the structure of the site?
- Is specific content placed too deeply in the structure from the home page?

WHOLENESS AND STRUCTURE

- Does the site structure seem apparent from the navigation tools, headers, and other repeated elements used in the top two levels of the site?
- Are site maps, indices, headers, or redundant navigation tools used consistently to help users identify the site's structure and major content areas?
- Do help pages merely assist users in finding content, or do they also aid users in understanding the organization of content in the site?
- Does the site use consistent labels for major content areas, pages, or sections of the site?

FIGURE 5-1. Visual-Spatial Analysis Questions for Site Structures

to users. There are a variety of methods of achieving this in a site design, including the use of redundant headers or navigation, a site map or index, and arrangement of content in the uppermost levels of the structure. All these methods help suggest how content is organized in the site. Figure 5-1 provides a list of questions to aid in the analysis of the visual-spatial aspects of a Web site structure.

Whether performing an analysis of an exiting structure for redesign, or evaluating initial ideas about developing a new one, these questions should help identify specifically how the site structure aids users in comprehending the overall site structure. They may also pinpoint missing features to include in the redesigned site. A visual-spatial analysis of the site structure is an effective evaluation tool that can help improve a poorly designed structure, or provide guidelines and ideas for creating an entirely new one.

Selecting Meaningful Labels

The task of labeling involves assigning specific labels to each major content area or function of the site. Start with the labels used to identify major content areas from the analysis step. In most cases, consider revising them and select more meaningful ones that describe each content area and page in the site. This is especially important for node pages, which serve as gateways to more specific content pages. The labels selected for content areas and individuals should be used throughout the site as headers, subheads, HTML page <TITLES>, and navigation links and toolbars.

Effective labeling often outlines content and functions available in the site, helping users understand both the structure and navigation choices in the site. Part of selecting meaningful labels is selecting a method of organization. Four types of labeling schemes commonly used are **functional**, **metaphorical**, **topical**, and **user-defined**. Functional labels suggest a specific use, or function, such as a shopping cart, search utility, or help utility. A metaphorical scheme involves using a specific theme for the site. For example, a site that uses a house metaphor might have links to the kitchen, library, great room, and attic as labels. Each of these labels has a very specific meaning within the context of the house metaphor to which most users would be familiar. When organizing pages by topic, it is important to use labels that will make sense within the current context. For example, avoid using technical jargon in labeling, unless each term is defined and explained for users. In the previous example of an automobile manufacturing Web site, it may be unwise to label sections solely by model number, which has meaning to the company, but nothing to the target users. In this case, include the make of each car and include a picture of it for users. If any of these methods of labeling don't seem to fit, consider a set of user-defined labels, or labels that are customized or organized to fit the subject, audience, or purpose. Figure 5-2 provides a list of labeling schemes and examples of how they are used in navigation toolbars to outline functions and major content areas.

When selecting a labeling scheme, the designer should consider the visual model that scheme suggests. This is particularly relevant when a site uses an index, table of contents, navigation menu, major content headers, or other elements that help users comprehend and visualize a site's structure.

Once labeling schemes and individual labels have been selected, it is useful to make an organized list of each label, its content area, page type, and brief sentence that describes the purpose and/or type of content on that page. Using the example of the automobile manufacturing Web site, a sample labeling list is provided in Table 5-2. Labeling lists provide an overall picture or outline of labels, content, and their arrangement. This helps identify trends and inconsistencies in the choice of labels. Use consistent labels to avoid confusion later on in the design process. When the list is complete, review it to ensure each label best fits the purpose and content of each page or section.

In some instances, users may not be familiar with the site or its content. In this case, provide contextual cues to help them comprehend the labels chosen. Users rely on these labels to help them outline content and comprehend the site's structure. Some methods of providing users with context include using text labels, descriptors, ALT attribute tags, icons, graphics, or glossary of terms. In the example in the previous paragraph, pairing graphics with text labels can be effective in providing users with context. If users don't recognize images, text labels or descriptions can help them understand the meaning and concepts more clearly. When all else fails, a variety of techniques such as textual descriptions, help pages, frequently asked questions section, or glossary help explain the use of labels in the structure. As part of this step, modify the list of labels to add the descriptors, images, or other contextual cues used with each label.

Functional

Labels describe the specific functions or use of the navigational tool.

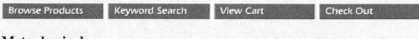

Metaphorical

Labels are based on a design metaphor used in the site. Each label suggests a specific concept that relates to the overall metaphor.

Topical

Labels represent the major topics or content areas found within the site.

User-defined

Labels are selected based on a specific purpose or need that fails to conform to other schemes. A user-defined scheme might use a combination of the other types.

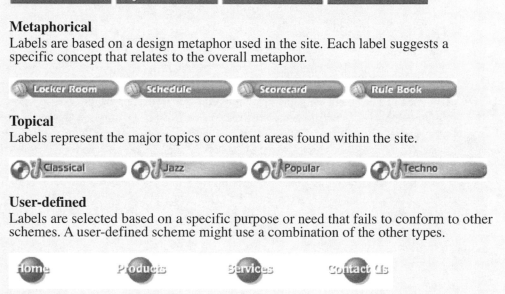

FIGURE 5-2. Labeling Schemes and Meaningful Labels

Graphic Source: Flashbuttons, http://www.flashbuttons.com.

TABLE 5-2. Sample Labeling List

Label	Content Area	Type of Page	Purpose
Cars	Cars	Node page	To provide a list and short description of each car model
Astra	Cars	Content page	To describe the Astra model's features and specs
Hypra	Cars	Content page	To describe the Hypra model's features and specs
Trucks	Trucks	Node page	To provide a list and short description of each truck model
Norstar	Trucks	Content page	To describe the Norstar model's features and specs
Westar	Trucks	Content page	To describe the Westar model's features and specs

Designing Site Structures

Designing the site structure, or blueprinting, involves deciding how many levels the structure has, in terms of both breadth and depth, as well as planning the overall layout. The site developer's job is to select a structure that best fits the rhetorical situation and user expectations. Select a structure that will make it easy for users to search, browse, and navigate. Based on the work of sorting content in the analysis stage, a skeleton structure, or basic arrangement of pages, may seem evident. Before committing to that arrangement, examine some of the types of basic site structures and how they're typically used, which might provide some ideas for which site structure works best. Site structures are often dynamic, in that their structure might combine different types, such as in a site that has multiple purposes, or in one that uses a database from which to construction pages and information pathways. For example, a search portal site constructs a different pathway and listing of pages based on each unique keyword search. These lists of pages and links are constructed from entries in a database, which are served up based on the search parameters. Four types of Web structures that serve as models for developing site structures are linear, hierarchical, hypertextual, and customized (see Figure 5-3).

Linear structures are used in sites that must follow a specific order or process. In these structures, spatially, one page follows the next in a sequence (i.e., page one, page two, page three). Linear structures require every user to read the same information in the same sequence. These structures teach users a linear process or order that must be followed. They offer less flexibility in navigation for users, since they must follow a rigid sequence or pathway. As such, they are used most commonly in Web-based training sites, online tutorials, and in a purchasing function used in a site that sells items. In the latter case, users typically deposit items in a virtual shopping cart and check out using a specific process or sequence of paying and confirming the order. Linear structures may only be used in a specific part of a site, such as the purchasing function, while other parts of a site's structure are organized differently.

Hierarchical structures organize pages into a spatial hierarchy of categories and subcategories that may resemble an outline or a table of contents in a book. This type of structure often works well for sites with large volumes of content that can be categorized easily. In this structural type, each major category may be provided as a navigation option on the home page and subcategories and related content are found in subsequent pages in the site. These structures are commonly used in education, business, and news Web sites (in the latter, individual news items may be organized into a hierarchy of categories such as World, Science, Law, and Education). Some news sites use a more complex structure that allow users to

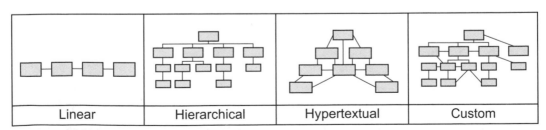

FIGURE 5-3. Four Types of Web Site Structures

search and browse more dynamically, by jumping from one subcategory to another one, but the basic overall arrangement of the site may still resemble a hierarchy. Hierarchies suggest a more logical or methodical organization of topics, although they can use flexible navigation, such as search features and links that help users quickly switch to a different pathway in the hierarchy.

Hypertextual structures are typically nonlinear structures, in which any content chunk or page can link to a single or multiple pages in the site. Hypertextual structures work well for sites with large databases of information that permit flexible searching or browsing. These sites customize content by piecing together individual content chunks from a database. Spatially, hypertextual structures are often complex, since they are unrestricted in both size and shape. Web search portal sites, such as Yahoo and Google, resemble a hypertextual structure since the results of keyword searches determine the relevant pathways and links for users. A hypertextual structure works well for sites that organize information associatively, where pages are often linked together based on the mutual relevance of content chunks. As such, hypertextual structures typically provide the most flexible navigation options for users. Other sites that use hypertextual structures are online reference guides, knowledge bases, and troubleshooting guides that link related content chunks to help users solve a problem. Hypertextual structures may help users visualize the relevance between individual pages, while the overall structure of the site may be more difficult to discern. In such a case, it is important to provide a visual means for users to comprehend the spatial organization more clearly.

Custom structures often combine multiple structural types, tailored to the specific subject or purpose of the site. Custom structures are typically used for sites with large databases or complex navigation systems. They work best for sites that aren't based on a hierarchical arrangement of content. A custom structure works best for sites with multiple purposes or a specific need for a unique structural type. These structures are spatially the most diverse of all the types, since they can incorporate other types and can be customized to fit multiple purposes or functions of the site. As such, sites with more than one function or purpose may benefit from the use of a custom structure. For example, an online university may need a hierarchical structure for its administration materials, such as policy statements, application guidelines, degree plans, and forms. It may use a linear structure for its online application process. And yet the same site might benefit from using a hypertextual structure for its course descriptions, which allows users to search a database of descriptions and titles in order to find those that best match their own academic interests. Many sites that sell products provide a hierarchical organization of products, a hypertextual search utility, and a linear process when purchasing items. Works of hyperfiction, or novels in hypertext form, may also have the need for a custom structure. Custom structures have the most flexibility, since they incorporate a variety of types, but they can also be the most difficult to discern. In this case, a site map, index, or other means should be provided to help users comprehend the site structure both visually and spatially.

Two important visual-spatial characteristics to consider in designing a site structure are breadth and depth. Breadth deals with the number of node pages, content areas or information pathways at any given level of the site structure, while depth deals with the number of levels in any given content area or information pathway. There are advantages and disadvantages to each of the types of structures commonly found in Web sites. For example, a site with eight major content areas would be considered broad, since it provides more

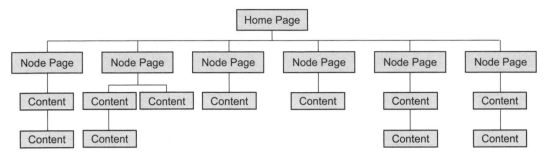

FIGURE 5-4. A Broader Hierarchical Site Structure

This structure has more content pathways in higher levels with variable levels of depth. This structure provides users with many content pathways, some of which are linear sequences of content pages.

categories or initial navigation pathways for users. A site with four major content areas is narrower, since it offers fewer pathways. The breadth will influence both the navigation and organization of your site. Sites with more levels in each content area have deeper pathways. Deeper site structures can require more search time by users, since there are more levels between the home page and the deepest content in the site, thereby requiring more mouse clicks by users. However, they can also accommodate larger volumes of content. Structures that are less deep place content closer to users, since they typically have fewer clicks or pages between the home page and content pages. However, they may also seem less organized into specific topics and subtopics. Four sample site structures are provided as examples in Figures 5-4, 5-5, 5-6, and 5-7. Note the unique characteristics of the sample structures as well as the advantages and disadvantages of each design.

Site Structure Layout

The next task in designing a structure is to sketch out a basic layout or blueprint of the structure. Use a single sheet of paper to draw a basic flowchart of the structure. Alternatively,

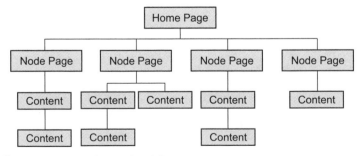

FIGURE 5-5. A Narrow Hierarchical Structure

This structure is simpler with few node pages, or content pathways and variable levels of depth. This site structure provides few content areas, most of which have linear sequences of content, and is relatively easy to comprehend.

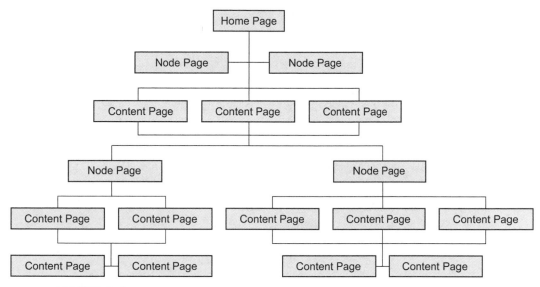

FIGURE 5-6. A Custom Structure

This structure resembles a network or web with multiple nodes throughout the structure, all of which may not be accessible from the home page. The layout is complex, which might make its spatial structure difficult to comprehend without other visual aids, such as site maps or indices.

use a stack of labeled index cards or Post-It notes and spread them out on a large surface. Alternately, some software programs that have flowcharting features can be used as a working space. The process of designing the site structure resembles developing a basic flowchart or organization chart. Draw boxes for individual pages and draw lines between each element in the structure to indicate how they will be accessed or linked, including page to page links, page to database links, and page to external site links. Regardless

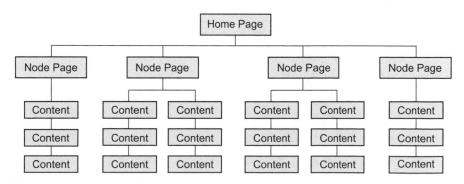

FIGURE 5-7. A Balanced Hierarchical Structure

This structure has the same number of levels of depth in the structure. Balancing the depth in each content pathway helps users anticipate how many mouse clicks away more specific content is placed in each pathway.

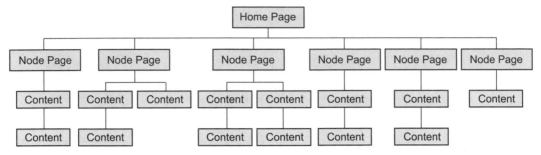

FIGURE 5-8. A Site Structure Sketch with Labeled Home, Node, and Content pages

of which methods are used to sketch the site structure, it may take several iterations before deciding on the right arrangement. Figure 5-8 is a sample site structure sketch that arranges the home page, node pages or major content pathways, and content pages. This sketch shows six major content areas and several content pages. Four content pathways use linear arrangements of content while the other two continue in a hierarchical arrangement.

For the next revision, use actual labels for each generic node page and content label in the site structure sketch. This will help visualize relationships between individual pages and sections and make revisions to create a more meaningful arrangement. For example, a car dealership Web site using a functional labeling scheme might use the following six content areas: browse, drive, purchase, service, repair, and contact. These six activities help define the major content areas or node pages of the site. As a result, the next revision might include these labels as the six node pages. Then, subsequent content page labels could be added to develop the structure, and so forth. One issue to consider in developing a site structure is scalability, or how flexible and accommodating the structure would be in adding future content. Since nearly all Web sites are evolving documents, consider how the structure will accommodate the addition of new content. If new content areas will be added in the future, mark each as shaded areas. While it may be difficult to fully plan for this, it is an important issue to consider in developing the initial site structure.

Communicating the Structure to Users

During the design of the site structure, consider how to make it easier for users to understand the organization of the site's pages. Part of the design stage involves planning methods of communicating the spatial organization of the site structure to users. One method is using contextual cues, which can act as visual signposts that provide contextual information for users. Contextual cues or information suggests the nature of content in a given page or pathway. Each page or object has its own unique center, which is balanced by individual visual elements on that page (Arnheim, 1988). When looking at a work of art, we often find a center point that we fixate on in that static image. In each Web page, our eyes are constantly changing their focus or center point, based on changing elements on the screen. In a Web site, whichever page we currently are viewing becomes our center point of focus, from which we plan subsequent searching and browsing within the site. One of the ways designers help users find their center point of focus is to provide contextual cues that tell the user where he or she

FIGURE 5-9.   Use of Breadcrumb Links

is at in the overall site structure at any given moment. These cues not only signal the nature of content and its arrangement, but it helps users plan where to go next. In terms of site navigation, this can be achieved through the use of site maps, indices, and breadcrumb links. Breadcrumb links show the succession of links chosen to reach a given page (see Figure 5-9).

Using a site map is another method of helping to communicate the structure of a Web site. Usability expert Jakob Nielsen suggests that a well-designed site map can help users visualize the structure (2002). Typically, site maps provide a structural layout of the site and links to all pages in the structure. They can be a textual outline or graphical map. They explicitly show the organization of pages, like an index, or table of contents. They help users plan paths through pages to find information. Site maps work well in sites with custom and/or complex site structures. Figure 5-10 shows a portion of the site map used

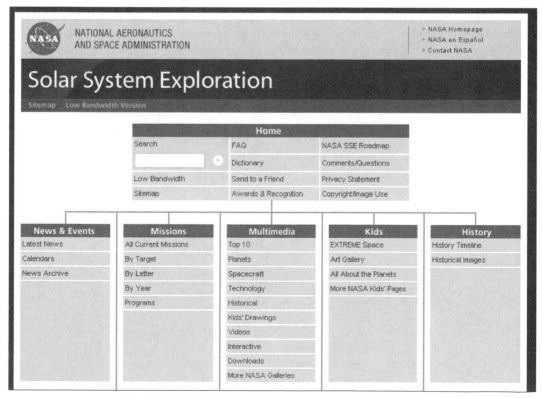

FIGURE 5-10.   An Excerpt of NASA's Solar Exploration Site Map

Source: NASA's Solar System Exploration: Sitemap, http://solarsystem.nasa.gov/sitemap/index.cfm.

ADVICE from PRACTITIONERS

Methods of Helping Users Visualize Site Structure

Andrew Eberhart • Senior Systems Programmer
Major Semiconductor Manufacturing Corporation

I typically use two features on a site to help the user understand the layout. The most common feature I will use is a site map. This will be a page that shows a visual image of the site layout so the users can see where information is located in the site. In addition, this page will usually have links to sections and pages on the map so that it can be used as a site index. Another feature I commonly use is a separate frame that lists all the content pages in the site with links. Once one of the content pages is accessed, this frame expands to show any content pages nested below it. This looks similar to a directory navigation tool under most operating systems, which provides a look and feel that is familiar for most users.

I believe the most effective feature in helping users visualize a site's structure or layout is the navigational frame. It provides a visual aid to the user that is always available to them. The site map feature is also a useful tool, but is only available when looking at that particular page. Typically, I will use both features on Web sites in order to provide the user with more than one option.

Being able to visualize the site structure and layout is important. The main objective of a Web site is to be useful for the users of the site. Humans are visual by nature. Showing them a picture allows them to better understand where the information they seek would be located and how they can get to it quickly. The quicker the users can get to the information, the more useful the site is to them.

in NASA's Solar System Exploration site. The site map uses interconnected boxes, lines, white space, color, and a text-based index to help users visualize the site's primarily hierarchical structure.

Other ways of communicating the site structure visually or textually include the use of headers, subheads, icons, graphics or descriptors, consistently or repeatedly on pages in the site. These types of cues tell users where they are, where they have been, and where they can go in the structure. When users notice these cues, they not only learn their navigation options but they get an overall concept of the whole structure.

Testing the Site Structure

It is important to test the site structure prior to implementing it and proceeding with other parts of the Web development process, such as navigation design, adding graphics, or developing an interface. Testing the structure allows a designer to see how well it fits users' mental models and expectations. Testing the site structure at this early phase of the entire Web development process can save valuable time in later phases of the work. Two effective methods for testing the site structure are card sorting and developing a mock-up version of the site structure.

Card Sort Test

A card sort test is a commonly used usability test for arranging and categorizing information. The purpose of a card sort is to test how the site structure fits users' perceptions of how information would be organized in the site. This simple testing method provides insight into how users visualize a whole structure based on the content provided. Since users are typically skilled searchers and browsers, a designer can learn a lot from the ways in which they might perceive how content is organized in the site by observing their process. Each user tested may have different ways of how to organize content in the site. The card sort test will help identify trends that might help improve a site's structure to fit the typical user's concepts of the site. This test requires a set of index cards and a small group of testing participants. Usability research suggests using a small number since results tend to repeat themselves beyond a testing population of about five users, so a small number will suffice for most tests.

In performing the card sort test, the tester can provide individual labels on each card for users or allow users to write their own labels, or change labels on the cards provided. Select whichever method best fits. To begin the sort, make a list of documents, headers and subheads, or even content sections that will be included in the site. Then, write the label of each listed item on a separate card. Shuffle the entire set and hand them to the testing subject. Provide the user with the subject, purpose, and any contextual information of the site. Then, have the user sort the cards into stacks, as if each card represented a different page in the Web site, based on how they might expect them to be organized. Ask users to write a sentence or two on the back of the card that explains their change. Record the results and repeat the process with each user. After completing all tests, analyze the results and attempt to identify any trends. Examine the structure, breadth and depth of stacks, the labels' use, and any consistencies across users. This analysis should provide valuable ideas in making changes to the site structure that fit the ways in which users think visually and spatially about the arrangement of content in a site.

Mock-Up Test

A mock-up is more involved than a card sort because it involves creating a skeleton of the site with sample pages that follow the actual blueprint of the site structure. Mock-ups integrate basic navigation links so users can explore the site structure. These mock-ups can be simple pages or fully developed drafts of the actual site, navigation links, and graphics. One benefit of using a mock-up version to test is that it allows users to visualize the site and developers to see how they think visually and spatially in using it. Many designers use a simple HTML mock-up, providing only basic information, such as a header, brief content description, and basic navigation links on each page. An alternate method would be to use Web development software to set up the mock-up structure, basic pages, and navigation links.

In developing the mock-up site, follow the blueprint of the site structure closely. Develop a separate basic Web page for each item on the blueprint. Place the label of each page as the major header on each page along with a purpose statement that describes the content found on the page. Create a basic navigation toolbar for the mock-up, which allows users to explore the pages in the site structure. This can be a simple list of text links to other pages in the site or even a simple site map.

Test the mock-up to ensure it is complete and functional and then write a short description of the subject, purpose, background information, and context in which the site will be used. Use this short description to introduce the site to the testing subjects before starting the test. Have testing subjects begin by browsing the site, following all of the links they find. Instruct them to read the information on every page so they understand what types of content found on each page. Observe their browsing and searching and make notes of important discoveries, problems, or errors they encounter. Provide them with a set of questions they can answer about the experience, some of which may include:

- What pages seem to be out of place and why?
- Where would these pages be more aptly placed and why?
- What labels would you change for links or page headers?
- Why would you make these changes?
- In what ways did the site seem to be unnecessarily complex in its organization?
- How would you make the arrangement of pages simpler?
- Based on your searching and browsing of the site, how would you sketch a site map that accurately illustrates the site structure?

The last question that asks users to sketch a site map can be very useful in seeing how users perceive the site structure based on their own visual and spatial thinking. Just like the card sort, collect the testing data and attempt to identify trends in responses. Certain responses might be particularly insightful even if they fail to respond to specific trends or expectations. Add any other appropriate questions to this list and consider providing time at the end of the testing for users to offer general comments. In either case, be sure to record their feedback for later use. The data collected should provide some general ideas of what users expect and suggest changes to be made in the site structure.

Revising the Site Structure

After testing site structure, consider the results in revising the site structure. This last step involves finding ways to condense it into a more efficient structure. Revising the site structure involves two things, editing and condensing. Editing involves making minor adjustments to the structure, such as moving a page from one content area to another. For example, a page may seem to fit better in one content area than other. Condensing involves finding ways to collapse or condense a structure. Sometimes in the development process, a structure can become unnecessarily large or complex. And most likely, a designer may not have created the ideal structure on the first try. Part of the task of condensing is to find ways of organizing pages more efficiently. In the development process, new threads or relationships between sections or pages may be discovered, which require making adjustments to the structure. In any case, some of the questions to consider when revising include:

- Are any content pathways only one page deep? Could these pages be placed under another area of the site structure?
- Which content sections could be combined?
- If there is a contact information page, does it provide minimal information that could be placed on the home page or in another location?

- Is there a content path that is significantly more shallow or deep than the others?
- Can the deepest information pathway be broken into separate sections?

The revising process may reveal better methods of modifying the structure, independent of the testing results. As adjustments are made to the structure, these changes may affect other aspects of the site structure. This is because when changes are made in the arrangement of pages, it changes the ways in which individual pages are grouped and relate. Revising can be a delicate task and can take great thought and time. Once revision is complete, perform a visual-spatial analysis (see Figure 5-1) of the revised site structure to determine how easy it is for users to comprehend the overall structure.

Conclusion

Building an efficient site structure is a complex task, which involves the arrangement of pages and the complex relationships between those pages in the overall structure. It is important to follow the process of developing a structure, since it will serve as the foundation for other parts of the site including navigation and interface design. The site structure performs more than the function of organizing pages; it suggests relationships between pages and can help users plan their searching and browsing of the site. Site structures give users a sense of the whole site and its structure, helping them determine where they are, where they have been, and where they can go in the site.

Chapter Summary

- The site structure development process involves organizing individual Web pages into a whole structure. It involves establishing relationships between pages and sections of a site.
- The process of developing a site structure involves analysis, labeling, design, testing, and aggregation.
- Methods of analysis used to determine major content areas in the site structure are content analysis and visual-spatial analysis.
- A visual-spatial analysis is important for two reasons: (1) it measures how well the site structure and related features help users comprehend the organization and layout of the site; (2) it helps identify areas of improvement in designing a more effective structure to fit user perception and need.
- It is important to select meaningful labels that outline major content areas for users. Four types of labeling schemes commonly used are functional, metaphorical, topical, and user-defined.
- Four types of Web structures that serve as models for developing site structures are linear, hierarchical, hypertextual, and customized.
- Site structures have visual-spatial characteristics, which include breadth, or the number content pathways, and depth, or the number of pages deep in a site structure.
- One method of communicating the site structure to users is through the use of contextual cues, which outline content for users and help them discern the site structure. They

signal to users where they are in the structure, where they have been, and where they can go.

- Two effective methods of testing site structures are card sorts and mock-up tests.
- Revising the site structure involves both editing and condensing the arrangement of pages in the structure.

Exercises

1. Browse a Web site for a professional or local organization that has a site map or index. Without viewing the site map or index, make note of the contextual cues used in the site. Look at navigation systems, textual elements, and graphic elements. Which elements are most effective in helping determine the organization or structure of the site? Sketch a basic site map, based on the time spent searching and browsing the site. Then, view the actual site map or index used in the site and compare it to the sketch.

2. In a small group, select a small or medium-sized Web site and make a list of the major navigation links found on the main navigation toolbar. Using index cards, write the name or label of each link on a separate card. Then, step away from the computer with the stack of cards and sort them into separate stacks based on how to best reorganize the links. The top card on each stack should be the major navigation link under which the other labeled cards would fall. Feel free to change the label or rename each card with a more appropriate label. Then, prepare a short paragraph that explains the rationale for making changes.

3. Select a Web site that uses either an index or site map and examine it. Make note of how information is organized using visual, spatial, or stylistic elements to help users comprehend the site structure. Draw a diagram of the site structure based on the information on the site map. Then, browse the site to determine the accuracy of the diagram. Identify any discrepancies found.

4. Using the questions in the section Aggregating the Site Structure, explore a familiar news or sports Web site and answer each question. If the site has an index or site map, examine it closely. Try to determine, based on the site structure (and perhaps navigation links), if there is a way to revise the site's structure. Draft a sample blueprint of the first level of the revised structure.

6

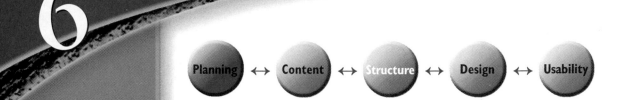

Planning ↔ Content ↔ Structure ↔ Design ↔ Usability

NAVIGATION SYSTEMS

Learning Objectives

After completing this chapter, you will understand:

- The relationship between navigation design and site structure

- The visual-spatial approach to navigation design

- The navigation design process

- The function of specific types of navigation tools

- Techniques for selecting labels for navigation

- Strategies for grouping and placing navigation tools

- The importance of providing contextual clues in navigation tools

Introduction

Navigation design is important to Web development because it involves designing tools that help users solve specific problems, and effectively search and browse a site. Navigation outlines the site structure, content, and functions, which allows users to make choices in finding specific information and performing tasks with sites. Navigation tools help users discern the organization of site content. For example, a navigation toolbar menu might suggest the major content areas, or nodes, available for searching and browsing. Web sites rely on a variety of visual tools such as toolbar menus, buttons, scrollbars, and hyperlinks for navigation. Effective navigation design depends largely on simplicity and ease of use. As such, designing navigation involves a careful balance of usability and aesthetics. Some designers are dazzled by the latest drop-down animated toolbar menu, but if a user has perceptual problems with its use, it will have defeated the purpose of providing easy access. A site's credibility is also partially based on the functionality and usefulness of site navigation. A site with broken links or overly complex tools will frustrate users and drive them away. For this reason, a designer must consider the perceptual habits and needs of users in the process of creating navigation tools. This process involves many other tasks, such as analyzing user preferences, selecting specific types of tools, developing meaningful labels, arranging tools, and testing each tool's functionality.

Navigation design and site structure share a close relationship since both outline how a site is organized into major content areas and functions. In effective site design, the navigation and site structure will mirror each other. Users should be able to look at the navigation tools to determine the major content areas and functions of the site, giving them an idea of the whole site structure. A site map is an example of when site structure and navigation work together. Site maps provide an outline of the site structure and navigation hyperlinks to various parts of the site. They demonstrate visually and spatially how content and pages connect and relate. They also allow users to see a bird's-eye view of the site structure and to use the map as a navigation tool. Other navigation tools, such as nested links and hyperlinked headers, can demonstrate how a site is organized into a coherent whole structure. The most effective navigation tools provide users access to site contents and help them understand the structure and organization of the site.

Visual-Spatial Approach to Navigation Design

Part of the designer's task is to develop navigation tools that help users solve problems and effectively search and browse the site. This is where visual-spatial principles can help designers anticipate the ways users perceive navigation tools and methods for searching and browsing sites. As readers attempt to discern contextual information in any document, printed or Web-based, designers should assume readers are on a quest for information, perhaps trying to solve a specific problem. In turn, users scan the page for elements or objects that we can use to plan our pathways through content. In many cases, these are navigation tools, search interfaces, headers, icons, site maps, and other visual objects that can be used to navigate or browse through content in a Web page. Other examples include grouping major site links into navigation toolbars, anchoring toolbars, and providing search and help systems and redundant textual navigation for users. During our initial Web searching process, we are looking for hyperlinks that we believe will eventually lead us to relevant information. Table 6-1 provides some navigation design guidelines that consider how users think visually and spatially in searching and browsing Web sites, which relate to Arnheim's five principles of visual thinking and the visual-spatial concepts from Chapter 1.

These guidelines apply generally to the entire navigation design process, while some specifically apply to one or two steps. They assist in designing effective navigation tools that help users locate themselves in the site structure and plan navigation paths through a site. A visual-spatial approach helps in the design of tools that assist users in solving problems and performing more efficient searches. Using these guidelines in the navigation design process helps designers consider the ways in which users think visually and spatially in Web sites.

Process of Navigation Design

The navigation design process involves analysis, type selection, labeling, grouping, and testing phases. Analysis involves revisiting previous research on the site's rhetorical situation, including analysis of audience or target users, purpose, and context. It involves making a list of navigation tools to use in the site. Type selection involves choosing which navigation tool best fits the purpose and function required. Labeling involves selecting a meaningful scheme for each tool

TABLE 6-1. Guidelines for Visual-Spatial Navigation Design

Concept	Navigation Guidelines
Visual focus	• Use figure-ground contrast to signal which elements readers should focus on, i.e., navigation tools, search interfaces, help. • Use animation or rollovers in navigation toolbars to indicate functional or meaningful items. • Visually emphasize navigation tools that are most important, to focus readers' attention. • Minimize the use of excessive animation, pop-up windows, and scrollbars, which can cause visual overload.
Problem solving	• Group navigation links into toolbars that suggest the major content areas or information pathways to users. • Provide multiple navigation tools and choices for readers, such as toolbars, drop-down menus, etc., to accommodate different methods of solving problems. • Allow users to sort search results by a variety of methods to facilitate their individual strategies of sorting and grouping information.
Contextual	• Use nested navigation, breadcrumb links, headers, graphic-text pairs to suggest the nature of information in a given pathway. • Use toolbars, buttons, icons, repeated links, and other navigation tools to group and organize content into broader conceptual categories.
Conceptual	• Use familiar shapes and icons in navigation to help users anticipate related content, themes or ideas. • Use shaded areas, boxes, lines, and other methods to group related navigation elements.
Wholeness	• Integrate hyperlinks into a site map that allows it to function as both a navigation tool and outline of site content. • Provide a help system, such as a frequently asked questions or knowledge base to help answer questions users might have about the site as a whole.

as well as individual labels. Grouping includes deciding how to cluster and arrange each tool. And, testing each tool is important to ensure proper functionality and usability. Table 6-2 summarizes the major steps of the navigation design process and purpose of each step.

Analysis

Analysis involves considering the site's audience, purpose, and any contextual issues, or constraints, as they relate to the process of selecting and designing each navigation tool.

TABLE 6-2 Process of Navigation Design

Process	Purpose	Tasks
Step 1: Analysis	To analyze the specific user needs and functions the site will have in planning the site's navigation	• Consider results of rhetorical analysis to determine user needs • Identify site functions
Step 2: Type Selection	To select the types of navigation tools, such as toolbars, site maps, and search features, that will be used in the site	• Select navigation tools that fit user needs and site functions • Consider visual-spatial concepts and principles
Step 3: Labeling	To select schemes and meaningful labels for navigation hyperlinks and tools	• Use site structure labels as guides for labeling • Select appropriate schemes and individual labels for each tool
Step 4: Grouping	To determine which strategies to use in grouping and arranging navigation tools	• Use visual-spatial principles to group navigation links • Plan arrangement and location of tools on individual pages
Step 5: Testing	To evaluate the functionality and usability of navigation tools	• Develop user tests and questionnaires to evaluate the use and function of tools • Revise tools based on test results

Start by reviewing the rhetorical analysis of your site, including information about the audience or target users, purpose, and contextual issues and constraints. Other issues to consider are the information needs and known technological limitations of the target users. Some questions that will help identify the important issues and design constraints include:

- What types of visual tools can be used to help users focus and solve problems?
- What types of functions will users need to perform?
- What known preferences or needs do the target users have with regard to navigation?
- What known technological limitations might they have?
- What types of tools do other sites with a similar purpose use?
- Does the site purpose suggest which types of tools might work best?
- Are there any contextual issues that might affect the choice of tools?

The answers to these questions will help identify specific guidelines to follow in the design of the site's navigation tools and in selecting the appropriate types of tools to use.

Type Selection

Web site navigation is usually comprised of four different types: hyperlinks, toolbar menus, site maps, and search utilities. Hyperlinks are the most basic type of site navigation and can be linked words, phrases, images, or buttons. Hyperlinks are clickable objects that allow users to access other pages, content, or to submit data, as in a form or using email. They are the basic foundation of all other navigation types. Toolbar menus are groups of navigation options that typically show the major content areas or functions of the site. They group hyperlinks together into a menu to help users plan their searching and browsing of content in the site. In many site designs, the navigation toolbar is located in the top, left-hand, and/or bottom margins. Toolbar menus are effective in communicating the site's structure, function, and organization of topics to users. Site maps provide the specific structural layout of the site, in graphical or outline form, and usually provide hyperlinks to most or all of the pages in a site. They can be a simple table of contents or a graphical map of the major sections and functions of the site's content. One advantage of using a site map is that it explicitly shows users the site structure and can help users quickly learn the site's organization. They function well in most sites that have complex structures and larger volumes of content. Many sites will include a hyperlink to the site map in a toolbar menu as a helpful tool for users. Search utilities allow users to search the entire site using keywords or phrases. This type of navigation is useful for sites with large volumes of searchable content or databases. Graphics are one example of nonsearchable content, since they are static images and not HTML-based text. Based on the keywords or phrases a user enters in a search field, a listing of pages and hyperlinks that matches is displayed for the user. Search utilities require users to filter these results to determine which page to select. They are less successful in smaller sites where it may be quicker to use a navigation toolbar to find a specific content chunk, rather than spending time sorting through results. Table 6-3 describes the four major types of navigation and functions and following, Figure 6-1 provides visual examples of each type.

Depending on the types used in a site design, navigation tools can provide users with visual and spatial characteristics of the overall layout and organization of the site's contents. Individual hyperlinks are visual, in that they typically stand out from normal text. However, they do little to demonstrate the spatial arrangement of overall content in a site. Toolbar menus can provide users with a visual outline of the major content areas of a site, while serving as a primary access point to the site's content. If the toolbar menu provides submenus, then it provides an even more detailed outline of the site. However, many toolbar menus suggest a hierarchical arrangement of the site's content, which may not be characteristic of the true spatial layout of pages in the site. Site maps can provide the most detail about the visual and spatial qualities of the site's layout, depending on its design. When they're as basic as a table of contents, they show the visual hierarchy and how pages are arranged spatially (i.e., from topic to subtopic). In some graphical site maps, users can see the visual and spatial arrangement of major content areas and individual pages, like in a topographic or a geographic map (see Figure 6-2). Users can click on an area on the map to get a more detailed map on related subtopics and sites to visit. This type of site map uses both visual and spatial characteristics to help users understand the organization and density of information on subjects.

TABLE 6-3. Navigation Types and Functions	
Navigation type	**Function**
Individual words or graphics	Hyperlinks can be individual words, phrases, or images that, when clicked, link to another page or chunk of related content. Users can click on these words, buttons or images to access the related page, chunk, or to submit data in a form. Hyperlinks are used in all site structures and are the foundation of other navigation types.
Toolbar menus	Toolbar menus are groups of multiple navigation choices that show major content areas and functions of the site. They can be drop-down, pullout, graphic-based, or text labels. Each item in the menu links to a related page or section of the site. In larger sites, submenus can provide links to more specific content. Toolbars work well in all sites, but are less effective in searching portal sites, which have large databases of searchable content.
Site maps	Site maps provide a structural layout of the site and links to all pages in the structure. They can be a graphic map or textual outline of the site structure. They explicitly show the organization of pages, like an index or table of contents. They help users plan paths through pages to find information. Site maps work well in sites with custom and/or complex site structures.
Search utilities	Search utilities allow users to type in key words or phrases in a search box and press a button to search the entire content of a site. Based on the results of the search, a list of possible pages that matches is displayed and links are provided. Search utilities typically work best in sites with large amounts of searchable content.

Most sites use a variety of the four types of navigation, but usually individual text links, graphic buttons, and toolbar menus are found in virtually all sites. Smaller sites will use the first two types, while larger, more complex sites may use all four types. Consider using individual hyperlinks for smaller content chunks that serve as references, such as definitions and links to other references. Words or images can be used within individual chunks to point users to related chunks or sites. Most sites will need to use a toolbar menu to help users plan methods of searching and browsing the site. If the site has a large volume of searchable content or uses database tables, add a search feature to help users locate information more quickly. If the site's structure is unusually complex, broad, and/or deep, develop a site map so users can more easily understand its organization. Some relevant guidelines based on the visual-spatial approach that apply to type selection are summarized in Figure 6-3.

One important rule for navigation design is to provide users with more than one type of tool to search and browse the site. Each user will have a different preference for how they search and browse a site and it's important to provide flexibility in the types of site navigation to accommodate the widest possible user base. Regardless of the combination of types used, effective navigation should help communicate the site's structure to users both visually and spatially, to help them search and browse the site more efficiently.

Hyperlinks	This is an example of a **textual hyperlink**. Images and buttons can also be used as hyperlinks. [Submit]
Toolbar menu	[Browse Products] [Keyword Search] [View Cart] [Check Out] (Source: Flashbuttons, http://www.flashbuttons.com)

Site map	**News**
	  Program Schedule
	  Training Center
	  Join Our Next Six Month Program
	  Email Questions
	  Email to Join
	Program
	Schedule
	Training
	  Strength
	  Cardiovascular
	  Nutrition
	  Wellness

Search utility	┌ Library Search ────────────── [ ] [SEARCH] ○ Author │ ○ Title │ ○ Subject

FIGURE 6-1. Examples of the Four Types of Navigation Tools

FIGURE 6-2. USGS National Cooperative Geologic Mapping Program—(NCGMP)

Source: Funded Geologic Mapping, and Related Studies Web page.
USGS NCGMP, http://ncgmp.usgs.gov./ncgmpactivities.

- Provide multiple navigation tools and choices for readers, such as toolbars, drop-down menus, etc., to accommodate different methods of solving problems.

- Use nested navigation, breadcrumb links, headers, graphic-text pairs to suggest the nature of information in a given pathway.

- Use toolbars, buttons, icons, repeated links, and other navigation tools to group and organize content into broader conceptual categories.

- Integrate hyperlinks into a site map that allows it to function as both a navigation tool and outline of site content.

- Provide a help system, such as a frequently asked questions or knowledge base to help answer questions users might have about the site as a whole.

FIGURE 6-3.   Visual-Spatial Guidelines for Navigation Type Selection

Labeling

After selecting individual types of navigation tools, the next step is to select a labeling scheme and develop individual labels. Ideas for labeling major content areas may come from the labels used to develop the site structure from Chapter 5. However, they may need to be revised in most cases to appeal to target users. A good labeling scheme can help in the selection of individual labels appropriate to the specific site purpose or design scheme. There are four types of navigation labeling schemes commonly used: functional, metaphorical, topical, and user-defined, illustrated in Figure 6-4.

A functional scheme involves using labels for navigation that suggest their function or use. For example, the label "shopping cart" suggests its function or use. A "submit" button suggests data or information will be sent when the button is clicked. Functional labels are typically verb-based and suggest an action. A **metaphorical** scheme is based on a specific

ADVICE from PRACTITIONERS

Decision Making and Navigation Type Selection
Tommy Petty • Software Engineer
Major Telecommunications Corporation

In deciding what types of navigation to use in a site, you always want to keep each navigation system as simple to use as possible. If it appears difficult or intimidating, users will be reluctant to use it. The type of navigation system I use often depends on the content the page is providing. A navigation system should be designed in such a way that it does not change from page to page, otherwise you will confuse some of your users. The navigation systems should function on all major browsers (at least one major browser for each popular operating system). You will not gain popularity among users of your site if the main navigation menu works great in Internet Explorer, but does not work in Safari or takes too long to load in Firefox. The visual aspect of navigation is also very important in navigation design, in that it must be attractive, but also simple enough for an average user to easily navigate. If its use and function is not obvious to the average user, you will get many phone calls asking how to navigate your site while many other potential users will simply give up.

Functional
Labels describe the specific function or use of the navigation tool.

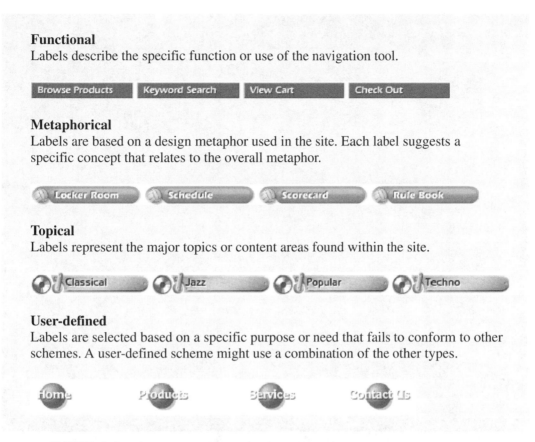

Metaphorical
Labels are based on a design metaphor used in the site. Each label suggests a specific concept that relates to the overall metaphor.

Topical
Labels represent the major topics or content areas found within the site.

User-defined
Labels are selected based on a specific purpose or need that fails to conform to other schemes. A user-defined scheme might use a combination of the other types.

FIGURE 6-4. Schemes and Examples for Labeling Navigation

Graphic Source: Flashbuttons, http://www.flashbuttons.com.

design metaphor used for the overall site design theme. For example, an office metaphor might use labels of objects found in an office, such as filing cabinet, bookshelf, and trash can. This scheme is a highly visual one, in that users can often visualize the concept behind the label and comprehend its use.

Metaphorical labels are typically noun-based since they represent objects within the metaphorical environment. A topical scheme most closely relates to labels selected for the site structure and is based on major content areas of the site's contents. Topical labeling schemes work well for sites that organize content by topic and subtopic, such as news and information sites. They might suggest the nature of the content found by following that particular hyperlink, such as a definition or external Web site. Topical schemes permit more flexibility in choice of labels since they are based broadly on the site's subject and purpose. User-defined schemes offer the most flexibility in choice of labels, since they are typically based on some type of exception or purpose. User-defined schemes can combine any of the other types and/or create a unique scheme. However, don't consider a user-defined scheme as a completely free-form scheme, rather try to select labels that will be meaningful in the context of the site's subject and purpose. Figures 6-5 and 6-6 provide two examples of labeling schemes used in Web sites.

FIGURE 6-5. The Conversive Web Site

This site uses a topical labeling scheme that uses color coded tabs and text labels to outline the site content. These labels suggest specific products, services, technologies, and audiences that help users conceptualize how information is organized in the site.

Source: Conversive, http://www.conversive.com/html/technology.php.

When selecting a labeling scheme, remember to consider the visual model that scheme suggests. Toolbar menus, major content headers, site maps, and other navigation should help users comprehend the concept or theme used in the navigation type. The visual-spatial principles of *vision is selective, fixation solves a problem,* and *shapes are concepts* suggest that readers actively focus on visual elements, use them to solve problems, navigate, and seek out visual shapes to help them. In functional schemes, the use of action verbs and/or a visual element might help users visualize the meaning more easily. Metaphorical schemes might require pairing a visual element with a text label to help users conceptualize the meaning of labels in that scheme. Topical labeling schemes often pair visuals, such as icons or pictures, with text labels to help users visualize the nature of content. User-defined labeling schemes might be more challenging since they have more variations possible and may not suggest a specific metaphor or set of topics already familiar to users. In any case, it is important to consider choice and

FIGURE 6-6.   The Vital Vinyl Dot Com Web Site

Two labeling schemes are used: main site navigation and submenu navigation menus. The main navigation has a user-defined labeling scheme that incorporates topics and functions. When selecting the CDs option, the submenu uses a topical labeling scheme based on the type of music. The labels selected have specific meaning to the site's target users.

Source: Vital Vinyl Dance Records, http://www.vitalvinyl.com.

design of labels that helps users visualize the nature of content in such a site. Some visual-spatial guidelines that can help pair visuals with labels are summarized in Figure 6-7.

Throughout the site navigation design process, multiple labeling schemes may be required based on the different navigation tools needed. Some sites design links based on the different major user groups. A university Web site may have one toolbar menu for students and another for faculty and staff. E-commerce sites may have separate toolbar menus or even site sections for distributors and end-users. Keep in mind the purpose of each link and the nature of the content or function when a hyperlink is clicked. That will help decide what type of scheme might be best for each navigation tool. When selecting individual labels for navigation hyperlinks and tools, make sure they are meaningful to users. "Click Here" only tells users these words are a hyperlink and fails to suggest the nature of content found by clicking on the hyperlink. When

- Use animation or rollovers in navigation toolbars to highlight individual labels, or choices, that indicate specific functions.

- Visually emphasize navigation tools and labels that are most important to focus readers' attention.

- Use familiar shapes and icons with navigation to help users anticipate related content, themes, or ideas.

- Group navigation links into toolbars that suggest the major content areas, information pathways, and meaning of labeling schemes.

- Use labeling schemes where appropriate to help users comprehend how topics and functions relate to the whole site.

- Use shaded areas, boxes, lines, and other methods to group related navigation elements.

FIGURE 6-7.   Visual-Spatial Guidelines for Labeling Navigation

using graphics or icons as part of navigation tools, provide meaningful text labels or descriptors so users understand the concept behind the visual object. A book icon may suggest many different concepts in a library Web site and nothing in a site that sells music CDs.

Grouping and Placement

Grouping and placing navigation tools in page layouts is essentially the first task in preparing to design the interface, which is discussed in detail in Chapter 8. But before laying out the entire screen interface, decide what rules will govern how tools are grouped, ordered, and placed. Navigation toolbars and site maps require more thought in planning their organization than individual hyperlinks, which may be placed in paragraphs or text chunks. This involves deciding the order of items, their visual characteristics, and their spacing. The scheme chosen for labels might dictate the order of links in a navigation toolbar or site map. A specific purpose or the importance of frequency of use might dictate the order. Figure 6-8 shows some frequently used methods of grouping navigation hyperlinks.

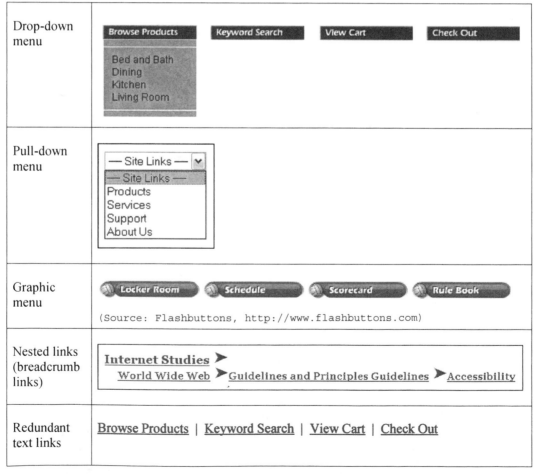

FIGURE 6-8.   Types of Grouped Navigation

Search utilities and site maps are two other types of grouped navigation shown in Figure 6-1. Search utilities vary in planning time and depend on the number of fields and options included. A basic text box and search button should be grouped in close proximity, but may not require much planning. However, for a more complex set of text boxes and searching options, try to sketch a draft of how each item will fit into the search form.

Navigation tools can provide important contextual clues to users as well. One example is the use of nested links, shown in Figure 6-8. They show the complete pathway a user has followed to reach his current location. In doing so, they help users understand the structure of the site by showing this pathway. Redundant text links provide context by reinforcing the major content areas and/or functions available to users in the site. They allow users to avoid scrolling back to the top of longer pages. Site maps provide context as well by explicitly identifying major content areas and functions, but often in more detail. Contextual clues help users visualize pathways that are possible when searching and browsing the site. They suggest the spatial relationships between individual content chunks and pages, as well as the overall organization of the whole site. Many sites use a variety of navigation tools and grouping strategies to help users find information. Two examples of sites that use different grouping strategies for navigation tools are shown in Figures 6-9 and 6-10.

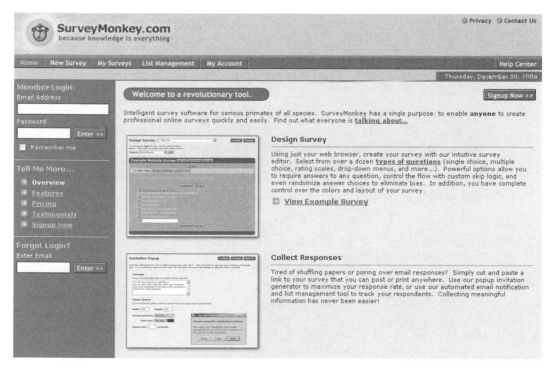

FIGURE 6-9.   The SurveyMonkey Web Site

This site groups main navigation links underneath the title banner, in a place most users will look. For other grouped site navigation, descriptive blue text headers are used against grey boxes to create contrast and focus. Members can easily locate the login form which is grouped with a "Member Login" header and informational links are provided under the "Tell Me More...."

Source: SurveyMonkey.com, http://www.surveymonkey.com.

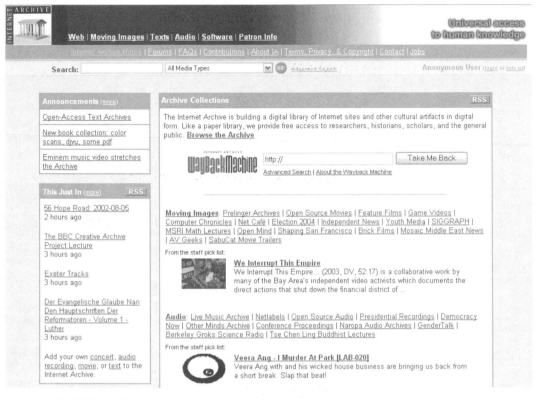

FIGURE 6-10.   The Internet Archive Web Site

This site uses shaded boxes and contrasting colors to highlight and group navigation, such as the "Announcements" and "This Just In" sections located in the left-hand margin. The main site navigation toolbar is organized by media type found in their collection, such as, Web, Moving Images, Texts, Audio, Software, and is placed near the site logo and inside the title banner. A search utility is also provided just below the main navigation toolbar.

Source: Internet Archive, http://www.archive.org.

Two principles to consider when deciding the placement of navigation tools are visual consistency and repetition. Visual consistency is based on user expectation. Once users learn and recognize patterns in sites, they depend on these new rules in searching and browsing pages. When they need to solve problems, make queries, or perform tasks, they will rely on what they already know to plan their actions. Visual consistency applies both to the grouping order and the placement of navigation tools in a site. Once users learn the location of key navigation tools, they can easily find and use them. When users learn the order of items in a toolbar menu or site map, they will be able to use that tool more efficiently. Users will expect to find individual hyperlinks or buttons in the same order and in the same location once encountered. Placing hyperlinks in new locations or in a different order would cause confusion. When deciding on the order and placement of navigation tools, use consistent methods to help improve the overall usability of these tools. Some

- Use figure-ground contrast to signal which elements readers should focus on, such as navigation tools, search interfaces, help.

- Group navigation links into toolbars that suggest the major content areas or information pathways to users.

- Allow users to sort search results by a variety of methods to facilitate their individual strategies of sorting and grouping information.

- Use toolbars, buttons, icons, repeated links, and other navigation tools to group and organize content into broader conceptual categories.

- In more complex sites, group hyperlinks into a site map that allows it to function as both a navigation tool and outline of site content.

- Repeat navigation links on pages that require scrolling to help users find navigation more quickly.

FIGURE 6-11.   Visual-Spatial Guidelines for Grouping and Placement of Navigation

visual-spatial guidelines that can be used in grouping and placement of navigation tools are provided in Figure 6-11.

Repeating navigation is important in grouping and placement, especially for longer pages that require users to scroll vertically or horizontally. Repetition is based on user expectation and helps users quickly learn the rules that govern the site. Repeating hyperlinks at the bottom of larger pages, or providing "back to top" links at the end of major sections on longer pages can help users return to navigation tools more quickly. If the site uses graphic navigation tools, consider providing a duplicate as text-only hyperlinks, for greater user accessibility. Some users may have graphics or certain scripts disabled in their browsers and providing descriptors for graphic navigation tools and a duplicate set of textual hyperlinks would enable them to still view and use the navigation tools. Another consideration is that sight-impaired users may be accessing the site using assistive software that provides an audio reading of Web content. This software can read the only descriptors, or ALT textual descriptions, assigned to each graphic. There might be subtle visual details, such as color, size, and other aspects not explained in textual descriptors. As such, descriptors only provide limited details to these sight-impaired users. Textual hyperlinks are read verbatim and ensure that all users have access to the same information.

Testing

Testing navigation tools helps you determine their overall functionality and usability. While a more thorough usability test for a completed site should be conducted, there are some initial tests that should be performed to determine the effectiveness of navigation tools. A functionality test involves testing all the hyperlinks, toolbar menus, site maps, and/or search features to see that they work as intended. To test their functionality, develop a few prototype pages, or mock-ups, with navigation tools. Only include the basics and avoid inserting other graphics, content, and backgrounds that do not affect the function of navigation tools. Consider designing a toolbar menu or basic form and test it in your prototype

- Using any site navigation tool contained in the site, find information on how to reach the site technical support team.
- Using only the main navigation toolbar, visit each of the main content section pages and then return to the home page.
- Examine the visual elements, such as graphics, icons, and colors used in the site navigation. Describe the concept, meaning, or function behind each.
- When visual elements are paired with text labels in site navigation, are they good matches? What other labels or visuals would be more appropriate to help users understand the meaning of these elements?
- Examine the use of repeated navigation links used in the site. Do the use of labels and their arrangement demonstrate consistency? If not, note any exceptions.

FIGURE 6-12.   Sample Practical Navigation Testing Questions

page to see that it functions properly. Developing and testing prototypes saves time since work can be saved and used in later page design layouts.

A basic navigation test can be performed with either a site prototype or on paper. The test can be performed with a small sample (about five users) and a series of short navigation problems for them to solve. Questions should address how users would solve a given problem, including the types of tools and navigation choices preferred. These problems can be practical that require the use of specific navigation tools to solve. Questions can address specific issues such as meaning, function, or consistent use. Some sample practical testing questions that might be used as a guideline are provided in Figure 6-12.

Since each site's purpose is unique, develop actual problems for individual questions that users might encounter when performing basic functions and searches of the site. Provide a combination of questions for testers to answer, including observation and post-test interview questions. This type of test helps determine the tools users prefer and if they are using tools correctly to solve problems. In turn, this information might be useful in redesigning existing tools or creating new ones to accommodate user preferences.

Conclusion

The primary focus of navigation tools should be on their functionality and usability. Aesthetics are important as well, but only if they conform to these two principles. It is important to consider user needs, the site purpose, and contextual issues as well in analyzing, selecting, labeling, grouping, and testing the navigation tools designed for a Web site. It is equally important to consider how navigation tools help users learn how the site structure and organization. Navigation hyperlinks and tools help define the site structure by connecting pages into a whole structure. They provide important contextual clues to readers to help them in searching and browsing sites.

Chapter Summary

- Navigation design is important to Web design because it allows users to interact with the site, and search, browse, control content and the sequence of pages displayed.

- Navigation design and site structure work together in a site design to communicate the site structure, major content areas, sections, and functions of the site. Together, they help users understand the visual and spatial relationships between pages and links that comprise the whole site.

- Designing usable navigation is important to site design because users assess the credibility of a site based on the functionality and usefulness of the tools provided.

- The five step process of navigation design includes analysis, type selection, labeling, grouping, and testing.

- Analysis involves considering the site's audience, purpose, and contextual issues in the overall process of selecting and designing each navigation tools.

- Four types of navigation used in site design include hyperlinks, toolbar menus, site maps, and search features.

- Effective navigation design should communicate the site structure, layout, or organization both visually and spatially to users.

- Four commonly used navigation labeling schemes are functional, metaphorical, topical, and user-defined.

- Graphics and icons, when used in navigation tools, should have meaningful text labels and/or descriptors to suggest the concept and meaning behind their use.

- Grouping navigation tools involves planning the order of individual hyperlinks in navigation toolbars, site maps, search utilities, and planning their placement on pages.

- Contextual clues help users visualize pathways that are possible when searching and browsing the site and are important to navigation design. They show users the spatial relationships and overall organization of pages in the whole site.

- Consistency and repetition are two principles to consider when creating usable and easily accessible navigation tools. Both rely on user expectation in the grouping and placing of navigation tools.

- Testing navigation tools helps determine their overall functionality and usability.

Exercises

1. Select an e-commerce site that enables users to buy products and services on the Web. Identify the types of navigation tools that are used to aid customers in searching and buying items. Which tools seem to be the most effective for searching and locating items and why? Which tools are used to actually purchase items? What other navigation tools could be used to aid potential customers?

2. Using the same e-commerce site from question #1, examine the main navigation toolbar menu and determine the labeling scheme used. If more than one toolbar menu is used, determine the labeling scheme used for each one. Assess the choice of schemes

and individual labels used. What changes could be made to improve the overall usability of each navigation toolbar menu?

3. Select a public information Web site, such as a government or nonprofit agency site, and examine the types of grouped navigation tools that are used. In addition, examine both the use of visual elements and space to group individual navigation tools. How effective are the grouping methods in helping users focus or comprehend the use of these navigation tools? Are problems created by the overuse or lack of visual and spatial elements to group site navigation tools?

4. Select a search portal site, such as Yahoo, and identify site navigation used to search the site other than the basic searching tool. Develop three sample user problems to test the usability of the search tool selected. Then, find two to five testing subjects to solve the sample problems. Based on the results, characterize the effectiveness of the navigation tool. What changes could be made to improve its usability?

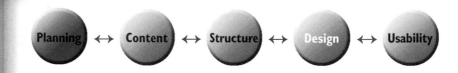

VISUAL DESIGN

Learning Objectives

After completing this chapter, you will understand:

- How user behavior and expectations affect design

- How user perception and visual-spatial thinking relate to design

- An overview of Web design principles and Web design conventions

- The process of designing visuals for Web sites

- Graphic file formats and important technical issues with regard to design

Introduction

Due to the highly visual nature of Web content, visual design is particularly important to the Web development process. Web designs rely heavily on the use of graphic elements for its organization, navigation, and content. When designing graphic content for Web sites, the design job involves much more than inserting images onto a static background. Web design work includes the use of animation, multimedia, audio, video, and other interactive graphics for navigation menus and forms. Visual design encompasses deciding what type of visual elements to use, their placement, usability, and readability. Design work should consider both visual and spatial aspects with regard to the emphasis, balance, symmetry, grouping, alignment, and use of space on pages, which are some of the discernable visual and spatial aspects to designing Web sites. Designers must consider the use of design conventions and principles as guides in developing effective visuals. Understanding the technical aspects of graphic design helps designers choose the file formats and methods that best achieve design goals.

Each graphic has its own unique visual and spatial qualities, such as the use of color, white space, or emphasis. In Web sites, the quality of the visual image can be as important as its placement on the page. Regardless of the type of visual, each shares certain characteristics, listed in Figure 7-1.

Each visual element has a target audience and purpose, as well as is situated in a specific context. A graphic not tailored to its audience or

- Each has a rhetorical function.
- Each suggests a specific function, meaning and/or use.
- Visual groups create a set of shared characteristics or traits.
- Each has unique visual and spatial qualities.

FIGURE 7-1.   Visual Design Characteristics

unique context, or without a purpose, has little use. Each visual element has interpretive value, which means that each user will not perceive its meaning in quite the same way. When designing visuals, this is an important issue to consider. Each visual should suggest a specific function or use within the Web site. Visuals are often grouped together and, subsequently, each group and its individual elements share specific characteristics.

The first step in visual design is to understand the importance and function of design principles and conventions. Design principles are based on theories of effective design and serve as broad guides for making design decisions. For example, consistency is a design principle that advocates the use of repeated elements throughout a page or site. Design conventions are more specific and prescriptive, often derived as practical tasks adapted from a specific principle or use. They are based on their tested use in a variety of site designs. One common design convention is to provide a navigation toolbar consistently on every page in a Web site. As such, design conventions can be considered a subset of design principles. Becoming familiar with these principles and conventions will lead to more usable visuals and page designs.

Understanding Web Design Principles

Web design principles serve as broad guides and are based on theories of design. Many Web design principles have been adapted from principles used to create print-based documents, such as newsletters and pamphlets. As we have gradually moved toward electronic forms of writing and publishing, we have borrowed from time-tested knowledge of designing printed documents. Since the Web has some distinct differences from print, principles used have to be adapted or modified to fit the Web's interactivity, use of multimedia, and other characteristics. Some design guides used in print just don't work as well on the Web. For example, italic print for citing book titles is used in print, using italicized text on a computer screen impairs its readability. The use of complex grids to format newsletter layouts can create a cluttered Web interface, offering users too many choices for navigation, content, and graphics. And the use of underlining titles suggests a header in print and often, a hyperlink on a Web page. One thing to consider when using design principles in Web development is how they may apply specifically to that medium or environment.

Design principles vary significantly; some apply specifically to printed page design or graphics, whereas others have more broad usage. Some design principles offer guidance on how information is placed, labeled, or organized (Rosenfeld and Moorville 2002). Others focus more on the unique characteristics of graphics, such as their alignment, contrast, proximity, and repetition (Williams and Tollett 2000). Some principles have a more rhetorical focus, stressing the importance of ethos, tone, and arrangement (Kostelnick and Roberts 1998). Others deal with how users perceive visual information, such as their figure-ground contrast, grouping, and similarity (Koffka 1935).

User Perception and Visual-Spatial Thinking

When considering a set of design principles that applies broadly to Web design, we must consider how users perceive design elements. The concept of visual thinking is based on an understanding of how humans perceive and respond to visual elements in a visual-textual landscape. Web browsing requires users to interact with content and to make choices. Visual thinking, based on the work of Rudolf Arnhiem and founded in Gestalt theory, is one approach to design that considers how *users as humans* act and interact with elements in their visual field. Visual thinking considers how users recognize patterns and respond in similar ways to visual information. For example, users may recognize a list of textual items in the left-hand margin of a Web page as a navigation toolbar. They might recognize the meaning and function of a shopping cart icon on a site that sells books. Visual thinking offers an approach that considers how users conceptualize, interpret, and respond in similar ways to these elements. Our interaction with visual information starts in the brain, where we visualize possible options and solutions before we act; in essence, this is visual thinking. Applying visual thinking to a Web environment requires that we consider the spatial qualities of design. In Web sites, our perception is as much a spatial activity as it is a visual one; in fact our own perception defies the notion that visual and spatial perception are separate (Johnson-Sheehan and Baehr 2001). Designing site structures, navigation systems, graphics, and interface page layouts are visual-spatial aspects of Web design that change the way we think and use Web site content.

Two Related Approaches

Visual thinking comes from the field of **Gestalt psychology**, which argues that humans respond, organize, and assign meaning to elements in their visual field. This approach considers how users conceptualize functional wholes from individual elements they perceive in the visual field. One principle, figure-ground, suggests that when two elements are placed in the same visual field, one will be perceived as the figure and the other as the ground. Depending on the level of contrast between the two objects, humans will tend to focus on the element in the foreground, the figure, and not the ground, or background. At any one instance, we focus on either the figure or the ground. The use of Gestalt principles, such as figure-ground contrast, can help designers signal to users which elements in the interface are most useful or significant. This includes how information is grouped and how visual elements are interrelated, to collectively function as a single, whole Web site. Other Gestalt principles include figure-ground, similarity, continuity, symmetry, proximity, area, and closure. For more information on these principles, perform a basic Web search on Gestalt principles, or seek out books written by key Gestalt theorists, such as Kurt Koffka, Wolfgang Kohler, and Max Wertheimer. Visual-spatial thinking builds on Gestalt theory and principles in its explanation of how users think and behave in visual-spatial environments, like Web sites. This approach considers how users focus, select, discern and conceptualize elements in their field of vision.

Another related discipline that focuses on user behavior and perception is **human–computer interaction (HCI)**. This discipline considers the design of human–computer interfaces, such as software and Web sites, which users interact with to perform tasks or find information. Its primary focus in the "design, evaluation and implementation of interactive computing systems for human use and with the study of major phenomena surrounding them" (Hewett et. al. 1996). It examines how computer products influence and persuade users to perform specific actions (Fogg 2003). HCI has evolved from a variety of disciplines, including computer graphics, programming languages, communication theory, industrial design, human performance, cognitive psychology, and human performance (Hewett et. al. 1996). HCI integrates the study of user performance and cognition, which are important to studying visual and spatial aspects of Web design.

Visual-Spatial Design Principles

Design principles are based on theories and research from a variety of fields. They offer broad based advice on design, rather than prescriptive rules. A design principle may suggest using elements consistently throughout a site, but they won't specifically tell a designer to use blue dots for bullet points on pages with light-colored backgrounds. It is up to the designer to decide how each design principle applies specifically to her work. Visual-spatial design is based on the concept that users think both visually and spatially in Web environments. Users actively focus their eyes, discern meaning, form concepts, and act based on the function and organization of visual and spatial aspects of what they see. Principles of visual-spatial design are important in helping designers understand how users think when searching and browsing Web sites. Five visual-spatial design principles that can be used to design visuals are contrast, concept, grouping, center, and consistency, summarized in Figure 7-2.

CONTRAST

Use of visuals or colors to create emphasis, which focuses the eye for a specific purpose

CONCEPT

Use of shapes, icons, or graphics that suggests a specific meaning or organization, which is context sensitive

GROUPING

Arranging elements together to suggest meaningful relationships between them

CENTER

The balance and symmetry created by other objects in close proximity

CONSISTENCY

Consistent use of elements and styles that conveys a complete or whole object

FIGURE 7-2. A Summary of the Five Visual-Spatial Principles of Web Design

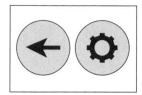

FIGURE 7-3a.   Example of Contrast

  Contrast deals with how visuals or colors look when layered, often on top of each other. Contrast is used to create emphasis or focus for the eye. It responds to the perceptual need to focus or fixate on elements in our visual field. Elements that have good contrast will make one element stand out more, such as white text on a black background. In this way, contrast can be used for emphasis. When colors have less contrast, they may seem to blend together, such as grey line on a dark grey background. But contrast doesn't just deal with the use of color, it also includes transparency. For example, when a watermark is used as a background, it has semitransparency that makes it only partially visible. Layering is a third aspect of contrast since it involves placing multiple visuals in the same space. Visuals in the background may have more or less contrast depending on its visibility. In Figure 7-3a, the use of a solid black border and shaded white background improves the visual contrast of the shapes, giving them added emphasis. In addition, solid black icons offer good contrast against the grey round buttons.

  Concept refers to the use of shapes, icons, or other graphics that suggest a specific meaning or function within a given context. It is based on the idea that each element has a specific rhetorical purpose or function. Concept responds to the cognitive aspect of user perception. As part of our perception of visual objects, we actively assign meaning to each, individually and as part of a larger whole. Certain objects might be categorized as placeholders, decorations, clickable buttons, or hyperlinks. Shaded regions or boxes used on a Web page suggest a concept—that items inside these elements are related. Icons and pictures, by themselves or paired with text, suggest concepts or specific meaning. They may suggest the function or category of a specific page or section of a Web site. For example, an icon of a house often represents the site's home page. A question mark may suggest a help feature. Designers can use these familiar shapes in sites to suggest the nature of content or function of objects. They can pair text tags with images or use elements repeatedly to suggest their purpose or function. Designing with concept in mind for visuals can greatly aid user comprehension of the functions of elements and layouts of sites. Figure 7-3b illustrates a header that pairs a graphic of a globe with text labels to suggest a "global" concept. This example from the U.S. Library of Congress Web site is used to convey visually one of the many sections in the site.

FIGURE 7-3b.   Example of Concept

Source: Library of Congress, http://www.loc.gov.

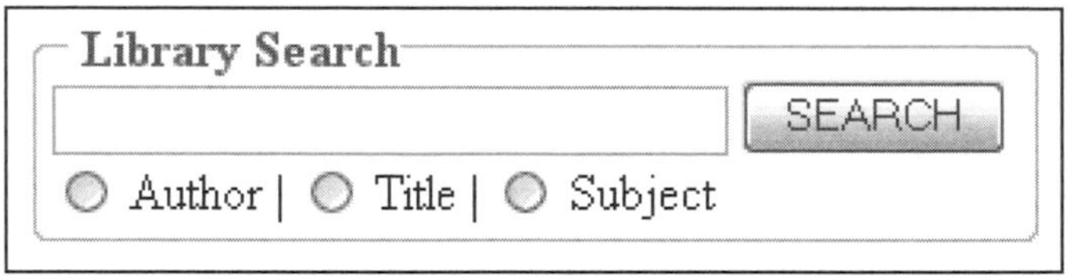

FIGURE 7-3c. Example of Grouping

Grouping is the arrangement of visuals to suggest a specific relationship among them. Grouping responds to our perceptual need to understand the relationships between elements in our visual field and our need to form conceptual wholes from our understanding. Grouping involves the arrangement of visual elements in close proximity using borders and spacing. Layering objects, like in the use of contrast, is another method of grouping elements. Elements that are grouped share a set of common characteristics and sometimes they share a function. For example, a Web form might group various boxes and buttons to suggest they function collectively as a single, whole form. Searching tools often group boxes and buttons together to comprise a whole search interface tool. Navigation buttons are often grouped to suggest a site navigation toolbar. The purpose of grouping is to suggest a relationship between elements to help users understand how individual elements in a page work together and share common characteristics. In Figure 7-3c, a library search utility uses spacing and graphic elements as visual grouping techniques. Users perceive that the text box, radio buttons, search button, and text labels function together to make up a whole search tool.

Center deals with the degree of balance and symmetry an image or page has. Each visual object when placed on a page affects all other objects. An object's center refers to the balance or imbalance created by its relation to other objects in close proximity. Visual objects have a degree of balance and imbalance as well as a degree of symmetry and asymmetry, individually and in relation to the whole. Balanced and symmetrical visuals tend to create a more organized appearance. Imbalanced and asymmetrical visuals tend to create more emphasis for specific elements and are found in more avant-garde designs. The level of balance refers to where the eye is naturally drawn to in the graphic, or what Rudolf Arnheim calls its "visual center" (1988). Graphics with good balance have visual centers that draw the eye toward the center of the graphic. Conversely, graphics that draw the eye to another feature not located in the center tend to be more imbalanced. Center is important to visual design because it can be used to focus the eye on or toward other elements placed on pages. When designing visuals, it is important to consider how they impact the overall visual balance and symmetry of the page as a whole. Sometimes not having balance isn't necessarily a bad choice, especially when there is a need to emphasize a specific area of a page or graphic. The overall design purpose and theme for a page will dictate the level of both balance and symmetry. Figure 7-3d shows the use of center in a graphic header used in the Research-Based Web Design and Usability Guidelines site. The visual center of the graphic draws the eye toward the text in the right side of the header, using both a directional arrow, gradient line, and bolded text.

Consistency refers to using elements repeatedly or similarly, which builds user expectation and demonstrates patterns that users can recognize in the design of visuals. As

FIGURE 7-3d.   Example of Center

Source: Research-Based Web Design & Usability Guidelines, http://www.usability.gov/guidelines.

part of user perception, we actively attempt to comprehend and make sense out of elements in our visual field. Consistency deals with using elements in similar contexts, styles, locations, or repeating them. This develops the rules that govern the entire organization of the site. Once users learn and can rely on consistent and repeated elements, they can more easily understand how visual elements are used in the site. Figure 7-3e, a basic navigation toolbar menu, demonstrates the principle of consistency. Consistent visual styles and icons are used for each element in the menu, including size, shape, border, icons, and color. Consistent text styles are used, which include the font face, color, spacing, and placement.

Figure 7-4 is a screenshot of the NASA Earth Observatory Natural Hazards page, which demonstrates the use of many of the five visual-spatial Web design principles. The site uses contrast by providing darker text colors and graphics that stand out against a plain white background. Concept is demonstrated by the use of icons and text labels. For example, a flame represents fire and a cloud with a thunderbolt represents severe storms. Grouping is used to pair images with navigation labels. Main navigation links are grouped across the top margin underneath the page header. A second navigation menu is provided in the lower right-hand corner based on the type of natural hazard. The site uses the principle of center to balance and organize the various navigation options for the site. The top half of the site balances the main navigation choices with the image of the world map. The bottom half of the page balances text chunks and events with a list of specific hazards. The use of dark colors and circle icon buttons are effective in focusing the eye on the symbols used in the site. The site uses the principle of consistency by pairing images with text labels and using consistent font and graphic styles.

Visual-spatial design principles address the use of emphasis, balance, symmetry, repetition, and grouping of visual elements in page designs. Using these principles will help design graphics that respond to the ways in which users perceive and conceptualize visual information in Web sites. Along with a good understanding of design principles, a designer should consider the use of Web design conventions, which provide more prescriptive guides for design work.

FIGURE 7-3e.   Example of Consistency

Source: Flashbuttons, http://www.flashbuttons.com.

e a r t h   o b s e r v a t o r y

home • data & images • features • news • reference • missions • experiments • search

NATURAL HAZARDS

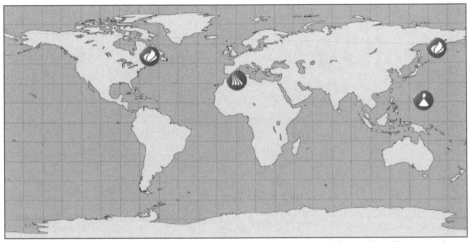

The icons on the above map show the locations of natural hazards observed by NASA satellites. Choose one to see the latest image associated with that natural hazard event, or select one of the sections from our topic list to learn more about these extreme events.

Earth scientists around the world use NASA satellite imagery to better understand the causes and effects of natural hazards. The goal in sharing these images is to help people visualize where and when natural hazards occur, and to help mitigate their effects. All images in this section are freely available to the public for re-use or re-publication (please use credits as indicated for each image). More images can be found in our archive of older events. Check out our related links.

This Week's Events

Fires: Fires in Quebec
At the end of May 2005, lightning triggered scores of wildfires across the Canadian province of Quebec. 2 Images, Updated: June 03, 2005

CROPS & DROUGHT

DUST & SMOKE

FIRES

FLOODS

SEVERE STORMS

VOLCANOES

UNIQUE IMAGERY

FIGURE 7-4.   NASA Earth Observatory Natural Hazards Web Page

Source: EO National Hazards: National Hazards Main Page, http://earthobservatory.nasa.gov/NaturalHazards/.

Understanding Web Design Conventions

Web design conventions are based on user expectations and are commonly found in many major Web sites. They differ from design principles in that design conventions offer prescriptive rules that refer to specific suggestions. Design conventions are often based on the work of experienced designs that have been tested and widely used. They may be based on a style sheet or known user preferences. For example, users of a specific site may expect to find grouped navigation tools, a keyword search field, a site map, or other graphic content that supplements the textual content in a site. When performing searches, they might seek out shaded boxes that permit them to search the site by keywords. The Research-Based Web Design and Usability Guidelines site, http://www.usability.gov/guidelines, provides design and usability conventions on the use of titles, headings, page layouts, link use, navigation, graphics, and content. One guideline specifies the use of external links to indicate when a link points to a page on a different Web site, since users normally expect links take them to pages in the same site. Many Web design conventions are based on user expectation and perception, or their repeated use. Since users respond and recognize these conventional elements from many popular Web sites, designers can use them to improve usability. What knowledge these users learn from one site, they can apply to other sites to aid their searching and browsing. For example, most users recognize a white rectangular box with a grey "Search" button close to it as a basic searching tool. Experienced users know that keywords can be typed in the rectangular box and by pressing the button, the site will provide them with a list of relevant pages. Once users learn how to use a search utility, they can use a similarly designed object in another site. The more users encounter similar objects or visuals across sites, the easier they will recognize them as conventions. Figure 7-5 lists some common Web design conventions found in many frequently visited sites.

- Use colors that contrast well to add emphasis to elements.
- Pair graphical navigation tabs or icons with text labels to make their meaning clear.
- Use drop shadows, boxes, lines, or shaded boxes to provide visual emphasis for graphics.
- Place navigation links on the left-hand side or top of pages to make them easy to find.
- Provide noticeable headers as hyperlinks, such as nested links or breadcrumb trails, to help users see visually where they are and where they have been in the site.
- Use visual elements such as arrows or boldface text, in site maps to illustrate relationships between pages.
- Minimize the use of dead space on pages.
- Place shopping cart, help, and search links at the upper right corner of pages.
- Provide redundant text navigation links to complement the graphic toolbars or image maps.
- Provide headers and logos on all site pages to help users clearly identify location and brand.
- Use graphics, icons, and styles consistently on pages in a site.

FIGURE 7-5. Common Web Design Conventions

Some of these conventions address specific strategies for designing graphics, while others suggest the design and placement of graphics on pages. Using good color contrast aids the readability of images, such as graphics or text on a background, and it is a visual-spatial design principle. Pairing graphic elements with text helps users notice them and understand their meaning or function, especially if used as navigation choices. Using drop shadows or boxes with graphics will provide more visual emphasis so they are noticed by users. Placing navigation and search utilities at the top or left-hand margins helps users notice them quickly, since scrolling is generally not required to find them when the page loads. For the most part, the placement of images overlaps with designing the Web site interface, which is the subject of the next chapter. Many of these conventions offer prescribed design guidelines, such as using icons or tabs for navigation, avoiding the use of too many font faces, or providing visual cues that help users see where they are in a site. According to usability expert Jakob Nielsen, when 60 to 90% of large commercial sites use similar design elements, it can be considered to be a convention; and when at least 90% use it, it is a design standard (Nielsen 2000). Although this may be a way of quantifying what determines a convention, each design convention does not apply to every site or situation. A site that sells font sets for download on their site would break the font face limit convention so it could show samples of all the font sets.

An advantage of using conventions is that once users recognize conventions in other sites, it can help them learn how other sites work. For example, when users see that clicking on the company logo will take them to the home page, they might try this behavior on other sites. While we can benefit from this knowledge of the user's experience, it may not guarantee how other users will act in every situation. Such a list of conventions may be useful, but select items from the list that best fit the purpose and specific goals for the site. Regardless, Web sites should be internally consistent with their use of design conventions and rules. Figure 7-6 the weather.org Web site, illustrates the use of Web design conventions. While there is no single definitive list of these conventions, many can be found in a variety of design books, Web sites and organization style sheets. Even though using conventions might contribute to the site's ethos, clarity, or readability, they're still based heavily on the expectations of experienced users. Design conventions can help designers meet user expectations by providing them with visuals they recognize and have experience with. Usability experts Nielsen and Barnum advocate the use of design conventions if they promote a high degree of usability (Barnum 2002; Nielsen 2000).

It would be easy to develop an equally valid list of conventions based on bad visual design. The use of flashing pop-up advertisements, multiple navigation menus, graphic-heavy designs, poor color contrast, and too many color and font choices are good examples. While user testing and other such research may confirm how users will respond, that knowledge may not always be used to benefit the user. While users may initially notice such flashy visuals, they may eventually learn to avoid them and seek their information elsewhere. Web conventions are not intended to be used unilaterally and there is no single definitive list appropriate for every design. Every convention will not be rhetorically suitable in every situation. For example, the use of a keyword search box might be better used in sites with large amounts of searchable content, but a drop-down list might be better suited to sites with less content, such as a library of Adobe PDF files. While many conventions are based on testing, experience, and research, there is not a definitive style guide for the Web (yet) or list of design conventions that can explain how users will interact with a

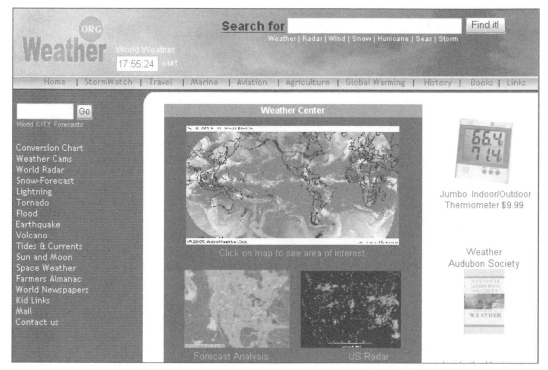

FIGURE 7-6. The Weather.org Web Site

This site demonstrates the use of many Web design conventions, including the use and placement of a logo in the upper left-hand corner, the use of dark and light contrasting colors and shaded boxes for navigation menus and links, and the use of colors to emphasize concepts, or specific warning areas, on the graphic maps.

Source: World Weather at Weather.org, http://www.weather.org.

site. Part of the task of a designer is to determine which design conventions apply to specific design tasks and projects.

Visual Design Process

When designing a visual graphic for a Web site, whether it is a site header, logo, map, navigation tool, or background, it is important to follow a design process. This process involves four important steps: (1) analyzing design characteristics, (2) benchmarking, (3) creating a graphic identity, and (4) design production.

Step 1: Analyzing Design Characteristics

Whether designing a navigation toolbar, background, page layout, or graphic, the initial step is to consider its unique design characteristics. This includes its purpose, how it will be interpreted by users, its function, and how it will be grouped with other visuals. Figure 7-7 lists some important questions to consider when designing graphics.

- What is the visual element's rhetorical purpose?
- How will the visual be interpreted by the user and in the context of the whole site?
- What use or function does the visual suggest to users?
- What other visuals will this one be grouped with? What characteristics will this visual group suggest to users?
- What are its unique visual and spatial characteristics?

FIGURE 7-7.   Design Analysis Questions

Step 2: Benchmarking

Benchmarking is a method of determining what design conventions are used in sites with a similar purpose or context as the site. In designing a bookselling Web site for a local store, consider what the competition has to offer. Examine the navigation tools found, colors used, graphics and icons, and the overall tone of the site. One advantage of benchmarking is that the knowledge gained can be used to help design to what users have come to expect. Alternately, if the goal is to take a unique design approach, take note of what has already been done both successfully and poorly by the competition. Figure 7-8 provides a list of useful benchmarking questions to consider. In addition, expand the research of sites to include larger, more popular book selling Web sites, since they are used by many people (if only for their extensive searchable database and sample pages). Examine how these sites use navigation tools, graphics, icons, and colors. Observe the use of subtle design elements that set each site apart from the rest. The goal of benchmarking should be to gather information about what users expect from similar sites, not to provide a means of copying the work others have done.

Step 3: Creating a Graphic Identity

Creating a graphic identity for a project is important because it lays the rules that will govern all aspects of designing the site. This includes the selection of design principles and design conventions used to govern the design work. It may include specific rules or guidelines

- What types of tasks can users perform?
- What types of navigation tools are used?
- How are graphics and icons used and what purpose do they serve?
- What colors and other design elements are used in the design?
- How are visuals used consistently in the site?
- What is the overall tone of the site?
- What does the site do well and not so well?

FIGURE 7-8.   Common Benchmarking Questions

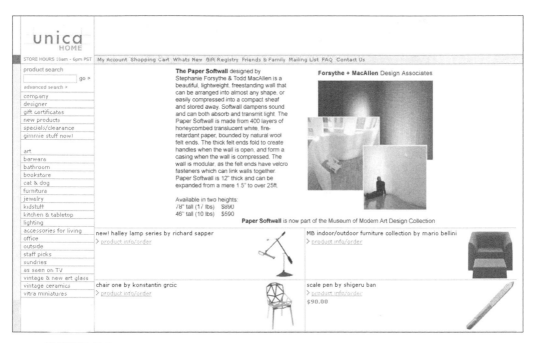

FIGURE 7-9.   The Unicahome Web Site

The site uses visual elements to create a subtle graphic identity, which allows specific products greater emphasis. The design uses soft colors that contrast well with the white background and clean lines to create visual separation between navigation links and individual products.

Source: Unicahome Featured Products, http://www.unicahome.com.

defined in the project scope or by the organization. It involves establishing the tone and color choices that will be used in the design. The project scope and rhetorical aspects should suggest the overall tone, whether it is professional, subdued, exciting, or organized. Benchmarking, research, and random browsing of other Web sites may provide ideas about color choices. The site's graphic identity is built on these things and includes the use of graphics, colors, icons, spacing, and other elements used repeatedly throughout the site that give it its own unique brand. A specific theme or design metaphor may help guide design choices and create the site's unique brand. For example, a site that sells kitchen appliances and implements might try using a kitchen theme or metaphor in the design. Or it may simply incorporate the use of familiar pictures as part of its design. Brainstorm and sketch out a few ideas to see what they may look like. Remember that sometimes a more subtle graphic identity may achieve what other flashy designs cannot (see Figure 7-9).

Once a design concept has been decided, make a list of specific rules and features to include in design. This list of rules is the style sheet, which provides detailed specifications for creating the graphics and overall site design. The list should include the use of colors, font faces, font sizes, spacing, justification, placement, file formats, graphic sizes, design conventions, and design principles. It should be as detailed as possible since it serves as the design blueprint, and it provides a consistent working guide. Table 7-1 is a worksheet that can be used to develop a basic style sheet for visual and textual styles in the Web site design.

TABLE 7-1. Sample Web Design Style Worksheet

Style Element	Specification
Font faces, sizes, and colors	
Heading level 1	Arial, 18 point, bold, black
Heading level 2	Times New Roman, 14 point, black
Text-based navigation	Times New Roman, 12 point, blue, underlined
Textual content	Times New Roman, 12 point
Other	
Spacing and alignment	
Headers	Left justification
Content chunks	Full justification, left indent 5 spaces, double-space between paragraphs
Other	
Color use	
Background	White
Bullets and symbols	Black
Other decorative	
Graphic size and file format	File: watermark.jpg
Background	File: logo.jpg
Banner	Standard grey, text labels
Buttons	
Navigation	Uniform size 300 $\times$ 200 pixels, .jpg format
Photographs	N/A
Sketches	Times New Roman, 12 point
Bullets and symbols	
Other	
Design conventions	• Use graphical navigation tabs or icons at the top of a page to signify global navigation. • Place navigation links on the left-hand side of the page. • Group search boxes at the top of pages, near the title banner or company logo. • Provide redundant navigation links to complement the graphic toolbars or image maps. • Hyperlink the company or site logo to the home page.
Design principles	Contrast, concept, grouping, center, and consistency, as defined in *Web Development: A Visual-Spatial Approach*
Other	Client wants to incorporate bee-themed graphics and colors.

Step 4: Design Production

Every designer has her own unique process for getting the actual production work accomplished. In many cases, the process will be based on past experiences of how to organize tasks and to make the best use of time. Designers often perfect their process and shape it as they accumulate project experience. Consider grouping the work into tasks, based on the function

---

ADVICE from PRACTITIONERS

Working within Specific Design Requirements

Arthur Oakley IV • Graphic Designer Texas A&M University College of Veterinary Medicine & Biomedical Sciences

The college's dean has requested, whenever possible and appropriate, that both the university and college seals be included on all official publications, both in print and online. The intention is to show that the college is part of a larger, research-focused academic entity. We also inevitably have to include some maroon in our work since it is the school's primary color. In addition, much of our work is based on tried-and-true design conventions—as a primarily conservative school, flashy, bleeding-edge designs are hardly ever used.

Also, as a veterinary medical teaching facility, we are limited in the type of photographs we can display in noneducational, public access promotional materials. Understandably, we cannot display animals in distress or in situations where they are experiencing pain and suffering; however, recovery photos are usually acceptable. In most cases, however, we try to use pleasant photos of people interacting with healthy animals that help convey the human–animal bond.

As an academic institution we admittedly have more freedom to produce our communications publications than most other organizations might, yet we are still guided by underlying design principles that place a strong emphasis on end-users. Experience has taught our staff that if something is not easy to understand, people simply won't use it.

Process of Creating Innovative Designs

Rather than pay costly subscriptions for design magazines or annuals, I tend to simply "take in" the world around me. Useful design resources and examples are everywhere you look—in department stores, on TV, on the Internet, and even in junk mail most people throw away. Like most graphic designers, I have a stack of attractive publications in a drawer as well as a folder of bookmarked Web sites I revisit every now to help generate layout ideas. The trick is to foster a sense of good taste and functional style from such examples. I'll also add that you can learn just as much from bad design as you can from good design.

As far as techniques, content drives design in my experience. Therefore, I always start with the end in mind before I begin any layout work. It is also easier to gain momentum for a project when I know what sort of deliverable I will ultimately produce. I generally try to get a sense of scope at the onset of a project so I won't have to rework major areas midway through the job. In fact, a major portion of my preliminary design work is to analyze and organize the initial content that gets handed over at the start of a project. All of this comes with experience, of course, and there is no substitute for practice and hands-on familiarity with the medium. The bottom line is that good design simply doesn't happen—it requires diligent forethought and planning, much like professional writing.

of the visuals needed for the site. For example, a designer might complete tasks in the following order: title banner, navigation graphics, clip art, icons, decorative elements, graphics for specific pages. This process places designing thematic graphics first, so the designer can test how well the design theme is working early on in the process. Once completed, design visuals for specific content pages and test how they fit the overall graphic identity and visual theme.

Graphic Formats

Three of the most common types of file formats used in Web sites are the Graphic Interchange Format (.GIF), the Joint Photographic Experts Group format (.JPG), and the Portable Network Graphic format (.PNG). Table 7-2 lists the individual characteristics of each graphic format in terms of their color depth, transparency, animation, and interlacing qualities and Figure 7-10 provides examples of each type. Each type has relatively good file compression capabilities, which means that they typically have smaller file sizes compared to other formats. Smaller file sizes mean shorter user download times on the Web. Commonly used formats that tend to have less compression include Windows Bitmap (.BMP), Encapsulated PostScript (.EPS), and Tagged Image File Format (.TIF). Other formats should only be used if there is a specific reason.

When deciding which format to use, consider four important aspects of graphics: color depth, transparency, animation, and interlacing. Color depths affect both the quality and file size of the image. True color images display up to 16.7 million colors and produce images of photographic quality. However, not all graphics require this level of color depth, such as clipart or images that use fewer than 256 unique colors. Transparency assigns a single color in a graphic to be transparent, which allows graphics to blend with different backgrounds. PNG files allow semitransparency that allows control over how well it blends into the background on which it is placed. Animation allows multiple images to be combined into a short movie. Some types of animations don't require special software plug-ins or programs to view them, such as animated .GIF files, while others may require a specific program, especially if they are longer and more complex. Interlacing allows users to see pieces of the graphic on the screen as they load, while noninterlaced graphics remain unseen until the entire image is downloaded.

Many other types of graphic formats are unique to different graphic design software and programs, such as animations, three-dimensional (3D) modeling, drafting files, video

TABLE 7-2. Characteristics of Graphic File Formats

File Format	Graphic Interchange Format (GIF)	Joint Photographic Experts Group (JPG)	Portable Network Graphic (PNG)
Color depth	• 256 colors	• 16.7 million colors	• 16.7 million colors
Transparency	• Transparency	• No transparency	• Transparency
Animation	• Animation	• No animation	• No animation
Interlacing	• Interlaced	• Noninterlaced	• Interlaced

GIF Graphic • 256 unique colors • Can set one transparent color • Can be animated images • Interlaced	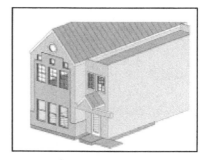
JPG Graphic • Up to 16.7 million unique colors • No transparency • No animation • Noninterlaced	
PNG Graphic • Up to 16.7 million unique colors • Semitransparency (i.e., house windows) • No animation • Interlaced	

FIGURE 7-10.   Examples of GIF, JPG, and PNG Graphics

Source: JafHomes, http://www.jafhomes.com.

clips. Most require specific software programs or plug-ins to view. If the site uses these types of files, instruct users on how to properly download and view them. Provide file formats that will not require them to purchase additional software or spend a lot of time downloading appropriate viewers. Be sure to consider the site's target users when making the choice.

In designing a site for a general audience, consider using file formats that can be viewed with free viewers or software plug-ins, or provide users with alternate versions. Sometimes simple scanned images, saved as JPG files, are good supplements that allow users to view static images or parts of dynamic content. If members of the design team lack the expertise to address some of these issues, it might be best to hire a graphic design consultant to help solve some of these issues.

Conclusion

Design considers both the unique visual and spatial aspects of graphics and page layouts as they pertain to the Web development process. With an understanding of user perception, design principles, and design conventions, we can tailor our design work more effectively to our users. Considering both the visual and spatial characteristics in design can improve the overall usability of our site designs by responding to the searching and browsing habits of users. When we begin to consider design aspects on a conceptual level, we can design to accommodate the ways in which users perceive and understand visual information in Web site designs.

Chapter Summary

- Visual design involves the use of design conventions and design principles to create visuals that deal with their appearance, placement, and function.
- Visual-spatial thinking is based on an understanding of how humans perceive and respond to visual elements in a visual-textual landscape. It considers both visual and spatial aspects of designing visual information and page layouts.
- Design principles are theoretically ground and involve both visual and spatial qualities. Five visual-spatial principles that can be used for design include contrast, concept, grouping, center, and consistency.
- Design conventions are based on user expectations and commonly used elements found in many major Web sites. They differ from design principles in that they offer prescriptive rules that refer to specific design suggestions.
- The design process involves four major steps: (1) analyzing design characteristics, (2) benchmarking, (3) creating a graphic identity, and (4) design production.
- Three of the most common types of file formats used in Web sites are the Graphic Interchange Format (.GIF), the Joint Photographic Experts Group format (.JPG), and the Portable Network Graphic format (.PNG). Each has unique characteristics such as color depth, transparency, animation, and interlacing that should be considered when selecting the type of format to use.

Exercises

1. Select a Web site that has a similar subject and purpose to one you are designing and answer the benchmarking questions (Figure 7-1) for the site. As part of this benchmarking research, make a list of conventions, or consistent use of visuals. Which of these conventions would be appropriate for use in your site design? Which would not?

2. Using the set of visual-spatial design principles (Figure 7-2), analyze their use in selected Web site's home page. Look for ways in which the site's home page adheres to each principle and make note of any violations. For each exception where a principle is not followed, provide a reason to explain the discrepancy.

3. Browse two or three other U.S. Government Web sites, making note of the use of visual information and page layouts. Then, return to the United States Library of Congress Web site, http://www.loc.gov. Make a list of design conventions that seem to be used consistently in all of these sites. How do these conventions aid users that may use all of these sites?

4. Select any Web site and identify elements used that comprise its graphic identity. What types of graphics and colors are used to establish its unique brand? What types of impressions does its graphic style suggest in terms of tone, reputation, credibility, and usefulness?

5. Select any Web site and perform an analysis of its unique style guidelines by examining at least five of the site's pages. Use Table 7-1, the Web Design Style Worksheet, to record any observations. Are styles used consistently throughout the site? If not, are there good reasons for violating the consistent use of styles?

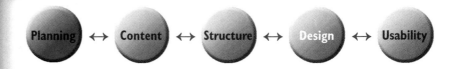

8

Planning ↔ Content ↔ Structure ↔ Design ↔ Usability

INTERFACE DESIGN

Learning Objectives

After completing this chapter, you will understand:

- How user behavior and expectations affect interface design

- How visual-spatial thinking can be used to develop interface layouts

- Elements that comprise a typical Web interface

- The importance of visual syntax

- Typical interface layouts

- How to perform a basic interface layout test

Introduction

Think of the Web interface as a virtual control panel with all sorts of buttons and knobs that allow the user to browse, search, and direct the flow of information in a Web site. Interface design involves the selection and arrangement of elements that make up the whole screen a user sees. In other words, it involves the dressing up, hanging, or arranging of visual and textual elements, such as the title banner, navigation tools, search features, text, and graphics, to help users see the whole picture of a Web site. The interface communicates to users where they are in the site, where they can go, and what tasks they can perform. Interface researcher Steven Johnson says "the interface is a way of seeing the whole" (238). In the case of a Web site, it includes the use of interactive features, such as buttons, links, search boxes, online help, forms, and dynamic toolbars. All of the controls, visual elements, text, and space displayed in a browser window comprise the interface. Instead of just a single browser or window, the interface may be comprised of multiple windows, such as frames or pop-up windows, to comprise the site. For example, in sites where the navigation toolbars are placed in a consistent location or frame, these toolbars can remain in the same location even though other frames and windows may be serving up different content as users navigate. Although there may be a variety of choices in terms of dressing up the screen interface, one thing is important: Design should focus on the perceptual habits and needs of the site's targeted users.

Designing the interface involves layering of graphics, icons, text chunks, interactive menus, and search fields into spatial arrangements. In a Web site, users learn by doing, or by experimenting with the interface by trial and error. Initially, they analyze the various visual, spatial, and textual elements to understand the audience, purpose, context, and function of the site. In essence, they are trying to learn the language of the interface. Since the interface has its own language, the designer must help users learn how it functions and communicates. Effective interface design uses elements that emphasize or signal to users what should be noticed, in the form of visual cues, which gives them contextual information about the nature of content found on the site and its arrangement. For example, specific headers, colors, and icons might be used to indicate which area, section, or subsite the user is currently browsing (see Figure 8-1). Grouping elements close together, using space, shaded areas, or text boxes are visual-spatial techniques that help users identify which items go together. A breadcrumb trail might signal to users which pathway they have followed to get to the current page. Hyperlinks and other visual objects help users

FIGURE 8-1.   The FirstGov Web Site

This site groups navigation links into categories with graphic headers that indicate the purpose, function, or nature of content. Lines, boxes, colors, and graphic headers are all used to group and outline navigation links, content, and specific functions, such as keyword search utilities.

Source: FirstGov, http://www.firstgov.gov.

navigate between pages and control the arrangement and delivery of information through tools in the interface.

The use of Web design conventions also helps users learn the language or functionality of the site. Many of these conventions are based on usability tests, user preferences, and are features commonly found in other sites. For example, the use of a white rectangular box with a button labeled "Search" suggests these elements function as a keyword search feature. Placing a navigation toolbar in the left-hand or top margin follows a common placement convention. Together, these cues and conventions can be used as visual signposts to help guide users and prevent them from getting lost or frustrated when navigating a site.

Conceptually, users create their own windows, or areas of focus, when viewing a site. In a Web site, we naturally fixate or focus on specific areas of the screen to solve problems, perform tasks, or find information. Kurt Koffka, a Gestalt psychologist, suggests humans naturally try to organize elements in their visual field to understand their characteristics and how they relate. This type of visual grouping is important to interface design, because it helps users understand the relationship between elements they see on the screen. For example, to help users understand the interface, we might use shaded boxes to group elements in the searching feature mentioned previously. Navigation tools are often grouped together, as are headers and textual chunks to signal relationships between individual titles and paragraphs of text. Effective interface design includes applying the knowledge of user perception, including how users respond to visual elements on the screen.

Understanding User Behavior

Few Web design texts and Web sites discuss the importance of studying user behavior and how it can inform specific design or style guidelines. When they do, mostly this understanding of how users interact and respond to the Web interface is applied to usability testing, building site indices, and developing help and searching systems. Some books stress the importance of getting to know target users through testing and various methods of inquiry. Others focus on the use of design principles and conventions that should always be used in site design. Few, however, focus on the importance of studying user perception and behavior to inform how our interfaces should be designed. The visual-spatial approach addresses the root of what makes one site more usable than another by focusing on user perception and needs.

Often, we can learn a lot about user behavior from our own design experience and feedback from users. Each Web designer may have differing ideas of dos and don'ts about arranging information on pages and what works best for their target users. What designers learn from user feedback contributes to our general knowledge of their searching and browsing preferences and habits. In a practical sense, design experience and user feedback can help create more aesthetic and clean designs. This helps enhance the usability and number of visitors to our sites.

The foundation of interface designer work lies in determining how best to design to accommodate those needs and perceptual habits. Designing with the user in mind is an inherently rhetorical practice, in that it is concerned with inventing, arranging, and delivering information to users for specific purposes and within given contexts. This chapter takes a combined approach of studying user needs, design conventions, and visual-spatial thinking to design interface layouts.

Identifying Target Users

The first step of interface design involves collecting specific information on users, their habits, information needs, and experience to give us a better understanding of them. This should precede any graphic or content development, scripting or interface layout sketches. It involves writing down what is known about the site's probable users. Another approach is to collect information on user needs, behaviors, and preferences, to create a profile of typical users. These user profiles can be developed from client interviews, usability testing results, surveys, site statistics, and other types of feedback obtained from site users. This will involve developing a specific set of questions and determining how to measure responses. Develop a list of site-specific questions to ask. For example, in using both a toolbar and drop-down menu as site navigation tools, ask which users prefer or find easiest to use. Ask users to rate their responses or ask them to provide written comments to each question or feature. Contacting users, via e-mail or other methods, can be a little more precarious. Do not mass-mail users without their permission, especially if they have indicated they do not want to be contacted. Provide users an incentive or even the option to decline and they may be more likely to respond. Start with a basic questionnaire that inventories general knowledge of users. Include these five basic questions in your inquiry:

1. Who will be the site's primary users?
2. What tasks will users typically perform on the site?
3. In what ways will they use information on the site?
4. What specific requirements will users have to meet (technological constraints, language constraints, etc.) to view content or navigate the site?
5. How will users be able to offer feedback?

When working on a redesign project with some knowledge of users, consider these additional questions:

- When users seek help, what methods do they typically use (email, feedback forms, FAQs, etc.)?
- What types of compliments or complaints are most common among users?
- Which browsers (and versions) do your users have?
- How frequently is e-mail received from users and on what subjects?
- What suggestions have users provided?

These questions can be rewritten to address potential users. Adapt and rewrite these questions to fit the project scope. Include questions that deal with specific types of content or formats under consideration for use in the site. Ask questions that address their preferences and limitations from a variety of standpoints: navigation, content, technology, and expertise. Table 8-1 provides a sample user questionnaire that responds to user preferences and limitations on these four categories.

A good analysis of your users will typically include an assessment of their preferences and limitations with regard to their navigation, content, technology preferences, and level of expertise. Existing sites can collect user feedback through the use of a feedback page, form, or e-mail support links for the user. Preferences can be obtained by collecting site statistics that record the browser types and choices users make.

The information collected about users, their needs, and habits can be used to create user profiles, or short descriptions of typical user habits, preferences, and skills. These short narrative sketches can help identify specific characteristics of users. Since most sites

TABLE 8-1.	User Preferences and Limitations Matrix			
	Navigation	**Content**	**Technology**	**Expertise**
Preferences	What types of navigation tools do you prefer using? Which types of navigation tools do you dislike?	What types of document formats do you prefer reading (HTML, DOC, PDF)?	What types of interactive graphic features do you dislike?	How would you characterize your experience with browsing Web sites?
		In extended descriptions, do you prefer reading them in HTML or other formats available for download?	What types do you find easiest to use?	
Limitations	What types of navigation tools have not worked successfully for you when visiting Web sites?	Which word processing software package do you have installed on your computer?	What browser and version do you use for most Web browsing?	What do you find to be most difficult about navigating most Web sites?
		Which document viewers do you have installed?	What screen resolution and color settings do you have on your monitor?	
			What type of computer do you use (PC, MAC)?	
			What known software plug-ins are installed on your computer?	
			What method is used to connect to the Internet?	

will have more than one type of user, multiple sketches can help distinguish between the varied needs and habits of different types of users. For example, a bookselling Web site may have the following types of users: student, teacher, collector, and browser. As part of the description for each user type, list the specific needs and tasks each user type may seek and perform. User profiles help designers put a face on or characterize typical users. They help designers visualize a specific person and how they might react to certain design elements or features. While user profiles may seem somewhat stereotypical, they can provide general insight into the specific needs of user types.

Designing the Interface

The process of designing the interface is one of the most exciting and challenging aspects of the Web development process. The first of two major tasks to consider is deciding what features or tools to integrate into the screen interface. These elements might include a title banner, logo, navigation toolbars, searching systems, help systems, and other features. Some technically competent developers and designers alike do not like this part, because a lot of it forces them to choose between satisfying user preferences, design principles, conventions, and personal preferences. It relies on making some aesthetic choices, which may not be everyone's forte. Web interface design, like most design work, should consider the primary audience, purpose, and should stay within the design constraints. Web interface design is a balancing act that involves pleasing users, clients, and (often the worst critic) the designer. Visual-spatial thinking can help make some of these tough choices easier by focusing decisions on basic user perception and expectations.

Visual-Spatial Interfaces

Users actively seek out navigation tools on the browser interface and home page to solve problems and plan information searches. Part of interface design work involves developing and arranging navigation tools and contextual cues that support both the site structure of information and user needs. The interface is the user's primary medium to interact, navigate and observe meaningful connections between pages and elements on the screen. Each user typically follows a unique pathway through Web sites when searching and browsing. In any given instant, that user occupies a specific location or center within an information structure, relative to other pages. As users attempt to situate themselves in the whole structure, they examine which pathways and navigation tools exist to plan their searches to solve problems and information needs. As users plan their pathways through texts, the Web reading experience becomes as much a spatial experience as a visual one. This helps explain why visual-spatial thinking is important to the design of Web interfaces. Table 8-2 provides some useful interface design guidelines that relate to Arnheim's five principles of visual thinking and the visual-spatial concepts from Chapter 1.

While these examples offer some practical guidelines, there may be other useful applications of these principles as well. The visual-spatial approach helps design interfaces as integrated wholes that arrange and use elements consistently. These design guidelines explain how users look for elements to focus on to help them solve problems or aid in searching and navigating pages in the site. This approach also considers how we collectively perceive visual elements in Web sites and offers specific guidance for designing the interface.

TABLE 8-2. Guidelines for Visual-Spatial Interface Design

Concept	Interface Guidelines
Visual focus	• Use improved figure-ground contrast to signal which elements users should focus on. • Use animation and rollovers in navigation toolbars to indicate functional or clickable items. • Give contextual and visual cues greater visual distinction. • Develop style sheets that specify similar formats for level headings and spacing between text chunks.
Problem solving	• Highlight potential pathways to readers by using breadcrumb trails, site maps, indices, and headers. • Develop navigation toolbars that suggest information pathways to users, which don't just outline content. • Provide multiple navigation tools and choices for readers, such as toolbars, search fields, drop-down lists, site maps, etc.
Contextual	• Place more contextual information, such as visual cues, in higher site levels. • Provide detailed content in lower site levels. • Use shaded regions, tables, frames, or other methods to anchor navigation tools in consistent locations. • Place content no more than five to seven links or clicks from users, so content is not placed too far from users.
Conceptual	• Use familiar icons, shapes, and graphics that rely on prior user knowledge. • Place graphics in familiar contexts. • Provide text tags for images used in new contexts. • Use design metaphors to help users comprehend the arrangement and content of visual spaces.
Wholeness	• Group related content using visual shapes, such as shaded boxes or rules, or by using space. • Use figure-ground contrast and grouping to help users identify relationships between elements. • Use breadcrumbs, site maps, indices, etc., to help users identify the site's structure. • Provide a help system, such as a FAQ or knowledge base to answer common questions.

Elements of a Web Interface

Almost all Web sites use similar elements in their interfaces, including a site header, logo, navigation tools, search and help utilities, graphic elements, and textual content. In most cases, many of these common elements will be used in developing the interface. Include elements specifically tailored to target users. Consider which elements are appropriate or consistent with the site's audience, purpose, and design constraints. Figure 8-2 illustrates a site that incorporates many of these elements. Each of these elements is an important feature of Web interfaces, and using visual-spatial techniques are useful guides for incorporating each.

Site Header

The site header usually includes the title of the site, company logo, and sometimes a navigation toolbar, search utility, or help utility. Site headers are usually placed as the name

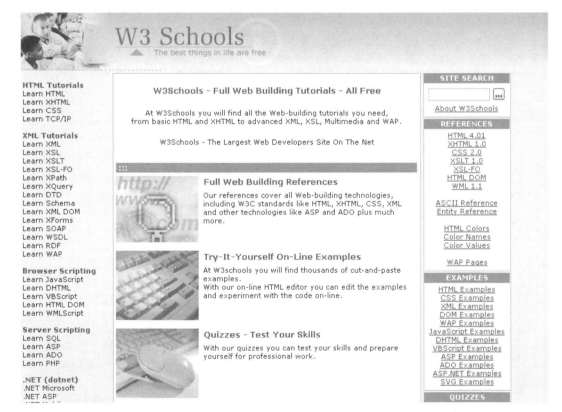

FIGURE 8-2.   The W3Schools Web Site

The interface includes a site header and logo (top margin), navigation tools (left and right margins), search utility (upper right), and content window (center margin). The use of consistent colors for shading, headers, and text, and use of graphics comprise the site's graphic identity. The interface uses shaded boxes, contrasting colors, and headings to outline lists of links, references, and examples.

Source: W3Schools Online Web Tutorials, http://www.w3schools.com.

suggests—at the top or head of a page. So, why should all this information be placed at the top? Two reasons: Visually distinct information is usually placed in a header, and most users will typically look at the top of a page while or after it loads. The header has an important function: It establishes the title, subject, and graphic identity of the site. Designers often use colors, shapes, logos, or other elements from the header in other areas of the site to create continuity and consistency in the use of design elements.

One important part of the header is the site <TITLE>. This is different from the graphic or text banner that appears on the page; it is displayed in the top status line of the browser window. It is important for search engines and assistive software to provide titles for each page, so they can be indexed and read properly. Most search engines, when indexing your site, will use the <TITLE> as the name of your site in the listing of your query. Set titles for your pages using the <TITLE> tag inside the header of your HTML code, or set it using your Web development software, as shown below.

```
<TITLE>Invericorp Industries</TITLE>
```

Sometimes, hyperlinks are used in site headers and/or logos. Usability expert Jakob Nielsen suggests that a hyperlink to the site home page be placed on a logo used throughout the site. This usability convention is often featured in many large commercial sites. Global navigation is sometimes used in the header, to allow users to access links to the Home Page, Site Map, Index, About Us, Contact Us, Help, or Search features. Placing a search box in the header can help users access site content by keyword or other methods. This can be a useful way of helping users locate links that will help them navigate a particularly complex site architecture or large volume of textual content. Navigation hyperlinks use text and often times, icons, graphics, or shapes that are paired with each text link. This helps users conceptualize or understand how each link functions. For example, an icon of a house is often used with a Home hyperlink and a question mark is paired with a Help link, and so forth.

Navigation Tools

Navigation toolbars and links are an important part of the interface functionality. Without them, users would only have scrollbars and browser controls to navigate pages. Providing navigation links as part of the interface serves to customize ways in which users can search, read, or browse information in the site. Navigation links are often grouped into toolbars, drop-down, pullout, sliding, or plain text menus to provide users with an index of the site content. Anchoring these menus in consistent locations can help users find them more easily. Embedded hyperlinks in paragraphs and text chunks can provide users with additional or related links to content. In addition, it is important to use the same labels, symbols, style, and so on, for navigation tools consistently throughout the site. Anchoring and consistent use are two essentials of interface usability with regard to navigation.

Search and Help Utilities

Search utilities allow users to search content by keyword, phrase, or other criteria used in many advanced searching features. Site maps or indices help users search from a bird's-eye perspective, by providing a list of the major site links and map of the site's structure. They serve as an organized outline, list, or map of links that shows users where they are and where they can go. And, some search features automatically generate a site map based on an index of the site's content. Not all sites require a search interface or site map, but the important thing to know is when to use and not to use them. Search utilities work best in sites with large volumes of searchable content. Search engines are less effective in searching sites with lots of static documents, such as some Adobe PDF files or graphic content. In addition, they won't search external documents in their native formats (i.e., Microsoft Word documents, etc.). When using a search feature, make sure the site uses searchable document formats.

As mentioned, search utilities are typically placed toward the top of a site page, so that users can locate them easily. Sometimes, if a search interface is integral to a site, it is often given some visual emphasis (i.e., placed in a shaded box or table) so it gets noticed. Setting up a search feature can be quite complicated, so without proper resources, you might want to consider embedding a free search interface into the site (just query any search engine for the words "free search feature"). When adding one, be sure to give it some emphasis and position it where it will be found, using appropriate visual styling and spacing.

Help utilities rescue lost users if designed properly. They can be as simple as a FAQ (Frequently Asked Questions) or troubleshooting page, or as interactive as agents (think of talking heads that can be scripted to answer questions for users). Help systems can be less obvious, such as breadcrumb links, a series of hyperlinked headers displayed toward the top of the page that shows the path a user has taken through the site. Add help systems to the global navigation toolbar, header, or in a consistent location throughout the site so users can always find these useful tools. And when all else fails, provide a simple e-mail link or feedback form for users to receive help from the technical support staff, although this may not be ideal as the only means of helping users. Before designing a feedback form, plan and design the form to solicit very specific types of feedback to avoid answering a number of e-mails on a consistent basis.

Content Window

Another important decision to make when designing the interface is the size, layout, and location of the main content window. This area of the interface is where most of the text chunks, supporting content, and embedded, redundant, or local navigation links are placed. When users click on hyperlinks, this is where the primary content is displayed. Usually, this area should be the largest part of the interface, because content is why most users have come to the site (not for just the dynamic drop-down menus, soundtrack, splash page, and animated graphics). Some decisions to be made for designing and arranging elements in the content window include:

- Where to put the local navigation links, if they are used
- How to arrange headers, subheads, and textual content consistently from page to page using a style sheet
- What size text chunks, or granularity, will be used on pages
- What contextual information will help readers understand what page they're currently viewing (i.e., headers, subheads, icons, graphics)
- Where and how dynamic content retrieved from databases or searches should be displayed

Place local navigation links or breadcrumb links at the top of content pages, unless they will be nested in the main navigation toolbar. For the style sheet, specify font faces, styles, sizes, spacing, and colors for headers, subheads, and regular text. Determine how large or small individual text chunks (or paragraphs) should be on the page. Then, decide what type of contextual information to provide for content (i.e., headers, icons, or graphics used with headers, embedded hyperlinks, etc.) described in the next section. Consider using redundant navigation links at the end of sections and/or at the bottom of each page, such as "Top of Page" for longer pages or links to major content sections. Creating a style sheet that includes design and style choices ensures they will be used consistently throughout the entire site, to enhance its usability and ethos. Consistency is always the best rule, especially for good Web usability.

Visual Context

In addition to arranging the visual and textual content, it is important to consider the context in which information is situated in a site. While this is not a specific element found in a consistent location on each page, providing contextual cues helps users understand more about the content, its arrangement, and relationship to other content in the site. A good Web interface will provide the user with a number of contextual cues on each page to

---

Breadcrumb links illustrate the pathway the user has taken to reach the current page, showing part of the site's structure.

BOOKS >>> FICTION >>> MYSTERY

Icons can signify concepts to users. A house icon might suggest a home page, or a question mark might suggest a help feature or FAQ list.

    ?

Headers and subheaders outline content on a page and can suggest the relationship between individual sections of content.

Popular Fiction
Mystery
Romance
Science Fiction

Rollovers, or mouseovers, are graphic navigation images that change when the mouse pointer is placed on them, and may suggest clickable buttons.

(Continued)

ALT attribute tags, when used with images, provide textual labels or descriptions to supplement the visual image.

<IMG SRC="photo.gif" ALT='Picture of two small stuffed animals, a panda bear and pig, in a spotlight.'>

Repeated graphic elements can suggest relationships between text chunks or pages that use them repeatedly.

⚒ Helpful Hints

- ⚒ Click RESET to clear your options.
- ⚒ Remeber to click SAVE before logging off.

Lines, tables, and shaded areas provide visual grouping, so users understand which elements are related or go together.

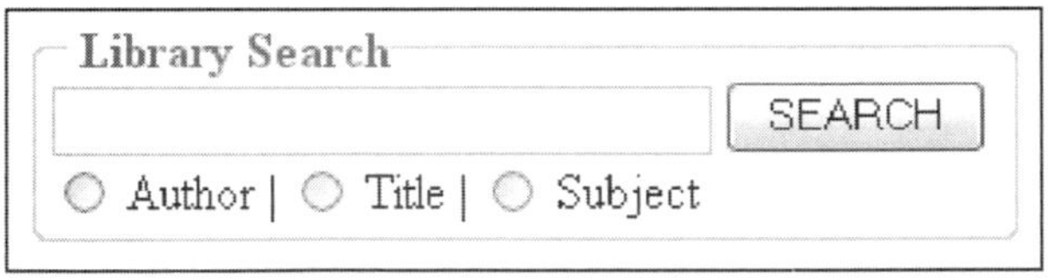

Consistent use of colors can suggest major sections or individual themes within a site.

Fiction
Non-fiction
Reference
Textbooks

FIGURE 8-3. Visual Examples of Providing Context

Source: Flash buttons, http://www.flashbuttons.com.

outline content and/or show relation between individual elements on the screen. Figure 8-3 provides some examples of providing visual context with a brief explanation of how each provides context for the site's content. This list is not all-inclusive, but it does provide some suggestions of how to use context cues to help users understand the relationship of chunks, graphics, and pages within the site. These cues act as signposts, signaling clues to users about the relatedness of elements in the interface. They also signal the relatedness and/or nature of content provided in the site.

Graphic Identity

The graphic identity refers to the consistent use of graphic (and spatial) elements throughout a site to suggest a specific scheme, theme, or identity in its style and appearance. This can include the use of colors, logos, graphics, shapes, icons, shading, negative space, or other elements consistently that gives users a sense of the whole site and its overall design. When using a design metaphor in the site's design, the graphic identity will conform to that metaphor as closely as it is possible. For example, a house metaphor as the design scheme would most likely incorporate elements found in a house and its various rooms. The site might use graphic elements such as doors, windows, and familiar rooms for hyperlinks or content sections. It might even use colors and fixtures consistently throughout the site as one might find in a typical house. Whether using a design metaphor or a custom theme for the site design, be sure to make consistent choices for the site's graphic identity. This will give users a sense of the whole picture or design theme. In turn, users will recognize the consistencies and learn them as part of the interface. Figure 8-4 examines the use of visual elements that make up a site's unique graphic identity.

Interface Layout

Deciding where to place elements in the interface is the other major part of the process of designing an effective interface layout. Planning the layout is as important as selecting the right features, graphics, and functionality for the site interface design. In addition to user responses to visual elements in the interface, it is important to consider the **visual syntax**, or normal viewing pattern our eyes follow. In print-based publications, this pattern roughly follows a reverse letter "Z" pattern. For example, our eyes first focus on an area slightly to the left of center, then toward the upper left, across to the upper right, then to the lower left, and finally to the lower right. This pattern works well for individuals in Western cultures, but quite differently for members of other cultures who read right to left or top to bottom. For Web pages, the visual syntax is slightly different because of the variety of layouts, frames, windows, and media used. On every Web page, users typically have a variety of visual elements in their field of vision, all competing for attention. Since the visual syntax of a Web page depends heavily on the placement of visual information, visual-spatial principles can be useful in helping users learn how information is grouped or arranged, so they can conceptualize the whole site. Another important aspect of planning the layout of the interface is to be consistent in the arrangement or grouping of elements so users can learn the visual syntax of the site more quickly to aid their browsing and searching.

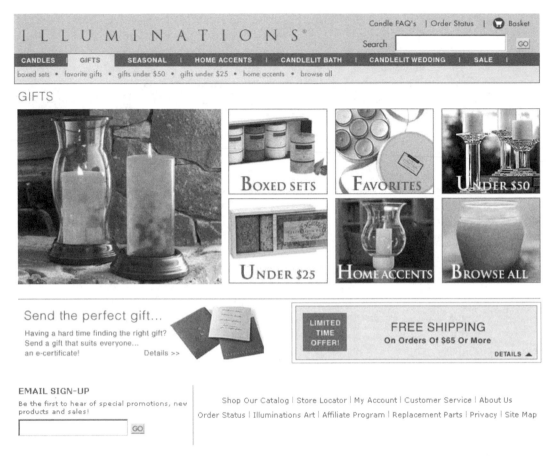

FIGURE 8-4. The Illuminations Gifts Web Page

The Illuminations Gifts page has a graphic identity that focuses on visual imagery and subtle background colors to emphasize the products sold on the site. Text labels are paired with graphics to suggest the concept or theme behind groups of gifts. The main site header, logo, navigation, and search feature are grouped in the top margin and use contrasting colors to emphasize navigation choices. The graphic identity is visually appealing, organized, and uses white space to help users distinguish between individual elements in the interface. This site is also a good example of a two-frame layout, which divides the interface between the header/navigation and primary site content and will be discussed in the next section.

Source: Illuminations—Living by Candlelight Gifts Web page, http://www.illuminations.com

Typical Interface Layouts

Most sites use the same layout for all pages, but some use two or more different layouts for pages in their sites. For example, sites that use splash pages, or introduction pages (often with short media clips or graphic navigation), sometimes use separate layouts for the introduction page and subsequent pages in the site. A site that has different functions or purposes may require separate layouts for certain sections of the site. For example, some real estate Web sites provide photo galleries of houses for sale that use unique layouts for the photo galleries. Other sites that use pop-up windows may create a different layout for those smaller customized windows. Whether using one, two, or multiple layouts, it's important to create consistency for users so they are not confronted with a new layout each time they click the mouse.

Single-Frame   This is often the most simple and commonly used layout. All of the information on the screen fills the entire browser window, without the use of internal or external frames or pop-up windows. Many introduction or splash pages, and smaller and simpler Web layouts use a single-frame layout. One advantage is that single-frame layouts always display in the entire browser window. This saves time in planning multiple or complex frames or pop-up windows in the layout. One disadvantage when working with a large amount of graphic content is that each time users click on a hyperlink, the entire page, graphics included, has to be loaded again. While many graphics are stored on the user's computer after they load to prevent longer downloads, each new page must be recached either from the computer's hard drive or server. When using a single-frame layout, it's best to minimize the use of graphics and multimedia used on pages to save the user valuable download time. Figures 8-5 and 8-6 depict examples of single-frame layouts.

Two-Frame   The two-frame, or two-pane layout splits the browser window into two separate areas, or frames, each of which displays a separate Web page. This is useful to display the navigation toolbar in one window and primary content in another window. This can be used to anchor navigation in one location, while only new content is updated in the other frame. Generally, two-frame layouts are used to provide the user with a stable header

FIGURE 8-5.   A Single-Frame Layout Occupies the Entire Screen

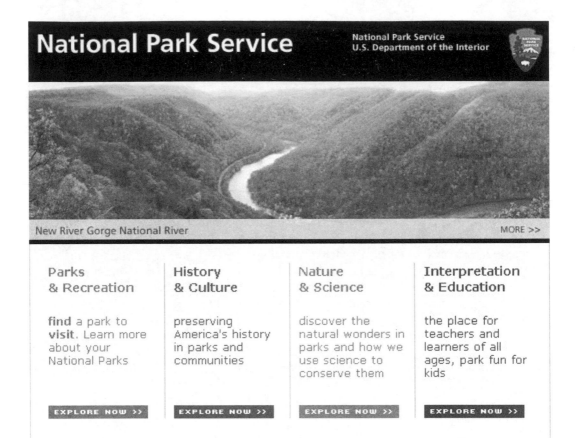

National Park Service

National Park Service
U.S. Department of the Interior

New River Gorge National River   MORE >>

**Parks
& Recreation**

find a park to
visit. Learn more
about your
National Parks

EXPLORE NOW >>

**History
& Culture**

preserving
America's history
in parks and
communities

EXPLORE NOW >>

**Nature
& Science**

discover the
natural wonders in
parks and how we
use science to
conserve them

EXPLORE NOW >>

**Interpretation
& Education**

the place for
teachers and
learners of all
ages, park fun for
kids

EXPLORE NOW >>

FIGURE 8-6. The National Park Service Web Site

This site interface is one example of a single-frame interface layout. All information is presented in a single window and simple, straightforward navigation is used. Shaded and bordered boxes and lines are used to group content in the layout.

Source: National Park Service, http://www.nps.gov.

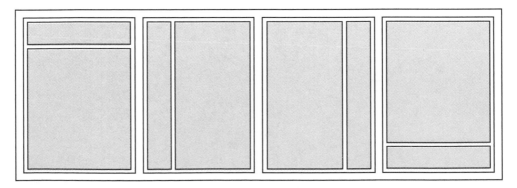

FIGURE 8-7. A two-frame layout typically divides the interface into two sections: one for content and the other for a logo, banner, and/or primary site navigation.

and/or navigation toolbar each time the user clicks on a new link. Figure 8-7 illustrates some different methods of using a two-frame layout.

Two-frame pages don't always have to use the same proportions as shown in Figure 8-7. The nature of the content, navigation, or other specific function of the site may require customization of the size and arrangement. In laying out a basic Web interface, a two-column or two-row table could be used as placeholders for content. Figure 8-4 is a good example of a two-frame layout that divides the header, main navigation, and logo from the content window.

Three-Frame   One standard Web interface layout is the three-frame, or three-pane layout used in a wide variety of Web sites, including many popular news sites. In these layouts, the logo and title banner appear in the upper portion of the screen, toward the left margin. A navigation toolbar is commonly placed in the top or left-hand margins toward the top of the screen interface. The largest of the three frames often displays the site's main content, making it the most visually dominant element in the interface based on sheer size. Figure 8-8 provides examples of three-frame layouts and Figure 8-9 illustrates one example Web page.

Custom   On the Web, there are a variety of custom interface layouts that use multiple frames, pop-up windows, and other features. Custom layouts are typically created for a specific subject, audience, purpose, function, or other reason. They are often used for sites that serve content dynamically by retrieving content from a database based on user input or preference. The advantage to using some of the more commonly found layouts is that they are more common and most users have seen them before. Remember, what users learn from one interface they can apply to others. Custom layouts are typically unique and may require more time for users to comprehend how the whole site is organized. In such a case, consider including more contextual cues for users to help orient them in the layout

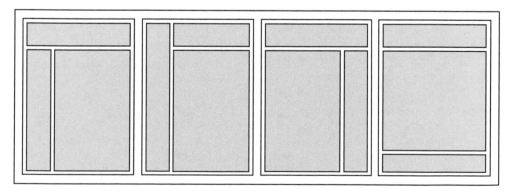

FIGURE 8-8.   A three-frame layout divides the interface into three sections: the site header, primary navigation or login, and content window.

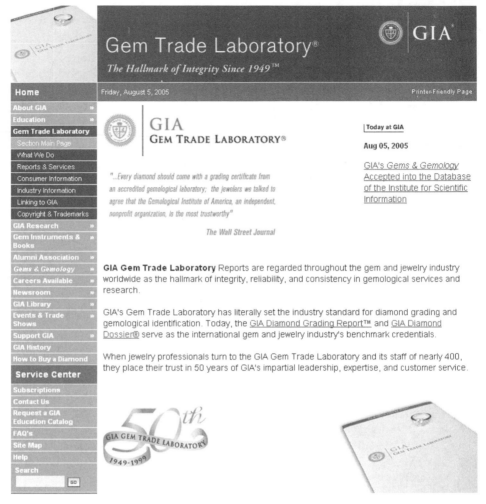

FIGURE 8-9.   The GIA Gem Trade Laboratory Web Page

This page uses a three-frame interface layout that divides the page into three regions that display the site header, left-margin navigation, and featured content.

Source: GIA Gem Trade Laboratory Section Main Page, http://www.gia.edu/gemtradelab/66/ section_main_page.cfm.

and structure of the interface layout. Arrange, emphasize, and group elements in ways that demonstrate consistency to users and that follow the visual-spatial approach. This will help users more quickly learn the language or layout of the interface. And most important, make sure there's a good reason to use a custom layout rather than just to show off. Figure 8-10 shows examples of possible custom frame layouts and Figure 8-2 provides an example of one.

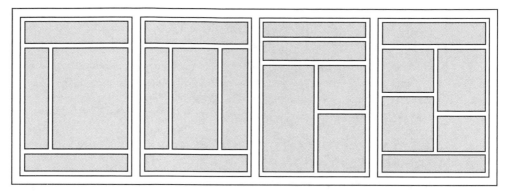

FIGURE 8-10.   Some examples of custom layouts use multiple panes in the interface design. If a custom interface layout is necessary, be sure it satisfies a specific purpose or need.

Testing the Interface Layout

After designing an interface that meets user, design, and personal standards, it should be tested on a variety of system settings and using the visual-spatial principles used in design. The interface design may look great on one computer system, but the layout might look slightly different on other systems with different settings. Two important system settings that affect interface design are screen resolution and color depth. Screen resolution is measured in pixels per square inch, which compose the picture you see on your monitor. Some common screen resolution settings include 640 × 480, 800 × 600, 1024 × 768, 1280 × 1024, and 1600 × 1200, which range from lower to higher. Color depth is the number of unique colors that are displayed on a screen. Common color depth settings are 16 colors, 256 colors, 16-bit (or 65,356 colors), and 32-bit (16.7 million colors). The brand and version of Web browser used to view a page sometimes affects the appearance. Test view a Web site in two different brands of browsers and examine the subtle differences in layout, style, or text size. These differences in system settings and browser type can affect the overall appearance and function of Web interfaces. For example, if the interface design uses a custom layout with a style sheet or multiple frames, it may appear perfectly aligned on a PC system that uses Internet Explorer 6.0, with a screen resolution of 1024 × 768, and a color depth setting at 16-bit color. It might look slightly misaligned on a Mac system, using Safari 1.0, with a screen resolution of 800 × 600 and color depth of 256 colors.

Since every user has different system settings, including platform, browser type and version, screen resolution, and color depth preferences, it is essential to test the site's interface on a variety of system settings. Figure 8-11 provides some general guidelines that are helpful in designing interfaces for users across platforms, browsers, and system settings. Since every site has unique features and layouts, certain guidelines will work better than others. It's best to test a strategy to get an idea of what will work for each site layout.

Part of the Web designer's job is to ensure a consistent product for all users. While insufficient time or resources may be available to test every possible system configuration and

USE RELATIVE SIZE VALUES FOR TABLES, FRAMES, AND DIVISIONS.

Relative values are expressed in percentages of the browser window size. As the browser window shrinks, objects that use relative sizes shrink as well. For example, a table might have a width of 40% of the screen size. Regardless of how the browser is resized, the table will always be exactly 40% of the total browser window size.

PROVIDE ALTERNATE VERSIONS FOR DIFFERENT SYSTEM SETTINGS.

Some sites provide alternate versions for different browsers and screen resolutions. Links can be provided to each version, or a script (i.e., JavaScript) can be used to detect the user's settings and redirect them to the correct version.

DESIGN A SITE USING LOWER SCREEN RESOLUTION AND COLOR DEPTH SETTINGS.

Some designers suggest using a low resolution setting, such as 800×600 to accommodate the widest possible user base. Due to the rapid evolution of screen and graphic display technologies, what is considered to be a lower resolution has changed rapidly. User statistics on one setting lower than most office or computer laboratory computers may help determine what settings should be used.

USE RESIZABLE WINDOWS AND FRAMES.

Resizable windows and frames allow users to customize the size of screen elements to best fit their needs. These resizable elements can provide users with scrollbars and the ability to change the height and width of windows and frames, so it is important to enable these features for users. Using vertical scrollbars where needed also helps users control the flow of content when reading.

FIGURE 8-11. Guidelines for Designing across System Settings

setting, doing some spot tests will help the overall usability of the interface. Site interfaces should also be tested using the same principles used to design it, namely the visual-spatial techniques and guidelines from earlier in the chapter. Chapter 9 outlines more detailed methods of usability testing which can be used to test the site's interface and overall functionality.

Conclusion

A number of sites and their interfaces are developed and published sometimes with little thought to how users perceive individual elements and their arrangement in the Web interface. Even the use of Web conventions, common among larger, more popular sites, can be helpful guidelines in designing interface layouts, but many rely on the knowledge of experienced users. Only by combining knowledge of users, their expectations, and how they perceive information can designers best develop effective interface designs.

ADVICE from PRACTITIONERS

Use of Company Specific Conventions in Interface Layouts

**Marc Bessent • Senior Operations Support Specialist
Major Internet Service Provider**

Absolutely! Standards are important to any organization as they are typically the foundation for how work is accomplished. The use of advertising banners and some scrolling banners are highly discouraged as they are distracting and typically detract from the page. Navigation placement in our organization requires a standardized menu on the left column of the page. It may be placed inside a frame and use Hypertext Markup Language (HTML), Dynamic Hypertext Markup Language (DHTML), or another form of interactive menu containing an index list of links. Pages on our larger sites tend to include a search element in the upper right hand corner of the page. As a large company we tend to use Cascading Style Sheets (CSS) to help create a uniform look and feel for the site. Global style sheets create a uniform style for pages in specific areas of the site, so users can recognize them. They also allow for quick and sweeping changes to be made during redesigns by the site administrators and developers.

Importance of Visual Elements to Guide Users

Clearly defined regions of uniform color that ties in with the site helps us define the different functions of the areas on a Web page. In my experience with usability testing, users tend to notice contrasts first and then move into the content of the page. It is best not to have your user searching around for how to get more information from your site or spend a lot of time trying to find the actual content. In any sales business, as an example, if users have to figure out how to find your products, or click several times and wait through page loads to get closer and closer to the information they seek, they are more likely to go to another site.

Chapter Summary

- Interface design involves the selection and arrangement of elements that make up the whole layout of a Web page.
- Interface design involves understanding user behavior and clearly identifying potential users. Designers must clearly identify the audience(s), purpose(s), and context(s) of their site to identify users. User preferences and limitations should be assessed with respect to navigation, content, technology, and expertise levels.
- Visual-spatial thinking provides a unique understanding of user perception and can be applied specifically to interface design. Visual-spatial thinking considers how users focus, select, discern, and conceptualize elements in their field of vision.
- The major elements in a Web interface include the site header, navigation, search, help, content, contextual cues, and graphic identity. Most of these elements are found explicitly or implicitly in a typical interface design.
- Visual syntax is the normal viewing pattern used by our eyes when scanning a page or a screen.

- The major types of Web interface layouts include: single-frame, two-frame, three-frame, and custom.
- A basic interface test should involve viewing a site using a variety of platforms, browsers and versions, screen resolution settings, and color depth settings to ensure consistency in design and layout. In addition, the interface should be tested with the same visual-spatial principles used in its design.

Exercises

1. Select a Web site and try to determine the typical users of the site, based on the visual and textual content. Observe the use of jargon, syntax, and granularity of text chunks to help give you a clear idea. Then, write two or three short sketches of typical users, identifying some of their preferences, limitations, and perceived uses of information from the site.

2. Select a Web site and make a list of the ways in which information is grouped or organized using both visual elements and negative space. Then, determine how these uses are effective in helping users understand information better in the site. How might certain elements be regrouped or redesigned to improve user comprehension?

3. Using the same Web site in Exercise #2, make a list of the contextual cues on the home page. What elements provide users with contextual information about the site, its structure, and content? Then, browse the site for about three to five minutes, making note of elements that make up the graphic identity. Which elements seem to suggest a brand, theme, or identity for the site? Is a design metaphor used? How effective is it?

4. Pick one of the popular news Web sites and determine the layouts that are used. Then, select and sketch a new and different layout which you feel would be an improvement over the original. Determine where you might place titles, headers, graphic elements, navigation systems, search boxes, and so on. Try to incorporate the use of visual-spatial principles in your redesign of the layout.

9

Planning ↔ Content ↔ Structure ↔ Design ↔ Usability

USABILITY and ACCESSIBILITY

Learning Objectives

After completing this chapter, you will understand:

- The importance of usability and accessibility testing

- Three methods of usability testing that can be used to test Web sites

- A basic four-step usability process to follow

- How to test technical issues for usability

- How to conduct a usability test using a visual-spatial approach

- Important accessibility guidelines and testing methods

Introduction

The fifth phase of developing Web sites is usability, which involves testing the site and making subsequent revisions so that it is readable, accessible, and usable. Considering usability as part of the process throughout the development of a site helps minimize problems with the site as it evolves. During the design of navigation tools, graphics, content chunks, site structure, and interface layouts, designers should always keep usability in mind and make choices that demonstrate good usability. As an iterative process, Web development requires constant revision of previous work and testing. Formal testing is important to help identify any final problems users may have with the site content, navigation, design, or functionality.

A wide variety of usability testing methods are used in testing Web sites. Some methods used include task-based tests, user scenarios, browser tests, heuristic evaluations, and accessibility tests. Usability testing often involves a set of heuristics, or measures, used to evaluate specific aspects of a Web site, such as the navigation, readability, or functionality. This chapter will discuss three usability testing methods, specifically technical usability checks, visual-spatial usability testing, and accessibility checks. These three types of usability tests address important usability issues, which include visual quality, access to content, organization, function, and user perception. For more detailed information on other methods of usability testing, three informative books on the subject are Jakob Nielsen's

Usability Engineering (1993), Mark Pearrow's *Web Usability Handbook* (2000), and Carol Barnum's *Usability Testing and Research* (2002).

Technical usability tests involve testing the site on a variety of system settings including operating systems, screen resolution, color depths, and browser types and versions. This type of testing is important because of the slight variations in display and function that result from different computer and browser system settings. These tests help identify issues that may prompt slight changes in the site design and layout to ensure pages can be properly accessed and viewed across a wide range of systems and settings. This test can involve any number of participants, which include the developer, design team, and actual users.

A usability test that incorporates the visual-spatial principles will help determine how well the site fits user perceptual habits, needs, and actions when searching and browsing Web sites. Specifically, the visual-spatial principles can be used as heuristics to develop test scenarios that measure how well a site supports the ways in which users focus, solve problems, discern organization, understand concepts, and perform tasks. These principles can be used to evaluate the major site components, including its navigation, interface, visual design, and content. This test involves having actual users perform basics tasks using a site prototype and its functions and features.

Accessibility tests are important to overall usability because they help ensure that the site's graphics, features, and functions are viewable and accessible to a broad user base, particularly individuals with specific disabilities or with technology limitations. Accessibility standards provide design guidelines that help make pages more easily read by assistive software and/or by systems with limited graphic capabilities. This test can involve the designer, design team, and actual users as participants.

All members of a design team should participate in the usability process, especially in evaluating and interpreting testing results. Designers, team members, and users should participate in the technical usability tests and accessibility tests, to evaluate those aspects of the site. Involving users in visual-spatial usability tests is essential to identify their perceptual habits, needs, and expectations. This chapter will discuss the usability process, three testing methods, and will provide step-by-step instructions, testing instruments, worksheets, and guidelines for interpreting results in planning necessary changes to a Web site.

Usability Testing Process

Usability testing involves a number of complex planning and preparatory actions, which include developing goals, methods, heuristics, testing instruments, and data collection procedures. It involves selecting participants, a testing environment, types of questions to ask, and determining how testing data can be used in improving a Web site. With all of these important details to manage, it is important to follow a testing process to ensure consistency in how a test is developed and administered. A process helps organize tasks and ensure that all of the important testing issues are addressed, which contributes to the quality of results. The basic usability testing process involves four major steps: establishing goals, developing instruments, conducting the test, and analyzing results (see Figure 9-1). Although formal usability testing performed in a laboratory setting may involve a more detailed and lengthy process, this simplified process can be used for the types of tests described in this chapter.

The first step of the process is to set testing goals and parameters. This includes what the test should measure, its methods, test population, and heuristics, or criteria, used in the

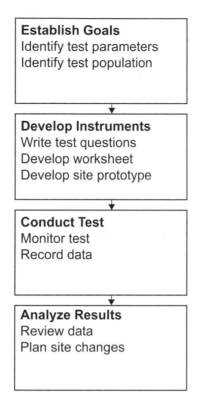

Establish Goals
Identify test parameters
Identify test population

Develop Instruments
Write test questions
Develop worksheet
Develop site prototype

Conduct Test
Monitor test
Record data

Analyze Results
Review data
Plan site changes

FIGURE 9-1.   Four-Step Usability Testing Process

test. Methods include planning for data recording, testing environment, and identifying participants. Usability research indicates most tests can be performed using a relatively small population of about five to seven users, since trends in the results tend to repeat themselves using higher populations (Nielsen 2000).

The second step involves developing the instruments for the test, which include writing test questions, developing a worksheet to record data, and creating a site prototype to test. Some types of test questions often used in usability testing are task-based, scenario-based, objective, or process-oriented questions (see Table 9-1). These questions can be used to develop worksheets, interviews, or user prompts for observational data collection. Other important instruments that are used include orientation scripts and descriptions of the site and its purpose. The purpose of these instruments is to provide a user with the necessary background information and context of the site and testing guidelines. In addition to developing testing instruments, a working copy of the Web site, or prototype of the site, should be published on a Web server or made available on a stand-alone system for the test. It is preferable to test the site online and on a computer not used to develop the actual site. Be sure the working copy of the site is fully functional on a single system before using it in the test.

The third step is conducting the test, which includes monitoring the test and recording data. In some cases, a test might need to be timed or observed to record data based on testing goals. Users will provide the data, which can be recorded by them on a worksheet, or by a test proctor that serves as interviewer or observer to collect data. To begin the test, provide test

TABLE 9-1. Types of Usability Testing Questions	
Type of Question	**Purpose**
Scenario-based	Provide the user with a scenario, setting, or situation and ask questions based on that context
Task-based	Provide users with specific tasks to perform that test their responses and accuracy
Objective	Provide users with questions and a set of responses from which to choose to guide their responses
Process-oriented	Provide users with a task that requires them to describe the process they use to execute the task

participants with background information on the site, including its subject, purpose, location, and any testing guidelines. Explain the instructions of the test, including the allotted time, evaluation criteria, and any forms and worksheets to be used by participants. Then, allow participants to perform the test without distraction or interference. Have the test proctor record any data or answer questions the participant may have. As part of their evaluation, instruct participants to identify items that violate any of the evaluation criteria and have them distinguish specific problems from general comments, if this information is valuable to collect.

The fourth step is to analyze the test results, which includes reviewing the data, interpreting it, and identifying what changes need to be implemented based on the test results. After the testing is complete, compile the responses and meet with the team to devise solutions for each of the problems noted by the reviewers. Be sure to take a close look at specific problems identified and any comments provided. Identify problems or issues that require action, which in many cases will be most of the problems identified. Often, problems are ranked in terms of their severity and prioritized accordingly in redesign efforts. Identify what actions, if any, are required based on any general comments made by reviewers.

Following a usability testing process ensures consistency in the development, delivery, and review of tests and testing results. This basic usability testing process should be followed for each of the three usability tests described in this chapter. Each type of test described in this chapter will provide specific suggestions on developing goals, heuristics, methods, and instruments. Although the purpose and outcomes of each test may vary, using a consistent testing process will help organize tasks and ensure that the testing procedure runs smoothly.

Technical Usability Testing

Performing a technical usability test helps ensure that a Web site will be functional across a variety of platforms, browsers, and different system settings. Each user has different versions of software, system settings, and monitor resolution settings, all of which can affect the display and function of certain pages and layouts. Web developers Robin Williams and John Tollett stress the importance of performing basic browser checks since what one user sees on a screen may not match what other users see on theirs (2000). While it might not be possible to design a site that works optimally for every possible system, testing the site on a wide variety of settings will help designers make necessary adjustments to account for many of the differences in system settings. In turn, this helps ensure equal access to site content for the widest possible user base. To perform a technical usability test, follow the four-step usability testing process. This includes establishing goals, developing instruments, conducting the test, and analyzing results (see Figure 9-1).

A technical usability test can involve any number of participants, which include the developer, design team, and users. It will require the development of a worksheet to record data and a working prototype of the site. The testing parameters should include the operating system type, browser type, screen resolution, and color depth settings to be used in the test. Technical tests should be performed using different operating systems (Microsoft Windows, Macintosh OS, Linux, etc.), browser types or brands (Mozilla Firefox, Netscape Navigator, Microsoft Internet Explorer, Macintosh Safari, etc.), browser versions (version 1.0, 6.0, etc.), screen resolutions (1024 × 768, 1280 × 1024, etc.), and color depths (256 colors, 32-bit color or true color, etc.). These elements should be used to develop a testing worksheet. For the testing sheet, specify at least two different operating systems and with at least two different browsers, preferably a more recent version of each. Use at least two different screen resolutions, one higher-resolution setting for newer systems and one lower-resolution setting for older systems. Screen resolution is measured in pixels per square inch, which compose the picture you see on your monitor. Some common screen resolution settings include 640 × 480, 800 × 600, 1024 × 768, 1280 × 1024, and 1600 × 1200, which range from lower to higher. Common color depth settings are 16 color, 256 color, 16-bit (or 65,356 colors), and 32-bit (16.7 million colors). Use at least two color settings, including 256 colors, to see how any high-resolution graphics appear at lower color depths. Both screen resolution and color depth settings can be found in the system's control panel (Windows) or system preferences (Mac). While there is no standard setting for all systems, trends seem to favor higher resolution settings as screen and graphic capabilities and technologies advance.

As part of the test, participants should examine key elements of the prototype site, which include navigation, consistency of the interface page layouts, clarity of visual elements, readability of the textual and graphic content, and overall functionality. Participants should record problems as they are discovered. Once testing parameters have been chosen, a testing worksheet should be developed that lists the testing parameters. This worksheet will also be used to identify specific problems encountered and severity level of each. As part of the worksheet, devise a system to rank the severity of the problem to help establish your redesign tasks later. For example, consider using the following system shown in Table 9-2.

TABLE 9-2. Severity Ranking System for Technical Usability Tests

Ranking	Characteristics
(1) Severe	Affects the accessibility of pages, or is an issue common across multiple systems with different settings
(2) Serious	Affects the readability and legibility of pages on one or more set of system settings
(3) Concern	Affects the clarity of elements or pages on one or more set of system settings

SYSTEM SETTINGS DESCRIPTION

Windows XP Professional, Mozilla Firefox 1.0, 1024 × 768, 32-bit color

SITE ELEMENT	PROBLEM	SEVERITY	SOLUTION
Navigation	Contact page uses different color scheme for visited links	3	Check to see if style sheet is referenced on contact page
Interface	Skewed alignments of page headers with browser resize	2	Use absolute positioning to fix headers in consistent locations
Graphics	Site logo on home page appears fuzzy	3	Pixel edit graphic and save at a higher resolution
Content	Text on images is too small to read	2	Increase text legibility and test at higher screen resolutions
Functionality	Submit button on feedback form is nonfunctional	1	Check form action and form handling script for errors

FIGURE 9-2. Sample Technical Usability Worksheet

This simple three-level ranking system can be modified to include other levels or types of problems. Identifying and ranking the severity level of problems will help prioritize later work in editing and revision. Once specific system settings and a severity ranking system have been developed, a worksheet can be developed to use by participants in the technical usability test. Figure 9-2 provides a sample technical usability worksheet with some sample data that can be used as a testing instrument to record data.

For each unique set of system settings, a separate worksheet can be developed to test the same site elements. After completing the tests, compile the data and develop solutions for each problem. Prioritize problems and solutions based on their severity ranking and follow through on implementing changes. When working on a team, consult with other team members in devising appropriate solutions. After evaluating the results, a plan for retesting the revised site should be developed, particularly if major changes to the site are required.

Visual-Spatial Usability Testing

Performing a usability test using the visual-spatial principles as heuristics will help test how well the site fits user perceptual habits, needs, and actions when searching and browsing a Web site. Since visual-spatial principles have been used throughout the development process, it is important to use these same principles to assess the usability of a Web site. To perform a visual-spatial usability test, follow the four-step usability testing process, which includes establishing goals, developing instruments, conducting the test, and analyzing results (see Figure 9-1).

This test involves having a small group of actual users (approximately five to seven) interact with a prototype of the site. Arnheim's five principles of visual thinking and the visual-spatial concepts from Chapter 1 can be used to develop test questions to evaluate how well the site fits the ways users perceive, search, browse, and interact with a Web site. These principles can be used to develop test questions that evaluate major features of a Web site, such as navigation, interface, graphics, content, and functionality. Table 9-3 provides some sample usability test questions designed to identify broader site issues.

These principles help focus the usability testing process on how users perceive and act on their visual instincts. These questions address broader site issues regarding a site's navigation, interface, graphics, content, and function. They evaluate the effectiveness of specific site elements in helping users focus, solve problems, organize, comprehend, and form concepts about the overall site and its features. These questions ask users to identify specific difficulties with site elements, their meaning, or organization. Additional questions based on these principles can be developed to examine specific elements, such as feedback forms or advanced search features. These questions can be task-based, asking a user to perform a task, and/or evaluation-based, asking a user to evaluate their use of a tool. For example, a task-based question might ask a user to use a search utility to find a specific content chunk. An evaluation-based question might ask the user to rate or examine its usefulness, flexibility, and labeling. Develop test questions that address broader issues to identify trends of what is working and not working in a site. Develop site-specific questions to test the use of specific tools, functions, or site content. Once testing questions have been developed, create a usability test worksheet for test

TABLE 9-3. Sample Usability Test Questions	
Concept	**Usability Questions**
Visual focus	• What elements did your find your eye focusing on most? • Which visual elements most influenced your choice of navigating the site? • Which visual elements did you eventually ignore and why?
Problem solving	• What elements did you focus on that helped you search and browse the site? • What methods of outlining content helped you make choices of what to read and what to click on? • What elements did you focus on that seemed distracting or not useful?
Contextual	• What elements on the home page and in the site helped you understand the organization of the site content? • As you followed links through the site, how were you able to find more specific information? • What methods might make it easier to find content?
Conceptual	• Describe shapes or icons that you found in the site and their meaning. • Were these shapes or icons useful in helping guide your actions or understanding of site content? • How did these shapes affect your reading, searching, and browsing decisions?
Wholeness	• What stylistic or visual elements were used that helped you understand the overall layout or organization of the site? • What elements were used repeatedly throughout the site to help you navigate or understand how the site was organized? • What were specific benefits and limitations of the site layout that helped and/or hindered your overall understanding of the site?

participants to use. Testing worksheets should provide adequate space for participants to record comments, observations, and notes. Figure 9-3 is a sample usability worksheet that incorporates both broad and site-specific questions using the visual-spatial approach.

This sample worksheet can be modified using other criteria, task-based questions, site-specific details, and tailored to use in the usability testing of any Web site. Using the

DIRECTIONS

This usability test will ask you to perform a series of tasks and to evaluate specific areas of the site, including the navigation, interface, graphics, content, and function. For each section of the test, you will be asked to perform a task that requires an answer. You will have approximately five minutes to complete the task and record your answer. The testing proctor will record the time. After completing the task, you will be asked a series of questions related to your experience in using the site to complete the task. In answering these questions, consider all aspects of the site, including navigation, interface, graphics, content, and functionality. These terms are defined below to familiarize you with their specific meaning.

NAVIGATION

The links, search utilities, and toolbar menus used to search and browse the site

INTERFACE

The layout, grouping, and alignment of elements on pages that make up the site

GRAPHICS

The use of graphics, colors, styles, and other visual information in the site

CONTENT

Textual and graphic information found in the site

FUNCTIONALITY

The operation of links, buttons, and media used in the site

TASK #1

Find a description of the GT3000 and list three of its distinguishing features.

QUESTIONS

- What navigation tools did you consider using to answer the first question and which tool(s) did you actually use?
- What elements did your find your eye focusing on most?
- Which visual elements most influenced your choice of navigating the site?
- Which visual elements did you eventually ignore and why?

(Continued)

TASK #2

Find a copy of the installation instructions for the GT3000 in PDF and save the file.

QUESTIONS

- What elements did you focus on that helped you search and browse the site?
- What methods of outlining content helped you make choices of what to read and what to click on?
- What elements did you focus on that seemed distracting or not useful?

TASK #3

Download a copy of the software driver for the XT411.

QUESTIONS

- What elements on the home page and in the site helped you understand the organization of the site content?
- As you followed links through the site, how were you able to find more specific information?
- What methods might make it easier to find content?

TASK #4

Use the site map to find a copy of the company's product warranty information and record the number of days before a warranty expires.

QUESTIONS

- Describe shapes or icons that you found in the site and their meaning.
- Were these shapes or icons useful in helping guide your actions or understanding of site content?
- How did these shapes affect your reading, searching, and browsing decisions?

TASK #5

Use the site's feedback form on the help page to send a comment about the site and record the ticket number.

QUESTIONS

- What stylistic or visual elements were used that helped you understand the overall layout or organization of the site?
- What elements were used repeatedly throughout the site to help you navigate or understand how the site was organized?
- What were specific benefits and limitations of the site layout that helped and/or hindered your overall understanding of the site?

FIGURE 9-3. Visual-Spatial Usability Test Worksheet

ADVICE from PRACTITIONERS

Importance of Usability Testing

**Andrew Eberhart • Senior Systems Programmer
Major Semiconductor Manufacturing Corporation**

Testing a site is extremely important prior to its publication. Nothing disappoints and frustrates a user more than broken links and incomprehensible content. Web sites in my organization exist as a tool to provide users with information and to allow them to perform certain tasks. The same as using a mechanical tool like a screwdriver, the tool needs to work and it should not be broken. Testing the site ensures that the tool is in good working order and does the job it is designed to do.

Usability Process and End Product

In my workplace, testing is usually done throughout the design and creation of the Web site. This allows problems to be recognized and corrected during the site development. As pages are created, the content and technical aspects are constantly checked for accuracy and usability. Once the entire site is completed and ready for a final review, the prototype of the site is made accessible to a few end-users of the site. They are asked to trial use the site as if it were live and report back any technical, visible, or usability problems. A questionnaire is provided to them to fill out in order to provide them with focus on what to examine and test. Any issues reported are resolved and then verified by the user that reported them. Finally, the site is put into production. The biggest savings in time and money in a project is the up-front testing done during the site's development.

visual-spatial approach to develop a site usability test allows a site to be tested using the same criteria used to design the site. A testing worksheet can be used to evaluate both broad and site-specific issues in the development of a site. When reviewing the data from this type of usability test, evaluate the results and return to the visual-spatial principles to help devise strategies and solutions for improving the site. These principles can suggest other methods of improving a site that better fit the ways in which users perceive and interact with a Web site.

Accessibility Testing

Another important aspect of Web usability is checking the accessibility of a site's content. Whether its purpose is to solicit clients, sell products, or provide information, all users should have equal access to the content, regardless of any physical, mental, or technical limitations. Some users may have trouble accessing your content because of system settings or older versions of software viewers or players. Some may have trouble based on a specific disability, such as visual impairment. Many people with disabilities access the Web on a daily basis using a variety of hardware and software products that can assist them. For example, users with visual impairments can use software that converts textual content into live audio and reads content to users. Regardless of the reason, these limitations can affect the overall accessibility of the site. While the designer may not be able to control all of these issues, the best way to ensure that a site is accessible is to check its pages against at least one set of accessibility guidelines. Two sets most commonly used are the U.S. Government Section 508 Accessibility Guidelines and the World Wide Web Consortium Web Content Accessibility Guidelines. To perform an accessibility test, follow the four step usability testing process, which includes establishing goals, developing instruments, conducting the test, and analyzing results (see Figure 9-1). This test can involve the designer, design team, and actual users as participants, and will involve selecting a set of accessibility guidelines as measures to evaluate a Web site.

One set of accessibility guidelines is the U.S. Government Section 508 Accessibility Guidelines, http://www.section508.gov, enacted by the U.S. Congress in 1998. This set of guidelines serves as an amendment to the Rehabilitation Act, to ensure that all Government public information Web sites and electronic materials be made accessible to all users, regardless of their disability. While the law applies also to software programs, telecommunication products, and other electronic media, it provides a set of 16 guidelines for Web-based materials, including Web sites. Figure 9-4 summarizes the U.S. Government Section 508 Accessibility Guidelines.

In accordance with their Web Accessibility Initiative, the World Wide Web Consortium (W3C) maintains its own set of Web Content Accessibility Guidelines, which is another commonly used set of guidelines (http://www.w3.org/WAI/) and is summarized in Figure 9-5. The W3C is a group of institutions and individuals committed to creating accessible and consistent standards for Web development. The W3Cs set of guidelines is based mostly on recommendations about design proposed by the W3C, which are not mandated by any specific law. This set of guidelines spans versions of HTML and overlaps with some of the Section 508 guidelines. Since different versions are released of the Web Content Accessibility Guidelines, it is best to check the W3C Web site to consult the most recent version to use in testing.

Regardless of which set of accessibility guidelines is used, it is important to test Web sites to ensure you are providing equal access to your site to all users. Either of these sets of guidelines can be used to evaluate your site's level of accessibility, including its navigation, interface page layouts, graphics, textual content, and overall functionality. One quick way to check your site with either or both sets of guidelines is to visit the Bobby World Wide Web site, http://bobby.watchfire.com, which performs automated accessibility checks of individual Web pages. The site provides a free version of the Bobby scan utility, which allows a user to enter a URL and select one of the two sets of accessibility guidelines to scan pages. The scan generates a customized report that summarizes the exceptions found and the corresponding rules. Each individual page will have to be tested, but these tests are performed quite fast. This tool helps designers identify accessibility issues that can help them plan appropriate changes to the site. Another automated accessibility check can be performed by the Web development software used to develop the site. Microsoft FrontPage and Macromedia Dreamweaver are two Web authoring software programs that have accessibility checkers integrated into their programs, which can be used to test a site. Be cautioned that the results of any automated check should be examined closely, as these software tools may identify or miss important issues, due to some software limitations.

SECTION 508 ACCESSIBILITY GUIDELINES

1. A text equivalent for every nontext element shall be provided (e.g., via "alt," "longdesc," or in element content).

2. Equivalent alternatives for any multimedia presentation shall be synchronized with the presentation.

3. Web pages shall be designed so that all information conveyed with color is also available without color, for example, from context or markup.

4. Documents shall be organized so they are readable without requiring an associated style sheet.

5. Redundant text links shall be provided for each active region of a server-side image map.

6. Client-side image maps shall be provided instead of server-side image maps except where the regions cannot be defined with an available geometric shape.

7. Row and column headers shall be identified for data tables.

8. Markup shall be used to associate data cells and header cells for data tables that have two or more logical levels of row or column headers.

9. Frames shall be titled with text that facilitates frame identification and navigation.

10. Pages shall be designed to avoid causing the screen to flicker with a frequency greater than 2 Hz and lower than 55 Hz.

11. A text-only page, with equivalent information or functionality, shall be provided to make a Web site comply with the provisions of this part, when compliance cannot be accomplished in any other way. The content of the text-only page shall be updated whenever the primary page changes.

12. When pages utilize scripting languages to display content, or to create interface elements, the information provided by the script shall be identified with functional text that can be read by assistive technology.

13. When a Web page requires that an applet, plug-in, or other application be present on the client system to interpret page content, the page must provide a link to a plug-in or applet that complies with §1194.21(a) through (l).

14. When electronic forms are designed to be completed online, the form shall allow people using assistive technology to access the information, field elements, and functionality required for completion and submission of the form, including all directions and cues.

15. A method shall be provided that permits users to skip repetitive navigation links.

16. When a timed response is required, the user shall be alerted and given sufficient time to indicate more time is required.

FIGURE 9-4. Summary of the U.S. Government Section 508 Accessibility Guidelines

Source: U.S. Government Section 508 Accessibility Guidelines, http://www.section508.gov.

W3C WEB CONTENT ACCESSIBILITY GUIDELINES 1.0

1. Provide equivalent alternatives to auditory and visual content. Provide content that, when presented to the user, conveys essentially the same function or purpose as auditory or visual content.

2. Don't rely on color alone. Ensure that text and graphics are understandable when viewed without color.

3. Use markup and style sheets and do so properly. Mark up documents with the proper structural elements. Control presentation with style sheets rather than with presentation elements and attributes.

4. Clarify natural language usage. Use markup that facilitates pronunciation or interpretation of abbreviated or foreign text.

5. Create tables that transform gracefully. Ensure that tables have necessary markup to be transformed by accessible browsers and other user agents.

6. Ensure that pages featuring new technologies transform gracefully. Ensure that pages are accessible even when newer technologies are not supported or are turned off.

7. Ensure user control of time-sensitive content changes. Ensure that moving, blinking, scrolling, or auto-updating objects or pages may be paused or stopped.

8. Ensure direct accessibility of embedded user interfaces. Ensure that the user interface follows principles of accessible design: device-independent access to functionality, keyboard operability, self-voicing, etc.

9. Design for device-independence. Use features that enable activation of page elements via a variety of input devices.

10. Use interim solutions. Use interim accessibility solutions so that assistive technologies and older browsers will operate correctly.

11. Use W3C technologies and guidelines. Use W3C technologies (according to specification) and follow accessibility guidelines. Where it is not possible to use a W3C technology, or doing so results in material that does not transform gracefully, provide an alternative version of the content that is accessible.

12. Provide context and orientation information. Provide context and orientation information to help users understand complex pages or elements.

13. Provide clear navigation mechanisms. Provide clear and consistent navigation mechanisms—orientation information, navigation bars, a site map, etc.—to increase the likelihood that a person will find what they are looking for at a site.

14. Ensure that documents are clear and simple. Ensure that documents are clear and simple so they may be more easily understood.

FIGURE 9-5.   Summary of the W3C Web Content Accessibility Guidelines, 1.0

Source: World Wide Web Consortium Web Content Accessibility Guidelines 1.0, http://www.w3.org/TR/WCAG10.

Reviewing Accessibility Exceptions

It is important to review and compare the results of an automated accessibility report to the actual set of guidelines used to test a site. While automated systems assist developers in checking overall accessibility, these tools fail to consider the context in which site elements are used. For example, the use of tables to create a site layout may not require the use of marked headers as suggested by Guidelines 7 and 8 of the Section 508 Accessibility Guidelines. After reviewing the results of the accessibility testing, make a list of possible solutions and note exceptions that may not apply because of certain conditions. One common accessibility exception noted in such a report concerns the use of headers for tables. If tables are used for layout purposes rather than to display numeric data, it may be unnecessary to provide headers for columns. Interpreting how guidelines and exceptions apply to a specific site is not always straightforward, but may require careful consideration based on the site's audience, purpose, context, and other issues. In all cases, review the results of an accessibility test carefully to see which exceptions should be addressed in editing and revising the site and set clear goals that address each issue. Some issues to focus on in review deal with graphic content, layout, navigation and forms, and other issues.

Graphic Content

One major accessibility issue addressed by many of the standards deals with accessing graphic content in a site, including the use of color, media, screen settings, and styles. Graphic content cannot be translated into textual or audio descriptions by assistive software easily without some kind of markup. The first guideline of both the Section 508 Accessibility Guidelines and W3C Web Content Accessibility Guidelines specifically deal with this issue. Normally, graphic content includes ALT descriptors that provide textual descriptions of graphic content, like that shown in Figure 9-6. These descriptors are what assistive software reads back to the user.

Some graphics are used as placeholders, rules, or as shapes, such as boxes. Unless there is a specific meaning or concept, these graphics can use a null value for the ALT descriptor. Partial color-blindness may be another vision impairment that affects a user's perception of color. If color is used in an essential way, then alternatives or descriptions should be provided to assist users. Guideline 3 from the Section 508 Accessibility Guidelines and Guideline 2 from the W3C Web Content Accessibility Guidelines 1.0 address this issue. In some cases, users might not be able to use software viewers or plug-ins to view video, audio, or other animated content, in which case a designer should plan a method of providing an alternate version of that content or link to access the plug-in. When all else fails, a text-only version of a page may be one of many possible options.

```
<IMG SRC="tech.gif' ALT='Technologies'>
```

FIGURE 9-6. Using ALT Descriptors

Layout   Two major issues with layout and accessibility standards deal with the use of tables or scripts for layout purposes and the use of titles for each independent HTML frame or window. Guidelines 7 to 9 of the Section 508 Accessibility Guidelines and Guidelines 3 and 5 of the W3C Web Content Accessibility Guidelines specifically deal with layout issues. Tables used to display data need headers for rows and columns, so these important descriptors can be read to vision-impaired users. If tables are used merely to organize elements on the page, then there is no need to identify rows and columns. Conversely, HTML frames must have unique titles so assistive software can help vision-impaired users identify each independent frame. Also, independent and descriptive titles can help users viewing pages outside of the normal frameset determine their location in the overall structure of the site.

Navigation and Forms   Interactive elements of sites, such as forms and navigation tools can create accessibility issues for users. Guidelines 14 to 16 of the Section 508 Accessibility Guidelines and Guidelines 7 and 13 of the W3C Web Content Accessibility Guidelines specifically deal with navigation and form issues. Redundant text links often provide easy-to-access alternatives to graphics versions, such as drop-down menus or image maps. They are also useful in sites that use HTML frames, so that users can access navigation tools on every page, in case they get separated from the main HTML frameset. Sometimes redundant navigation can get in the way and it is advisable to provide a means to skip over these features in some cases. Forms use similar elements to navigation, such as buttons and drop-down boxes, which can create similar accessibility problems. To maximize accessibility, develop simple, straightforward forms, with accessible and readable instructions and cues for users.

Other Issues   The best accessibility test for a Web site would be to have actual users with specific limitations test the site for other issues that may not easily be identified by a manual or automated accessibility test. If resources and time permit, it is recommended that formal tests by these users be conducted to verify the results and findings of accessibility testing using one of the sets of guidelines mentioned.

Conclusion

Web usability and accessibility are important aspects of the Web development process that ensure a site is readable, usable, and accessible by the broadest user base. Web usability should be something a designer focuses on throughout the development process and not just at the end of the project. Since the Web development process is an iterative one, it is important to test any revisions made during this process to save time and ensure a quality product. Usability testing is an iterative task as well, which may require a developer to revise previous work and to retest each subsequent version of a Web site as it evolves.

Chapter Summary

- The usability phase involves formal testing and editing of the site to ensure it is readable and accessible by the broadest user base.
- Although the visual-spatial approach to developing Web sites emphasizes a usability focus, formal testing is important to help identify any final problems users may have with the site content, navigation, design, or functionality.

- Three important usability tests that can be used to help identify potential problems are technical usability checks, visual-spatial usability testing, and accessibility checks.

- Following a usability testing process ensures consistency in the development, delivery, and review of tests and testing results. The basic four-step usability process includes establishing goals, developing instruments, conducting the test, and analyzing results.

- Technical usability checks involve testing the site on a variety of system settings including operating systems, screen resolution, color depths, and browser types and versions.

- Visual-spatial usability testing involves testing actual users to help determine how well the site fits user perceptual habits when searching and browsing a Web site.

- Accessibility checks are an important part of testing a site because they help ensure the site's graphics, layout, navigation, forms, and other functions are viewable and accessible to a broader user base, particularly individuals with specific disabilities.

- Accessibility results should be reviewed carefully to see which exceptions should be addressed in editing and revising the site.

Exercises

1. Select a familiar Web site and explore it for a few minutes making note of its layout, use of graphics, and elements in the interface. Then, change the computer's screen resolution and color depth settings in the system's display properties. Make note of the original settings and also for the new settings you select. Now, view the same site and make note of any usability problems with regard to the accessibility, functionality, readability, legibility, and clarity of elements used in the site. In addition, propose some alternatives for making changes to the site to improve the usability of the site regardless of system settings.

2. Using Figure 9-3, the Web Usability Checklist, perform a usability test of a school or organization's Web site. If a large site of more than 50 pages is selected, limit the test to a specific area of the site. Record notes for each item on the checklist that identify successful features or problem areas. Then, identify one potential solution for solving each problem identified.

3. Select a Web site that uses a large amount of graphic content on its home page or a site that has a complex interface layout. Examine the home page for a few minutes to become familiar with its layout and view the page's source markup code. Then, visit the Bobby Worldwide site at http://watchfire.bobby.com and test the site's home page using one of the sets of accessibility guidelines (either Section 508 or W3C Accessibility Guidelines). Carefully review the exception report to determine if there are valid accessibility issues with the site.

4. Using a familiar small Web site of fewer than 20 pages, test the site using one of the sets of accessibility guidelines and identify any exceptions on the home page only. Record any exceptions on a sheet of paper and identify them as graphic, layout, navigation/forms, or other issues. Then, perform an automated accessibility check using the Bobby Worldwide site at http://watchfire.bobby.com and one of the sets of accessibility guidelines (either Section 508 or W3C Accessibility Guidelines). Compare the results of your manual test to the automated test.

REFERENCES

Arnheim, Rudolf. *Visual Thinking*. Berkeley: University of California Press, 1969.

Arnheim, Rudolf. *The Power of the Center*. Berkeley: University of California Press, 1988.

Association of Teachers of Technical Writing, ATTW—ATTW Publications. 2005. http:// www.attw.org/publications/ATTWPubs.asp.

Baehr, Craig. *Conceptualizing the Whole: Using Visual-Spatial Thinking in the Interpretation and Design of Hypertext Systems*. Ann Arbor, MI: University of Michigan, 2002.

Baehr, Craig. "Web Pages and Writing for the Web", in Technical Communication: A Practical Approach, 6th ed. by William Sanborn Pfeiffer. Upper Saddle River: Pearson Prentice Hall, 2006.

Baehr, Craig, and John Logie, 2005. "The Need for New Ways of Thinking," in Visual Thinking, Online Documentation, and Hypertext, special issue, *Technical Communication Quarterly* 14, no. 1 (2005): 1–5.

Barnum, Carol. *Usability Testing and Research*. Boston: Allyn & Bacon, 2002.

Conversive, Inc. "Technology". 2005. http://www.conversive.com/html/technology.php.

DeVigal, Andrew. "Putting the Eyetrack Study to Good Use." Stanford-Poynter Project | EyeTracking Online News. http://www.poynterextra.org/et/i.htm.

Earth Observatory National Hazards. "National Hazards Main Page," http://earthobservatory.nasa.gov/NaturalHazards/.

FirstGov. http://www.firstgov.gov.

Flashbuttons.com, http://www.flashbuttons.com.

Fogg, B. J. *Persuasive Technology*. San Francisco: Morgan Kaufmann, 2003.

GIA—Gem Trade Laboratory. "Section Main Page." http://www.gia.edu/gemtradelab/66/section_main_page.cfm.

Hammerich, Irene, and Claire Harrison. *Developing Online Content*. New York: Wiley Computer Publishing, 2002.

Hewett, T., et. al. 1996. ACM SIGCHI Curriculum for Human–Computer Interaction, February 28, 2003. http://sigchi.org/cdg/cdg2.html.

Illuminations. http://www.illuminations.com.

Internet Archive. http://www.archive.org.

JafHomes. http://www.jafhomes.com.

JetBlue Airways. http://www.jetblue.com.

Johnson, Robert R. *User-Centered Technology*. Albany: State University of New York Press, 1998.

Johnson, Steven. *Interface Culture*. San Francisco: HarperCollins, 1997.

Johnson-Sheehan, Richard, and Craig Baehr. 2001. "Visual-Spatial Thinking in Hypertexts." *Technical Communication* 48 (1): 22–30.

Koffka, Kurt. *Principles of Gestalt Psychology*. New York: Harcourt, 1935.

Kostelnick, Charles, and David Roberts. *Designing Visual Language*. Boston: Allyn & Bacon, 1998.

Landow, George. "Hypertext and Critical Theory." In *Hypertext 2.0,* by Baltimore: John Hopkins University Press, 1997.

Lynch, Patrick, and Sarah Horton. *Web Style Guide*. 2nd ed. New Haven, CT: Yale University Press, 2002.

Mozilla. "Mozilla Products," http://www.mozilla.org/products.

NASA. "Solar System Exploration Sitemap," http://solarsystem.nasa.gov/sitemap/index.cfm.

National Park Service. http://www.nps.gov.

Nielsen, Jakob. *Usability Engineering*. San Diego, CA: Morgan Kaufmann, 1993.

Nielsen, Jakob. *Designing Web Usability*. Indianapolis: New Riders Press, 2000.

Nielsen, Jakob. "Content Creation for Average People." Useit.com. (October 2001.) http://www.useit.com/alertbox/20001001.html.

Nielsen, Jakob. "Site Map Usability." Useit.com. (January 2002.) http://www.useit.com/alertbox/20020106.html.

Norman, Donald. *The Design of Everyday Things*. New York: Basic Books, 2002.

Pearrow, Mark. *Web Site Usability Handbook*. Rockland, MA: Charles River Media, 2000.

Rosenfeld, Louis, and Moorville, Peter. 2002. *Information Architecture for the World Wide Web,* 2nd ed. Sebastopol, CA: O'Reilly and Associates.

SurveyMonkey.com. http://www.surveymonkey.com.

U.S. Department of Health and Human Services. Usability.gov. http://www.usability.gov/guidelines.

Unicahome Featured Products. http://www.unicahome.com.

United States Geological Survey. "Search Engine." http://search.usgs.gov/.

United States Geological Survey. "National Cooperative Geologic Mapping Program." http://ncgmp.usgs.gov/ncgmpactivities.

United States Government Section 508 Accessibility Guidelines. http://www.section508.gov.

United States Library of Congress. http://www.loc.gov.

Vital. Vinyl Records. http://www.vitalvinyl.com.

Williams, Robin, and John Tollett. *The Non-Designer's Web Book*. 2nd ed. Berkeley, CA: Peachpit Press, 2000.

World Weather @ Weather.org. http://www.weather.org.

World Wide Web Consortium. Web Content Accessibility Guidelines 1.0. http://www.w3.org/TR/WCAG10.

WorldSpace International Satellite Radio Network. "Overview." http://www.worldspace.com/whatisit/overview.html.

W3Schools Online Web Tutorials. http://www.w3schools.com.

Yahoo, "Directory Help." http://help.yahoo.com/help/us/dir/ctd/.

Index